Fine Art Printing for Photographers

Fine Art Printing for Photographers

Exhibition Quality Prints with Inkjet Printers

Uwe Steinmueller and Juergen Gulbins

rockynook

Uwe Steinmueller, ustein_outback@yahoo.com
Juergen Gulbins, jg@gulbins.de

Editor: Jimi DeRouen
Copy editor: Deborah Cooper
Layout and Type: Juergen Gulbins
Cover Design: Helmut Kraus, www.exclam.de
Cover Photo: Uwe Steinmueller
Printer: Friesens Corporation, Altona, Canada
Printed in Canada

ISBN 1-933952-00-8

1st Edition
© 2007 by Rocky Nook Inc.
26 West Mission Street Ste 3

Santa Barbara, CA 93101

www.rockynook.com

First published under the title "Fine Art Printing für Fotografen: Hochwertige
Fotodrucke mit Inkjet-Druckern" © dpunkt.verlag GmbH, Heidelberg, Germany

Library of Congress catalog application submitted

Distributed by O'Reilly Media
1005 Gravenstein Highway North
Sebastapool, CA 95472

This book is printed on acid-free paper.

Contents

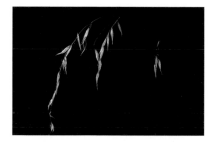

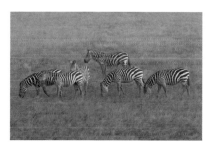

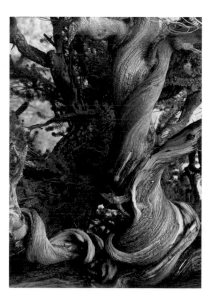

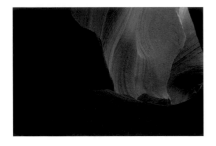

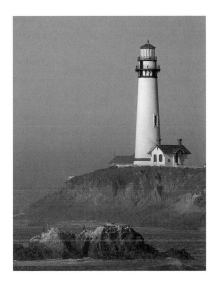

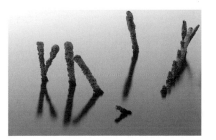

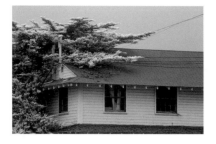

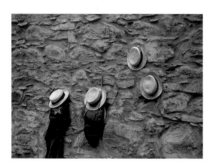

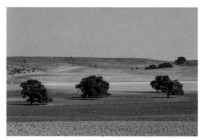

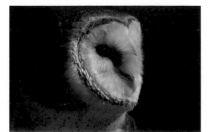

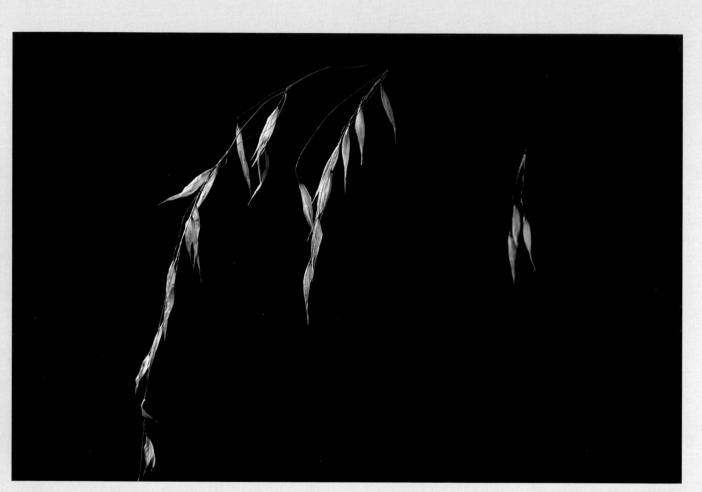

Kamera: Nikon D2X

Preface

A brief history

Inkjet printers have been around for more than 20 years, yet digital inkjet printing technology has only come of age in the past few years. The earliest consumer models lacked the technology and sophistication to print photographs similar in quality to common silver-halogenid prints (stereotypical photos printed on photographic paper), developed from film negatives or slides. Worse, inkjet prints lacked the lightfastness of silver-halogenid prints. For most users, the digital inkjet printers that delivered the desired image quality, e.g. Iris prints, were, unfortunately, rarely affordable. This economic obstacle has changed dramatically in the last few years, with the rise of digital photography. Thus, there is now a sizeable market for a new breed of inkjet printers from seasoned manufacturers like Epson, HP, Canon, Lexmark and Dell, among other newer brands.

Among the first A3+/Super B printers, suitable for both fine art printing and the budget of a broad range of buyers, were the Epson P2000 and P2200 (P2100 in Europe). The breakthrough of this line was based on quality, affordable price, and an Ultrachrome ink set.

Size matters

Many photographs impress viewers only when presented at an optimum viewing size; for example, the typical pocket-size 4 x 6 format is clearly unsuitable as a pleasing means of displaying a beautiful print. For most good shots, even the larger Letter, Legal and A4 sizes often leave viewers wanting more. Enter the A3+/ Super B prints, which measure an impressive 13 x 19 inches. In 2005, there was an explosion in the use of these large-format prints, an impressive statistic that promises to increase well into 2006 and beyond.

For some photographs, it is advisable to produce even larger prints. Printer manufacturers like Epson, HP and Canon market printers that promise high-quality prints up to 44 inches wide. There are many other large-format printer manufacturers out there, like Encad, Oce, Mutoh, and Roland, yet they are not designed for true, fine art printing. For this reason, we chose to focus on the moderately sized prints and printers, typically from Letter/A4 to C/A2. Most of the lessons of fine art printing, however, can be applied to both smaller and larger prints and printers.

Fine art printing is a sensuous endeavor

The highly technical nature of fine art printing should not overshadow its ability to awaken the senses. As the term "fine art printing" expresses, it is the printing of art in a highly artistic fashion. It allows you to project onto paper an image created with a simple digital or film camera, after enhancing the image with image-manipulation software to more accurately represent the original. Today's fine art printing, using a good digital inkjet printer, allows you to produce a quality of equal or higher value than that of traditional silver-halogenid prints, and clearly surpasses the quality of offset or rotogravure printing. When performed optimally, your printing can achieve a richer color gamut and finer tonal gradations than with traditional book- and magazine-printing techniques.

Experiment … and discover!

As with other genres of art, without proper knowledge and practical experience, the resulting print may not be as accurate as the image on your computer monitor, so you may have to try several different techniques, papers, paper sizes, borders, and matte styles. With careful practice, you will hopefully be on your way to producing museum-quality work with less effort than you had previously dreamed.

Though most prints are either displayed in frames behind glass or Plexiglas, often to reduce glare, this has the effect of reducing the visual appeal of the print and the fine art paper on which it is printed. Therefore, it is important to experiment with different types of fine art paper to achieve the desired result. Paper with a certain texture and tactile essence can be very sensuous indeed, so take your time to find the paper that best suits your taste and needs and to achieve the result you like.

A printing paper's color, surface, texture, and gloss will determine the kind of print you will produce, and must be carefully chosen to match the feeling you wish to project. An architectural shot may require a different printing paper than a photograph of nature or a landscape. A black-and-white print calls for a certain type of paper that would be unsuitable to a full-color shot. A certain print displayed without glass or Plexiglas will appear entirely different than one framed behind these types of transparent coverings.

Kamera: Nikon D2X

Both authors use digital cameras – Uwe Steinmueller as a professional and Jürgen Gulbins as a serious amateur. They were both led to fine art printing by the desire to control their workflow from start to finish, from the shooting of photos to the finished print. Printing with a fine art printer for them, is not a simple, tiresome task, but the final step , and a very important one – toward producing a pleasing image.

Planning for printing and printing itself takes time, but, in most cases, only a perfect, finished print gives full value to a good shot. Normally, only a few of all the photos you take will make it into a perfect, fine art print, but in many cases, this print will be the crowning glory of your photographic shooting. With the techniques shown in this book (together with others books we have published), you should be in complete control from start to finish.

We hope that the control of this process and the creative tasks along the way give you the same satisfaction and relaxation we found while doing it. Producing a satisfying print from your work has similarities to Christmas: the work is finished, and the present is unwrapped. You must still find a place to keep or present it, a place where it can be enjoyed for years to come.

Matting, framing, and hanging of prints is its own subject, and we go into it only briefly. We do, however, give some advice on how to keep and store your prints.

Acknowledgements

Thanks to our many influencers and friends like Bill Attkinson, Jim Collum, Charles Cramer, Brad Hinkel, Mac Holbert and Ben Willmore

Uwe Steinmueller, San José (California)   August 2006
Jürgen Gulbins, Keltern (Germany)

Foreword by Mac Holbert (Nash Editions)

Read our brief introduction to Nash Editions in our Printing Insights #22: "Digital Printmaking & Printmakers" at www.outbackphoto.com/printinginsights/pio22/essay.html

In 1989 my partner, Graham Nash, and I embarked on a search for a way to save a large body of his photographic work. The original negatives had been lost while being shipped from Los Angeles to Graham's home in San Francisco. All that was left was a box of "jumbo" contact sheets. Graham had been offered a show at the Parco Galleries in Tokyo and without his negatives he was unable to put together an exhibit. In solving the "problem" we ended up creating a method and a studio that has been recognized by many as the first fine art digital photography studio in the world. With the help of our friends, David Coons and Charles Wehrenberg, Jack Duganne and I experimented with hardware and software and by 1991 had developed a product that we felt was ready for the world. As it turned out we still had much to learn.

The only source of information in those days was from the few individuals that were involved in the technology. When I opened the door to Nash Editions in July of 1991, I had basic working knowledge of word processing and database management but I didn't have a clue what the difference was between a pixel and a raster. I asked a lot of questions, nurtured a lot of friendships and slowly I began to develop an overview of image processing and image output. By the mid 1990's the Internet had become an excellent source of information exchange and I began to frequent the online forums that focused on imaging and printing. I can't remember specifically when I first saw the name Uwe Steinmueller but I believe it was either 2000 or 2001. Suddenly I noticed his name appearing everywhere. Not only was he in quest of information but he was, more importantly, sharing it with anyone and everyone who would listen.

www.nasheditions.com

I finally got to meet Uwe in 2003 when he and his wife Bettina visited my studio. Their enthusiasm for the digital photography revolution was obvious. I have seen many "experts" come and go over the past 16 years. Uwe's expertise and his openness have gained him a high level of respect and admiration in the evolving world of digital photography.

I am very impressed with the book you are about to read. It's information like this that has helped to raise the quality of digital output and reduce the traditional art world's resistance to the use of digital tools in art. It is a book written by someone who KNOWS fine art digital printmaking. Uwe's style is concise and to the point. This comprehensive and complete guide to fine art digital printmaking should be included in the library of anyone who is serious about making fine art digital prints.

I only wish that all this excellent information had been available to me back in 1989 when I embarked on my digital journey. The hours I wasted … The ink and paper I wasted … The late nights …The cold suppers …

Mac Holbert   April 2006

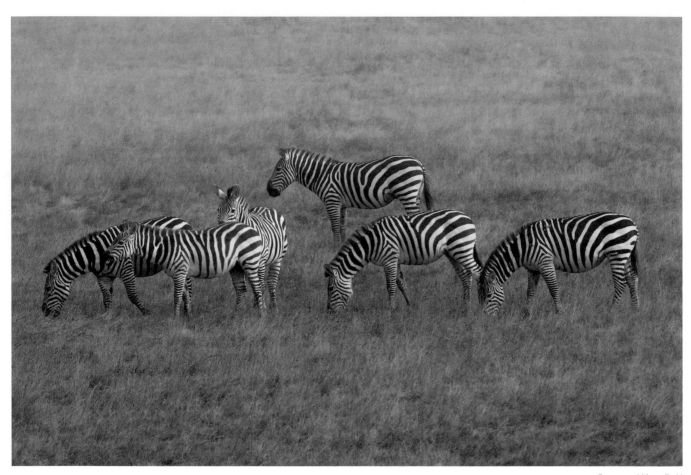

Camera: Nikon D2X

Printing Techniques

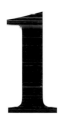

There are various methods of printing your own photographs. We only address one method in detail – printing using inkjet printers. In this chapter, we take a glance at different printing methods and discuss which are good and why. Most are not recommended for fine art printing.

The special focus of this chapter – and the focus of the entire book – is fine art printing, and our reader is the ambitious amateur, as well as the professional photographer. There are many reasonably good books on prepress work and commercial printing of books, magazines, brochures, or posters using offset printing, silkscreen printing, rotogravure or intaglio printing. We do not cover these methods, as they are either too complicated or too cost-intensive for the reader we target. Nor do they deliver the kind of quality that may be achieved with today's photo inkjet printers.

1.1   **Basic printing techniques**

The journey from a pixel to a printed point

In image processing, there are many terms used with a similar meaning, often used interchangeably for image and print resolution: **dpi** (*dots per inch*), **ppi** (*pixel (or points) per inch*), **lpi** (*lines per inch*). Apart from this, the resolution of an image is stated by its dimensions in pixels or in inches (at a certain ppi or dpi resolution). So let's try to clean-up this mess:

When an image is captured by a camera or scanner, the result is a digital image consisting of an array (rows) of separate picture elements (called pixels). This array has a horizontal and vertical dimension. The horizontal size is defined by the number of pixels in a single row (say 1,280) and the number of rows (say 1,024), giving the image a horizontal orientation. That picture would have a "resolution" of "1,024 × 1,280 pixels" (yes, some years ago, there were digital cameras around with such a resolution).

* A 17″ display is diagonally roughly 17 inches

This is not a physical size yet. You could, for example, display this image on a 17″ display (it would comfortably fill most such displays with each pixel of the image representing one pixel of the LCD monitor). It would probably have a display dimension of roughly 13.3 by 10.6 inches.* If you display this same image on a 19″ monitor, its displayed size would be approximately 14.8 by 11.9 inches.

The size of the image displayed is dependent on the number of pixels the monitor displays per inch. The "pixel per inch" resolutions (ppi) of monitors vary, and are usually in the range of 72 ppi to 120 ppi (the latter, larger 21.4″ monitors). In most cases, however, with monitors the resolution is given as the number of pixels horizontally and vertically (e.g. 1,0240 × 1,280 or 1,280 × 1,600). So the "size" of an image very much depends on how many pixels are displayed per inch. Thus, we come to a resolution given in 'pixels per inch' or ppi for short.

In Europe often "pixel per centimeter" (ppc) is used instead of ppi.

With LCD monitors, their ppi resolution is fixed and can't be adjusted (at least not without a loss of display quality). With CRT monitors you have more flexibility (we won't go into this further).

When an image is printed, its physical size depends upon how many image pixels we put down on paper, but also how an individual image pixel is laid down on the paper.

How image pixels are reproduced by printer dots

There are only a few printing technologies where a printer can directly produce a continuous color range within an individual image pixel printed. Most other types of printers reproduce the color of a pixel in an image by approximating the color by an $n \times n$ matrix of fine dots using a specific pattern and a certain combination of the basic colors available to the printer.**

Printing techniques that can produce continuous tone values are dye-sublimations, rotogravure and lightjet printing

** *These "basic colors" (or inks) of the printer are called 'primary colors'.*

If we want to reproduce a pixel of an image on paper, we not only have to place a physical printer's 'dot' on paper, but also have to give that 'dot' the tonal value of the original pixel. With bitonal images, that is easy. If the pixel value is 0, you lay down a black printed dot, and if the pixel is 1, you omit the dot. However, if the pixel has a gray value (say 128 out of 256), and you print with a black-and-white laser printer (just to make the explanation a bit simpler), we must find a different way. This technique is called *rasterization* or *dithering*.

To simulate different tonal values (let's just stick to black-and-white for the moment), a number of printed dots are placed in a certain pattern on the paper to reproduce a single pixel of the image. In a low-resolution solution, we could use a matrix of 3 printed dots by 3 printed dots per pixel. Using this scheme, we could produce 10 different gray values, as may be seen in Figure 1-1:

"Bi-tonal" means that there are only two colors in your image: pure black and pure white (or any other two colors) but no tonal values in between.

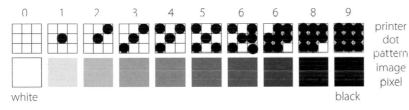

printer dot pattern
image pixel

white   black

◄ *Figure 1-1:*

Different tonal values simulated by a pattern of singe printed dots

Using more printed dots per image pixel allows for more different tonal values. With a pattern of 6 × 6 dots, you get 37 tonal grades, with an 8 × 8 pattern, 257 tonal grades, (which is sufficient). For a better differentiation let's call the matrix of printer dots representing a pixel of the image a *raster cell*.

Now we see why a printer's "dot per inch" (dpi) resolution has to be much higher than the resolution of a display (where a single dot on a screen may be used to reproduce a single pixel in an image, as the individual screen dot (also called a *pixel*) may have different tonal (or brightness) values.

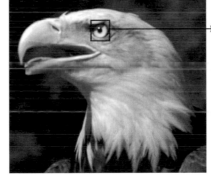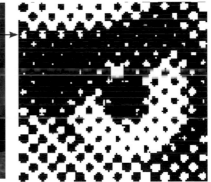

Figure 1-2: Enlarged printing raster of the eagle's eye in a printed image

When you print with a device using relatively low resolution for grayscale or colored images, you must make a trade-off between a high resolution image (having as many "raster cells per inch" as possible) and larger raster cells providing greater tonal value per cell.

The image impression may be improved when the printer is able to vary the size of its dots. This is done on some laser printers,[*] as well as with some of today's photo inkjet printers. If the dot size can be varied (also called *modulated*), fewer numbers of dots (*n* x *n*) are needed to create a certain number of different tonal values, (which results in a finer raster). You may achieve more tonal values from a fixed raster cell size.

* *E.g., HP calls the technique ProRes on laser printers or PhotoREt with inkjet printers.*

There are several different ways (patterns) to place the single printed dots in a raster cell, and the pattern for this dithering is partly a secret of the printer driver. The dithering dot pattern is less visible and more photo-like, when the pattern is not the same for all raster cells having the same tonal values, but is modified from raster cell to raster cell in some random way (this is called *stochastic dithering*).

What are 'lines per inch'?

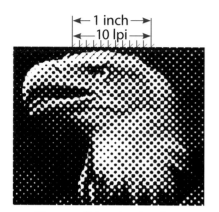

Figure 1-3: Enlarged version of very coarse raster of 10 lines per inch.

Using the technique described here to simulate different tonal pixel values, the rows of dots are not laid down exactly one below the other, rather the rows are slightly offset from one another. The macro-dots form a sort of line across an area. Raster cells and lines are not directly placed adjacent to each other, but have a slight gap (in most cases).

In black color, these lines are normally placed at an angle of 45°. The number of raster cells or lines in one inch (see Figure 1-3) defines another kind of resolution called '*lines per inch*' or lpi for short (using metric names it becomes '*lines per cm*' or 'l/cm' for short). When printing in color, a raster cell not only consists of a single color pattern, but the pattern process is repeated for all the basic (primary) colors found in the print.

Most color printers use cyan, magenta, yellow, and black as their basic colors (also called *primary colors*). Some printers (and almost all inkjet printers, that are titled *photo printers*) use some additional basic colors to achieve a richer color gamut and a finer raster, yet, basically, they use the same scheme as printers using only four basic colors. In color printers, the simulation of tonal values is represented using a pattern of primary colors (see Figure 1-4).

Figure 1-4: ▶

When printing color images tonal values (in inkjet and offset printing) are produced by a dot pattern of tiny colored ink dots. With inkjet printers, this dot pattern is not totally regular, but uses some randomness. This kind of dot pattern is also called 'stochastic pattern'.

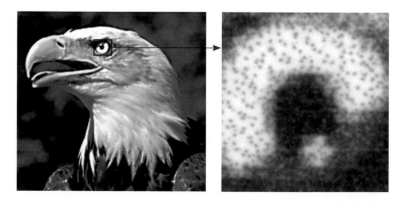

Different basic/primary colors (in a CMYK print there are four primary colors), raster cell lines are printed by using different line angles. In a normal CMYK print, those encountered in most colored books and magazines, cyan is printed at 71.6°, magenta at 18.4°, yellow at 0° and black at 45°. Other combinations are used, as well, but this is the common way to place lines of colored raster cells. To avoid moiré patterns stemming from overlapping rasters, line frequencies of colors vary slightly. Table 1.1 shows an example for a 106 lpi color raster.

	Cyan	Magenta	Yellow	Black
lpi	94,86	94.86	100.0	106.0
angle	71.56°	18.43°	0.0°	45.0°

Table 1.1: Example of a color raster using 106 lpi basic raster frequency

The number of lines per inch of a print depends upon:

1. the number of tonal values one wants (more tonal values require larger macro-dots as more printed dots are required to provide broader tonal values), and

2. the size of the individual printed dot,* and

3. the paper used. If you use newsprint paper, which absorbs a lot of ink, you would use a wider raster cell spacing to avoid the single macro-dots merging into one another. Using coated paper, raster cells may be placed closer together resulting in a finer printing raster and finer image impression.

The smaller the individual printed dot, the smaller the raster cell may be.

Table 1.2 provides a guideline at which resolution in pixels per inch and lines per inch is appropriate for different printing media – if you use a printing technique that works with a fixed raster (for inkjet printers, you don't use a fixed raster but a printer resolution setting in your printer driver or RIP).

Table 1.2: Recommended raster frequency for different printing situations

Raster width		Usage	image resolution
53 lpi	21 l/cm	Laser printer (600 dpi, 65 grey levels)	70–110 ppi
70 lpi	27 l/cm	Newspaper print, typical rough paper	90–140 ppi
90 lpi	35 l/cm	Good quality newspaper print	140–180 ppi
120 lpi	47 l/cm	Acceptable quality for books and magazines. Raster cells points can still be seen.	160–240 ppi
133 lpi	52 l/cm	Good quality for books and magazines. Raster cells points can still be seen.	170–265 ppi
150 lpi	59 l/cm	Good offset or silk printing, individual raster point may hardly be recognized	195–300 ppi
180 lpi	70 l/cm	Good offset and silk printing, very fine raster, individual raster point hardly recognizable; good inkjet printing, individual raster point no longer recognizable at a reading distance of 20–30 cm (9–12 inches)	250–360 ppi
200 lpi	79 l/cm	Very good book prints, you need a very smooth paper for printing. Raster cells points hardly recognizable.	300–400 ppi

When you use an inkjet printer for fine art printing, you do not have to concern yourself much with raster line width. The dithering pattern of your printer driver is more complex than just described. Don't worry. Learn the native printing resolution of your specific inkjet printer – usually between 240–360 ppi and scale (up- or upsize) your image to that size. The values do not have to be precise – close is good enough. In most cases, the printer driver (or Photoshop) will do the proper scaling when using a value close to the printer's native resolution. Using a modern inkjet printer, you need not bother much with color raster angles. This, too, is taken care of by the printer driver or the RIP. Inkjet drivers do not offer settings for raster width or color raster angles. For offset printing, however, this may (in very few situations) be of interest and may be dealt with in Photoshop when separating colors.

Printing using RIPs is described in more details in Chapter 6.

How many pixels or dots per inch do you really need?

There is no quick, general answer to that question. It depends on several factors:

▶ **Type of printing technique used:**
Are you using a continuous-tone printing method (such as lightjet or dye-sublimation printing) or a method that produces halftones by dithering (such as inkjet or offset printing)?

The ppi values you need will be roughly the same for both methods. However, the dpi values of the printers will have to change, as in dithering you need several printer points (or ink droplets) to build up a raster cell reproducing a pixel of the image.

▶ **Type of paper used:**
If you use a rough, absorptive paper (e. g., as used in common newspapers), printed dots will bleed a bit and you must reduce the dots per inch frequency (as indicated in table 1.2).[*] If you use a good, smooth-coated paper, you may increase your resolution and get a finer, more detailed image.

* The slightly increasing of the dot size caused by the bleeding is called 'dot gain'.

If you use glossy or luster paper, you will be able to reproduce even more details (allowing for higher ppi/dpi) than with matte paper or canvas.

▶ **Viewing distance:**
Viewing distance is an important factor, as the human eye can only differentiate single points up to a certain viewing angle (about 0.01–0.02°). If the viewing angle is less, two separate points can no longer be differentiated and visually merge. For a 'normal reading distance' of about 12 inches (30 cm), this minimal size is about 0.08 mm (0.0032 inch). Bright light may reduce this size a bit, low light increase it a bit. Consequently for an A4/letter-sized photo, a pixel size or raster cell size of 0.08 mm is a good value (equivalent to a 300 ppi raster size). If the

pixel size is smaller, visual image quality (in terms of visual differentiation of details) will not substantially improve.

If the photo is of ledger/A3 size, viewing distance is usually increased (in order to see the whole image at a glance). Thus for A3/ledger, the pixel size (or cell size if we use a dithering method), may increase the (raster) point size to 0,122 mm or about 210 ppi.

If you produce posters, the viewing distance will increase further, and the pixel size may increase accordingly (and the ppi may decrease accordingly). If you move up to large-format printing, your ppi may even go as low as 10–20 ppi. The viewing distance will usually be more than 10 yards (or meters). In a simplified formula, simply divide 300 into your viewing distance in feet and you have the required ppi value or:

$$resolution \text{ (in ppi)} = \frac{300}{viewing\ distance \text{ (in feet)}}$$

For this reason, a photo shot with a 12 megapixel camera may be enlarged to almost any size you want **if the image is viewed from the appropriate viewing distance.**

▶ **Type of printer** driver, driver **settings and interpolation used:**
For optimal results, you should use a ppi value close or even exactly that of the printer's native resolution. The printer's native resolution varies from manufacturer to manufacturer. Epson inkjet printers, for example, usually have a 'native resolution' of 720 ppi, while most HP inkjet printer use 600 ppi. Canon inkjets usually use 600 ppi, as well.

Do you really need an image resolution as high as stated? It contradicts a statement given before. Well, yes and no. For optimal results with an Epson inkjet printer, use either 720 ppi or 360 ppi; for an HP printer, either 600 ppi or 300 ppi.*

You may leave (automatic) scaling either to Photoshop (as part of the print dialog) or to the printer driver. However, in both cases, you really can't know exactly which algorithms are used for scaling and how well those algorithms will work with your image and your scaling factor (Photoshop will use the scaling algorithm you set in your basic Photoshop Preferences).

If your image is close to the native resolution given above (at the size you intend to print the image), the algorithm will not matter too much. If, however, the image has to be upsized or upsized considerably, the scaling algorithm does matter (it will also influence the effect of sharpening done for printing). In this case, you should either scale an image before calling up the print dialog (and you may have to do this for each individual printing size of the image) or you may use a RIP (see Chapter 6).

If you do your scaling in Photoshop, we recommend "Bicubic Smoother" for up-sizing and "Bicubic Sharper" for down-sizing.**

* Here, we assume, no further scaling is necessary.

** If you leave the sizing to Photoshop (via the Print with Preview dialog), Photoshop will use the upsizing method that was selected in your Preferences settings (Prefereneces ▶ General ▶ General).

1.2   Offset printing

Technically (as well as concerning ICC profiles), you differentiate between sheet fed offset printing and web offset printing. With the latter, the paper comes from a paper roll instead of separate sheets of paper. The basic printing technique however, is the same for both kinds of systems.

Offset printing is the technique used for most books, brochures, magazines, and newspapers. It is plate-based printing. The image is rasterized – as described under "*Basic printing techniques*" – for the print and transferred onto a printing plate. This projection currently is done with lasers or LED arrays. First, a plate is coated with a light-sensitive layer. The laser inscribes the image pattern onto this layer. Then, the printing plate is chemically developed. Those parts of the plate not printed are smooth and do not pick up water and ink when passing the wetting roller ①. When printing, the parts to be printed are rougher and pick up ink when passing an ink-soaked roller ②. This ink-pattern is transferred (by offset) to another rubber-coated rotating cylinder ④ (this is why the printing technique is called "offset printing"). The paper to be printed passes between this rubber cylinder and another roller ⑤ pressing the paper against the rubber cylinder. Thus, ink is transferred onto the paper and the image is also transferred. In color printing, this process is repeated in additional printing units – one for each primary color (normally C, M, Y, and K).

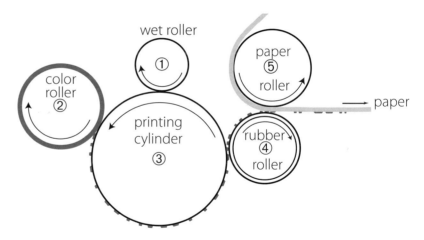

Figure 1-5: ▶
Functional model of offset printing (traditional analog offset printing)

The image quality achieved with this technology is quite good in terms of resolution and longevity – provided a good, coated, acid-free paper is used and the image is viewed from a correct (reading) distance. The richness of the color gamut is clearly below that of good photo inkjet printing (see Figure 1-6).

The gamut of an offset print may be enhanced if six rather than the normal four (CMYK) inks are used. Printing with six inks is also called *hexachrome printing* (in addition to CMYK, green and orange are used). This, however, requires special printing presses having additional print units. Hexachrome printing is far more expensive than CMYK (4C or 4-color) printing, and also requires a special color separation process and special plug-ins for Photoshop to prepare images or DTP documents).

Traditional offset printing might be considered if you intend to make a print run of 1,000 or more copies. As few, if any, home-users or small offices can justify printing equipment for offset printing, we will not discuss it any further (additionally, we have a very limited knowledge of the techniques involved).

In recent years, digital offset printing has come onto the market (e.g. HP Indigo press). These systems work with printing techniques similar to that of laser printers. These digital offset printers are mainly used for smaller print runs (typically 50–1,000). With most models, the maximum print size is restricted to A4 or A3. The resolution of digital offset printing is greatly inferior to that of analog offset printing (e.g. HP Indigo press 5000 has a resolution of 812 × 812 dpi, while analog offset printers work with typically 2,400 × 2,400 or even 3,200 × 3,200 dpi). Printing photos, this leads to a visible reduction of image quality. As for color gamut, some digital offset printers exceed the gamut of traditional CYMK offset presses. They, however, are still inadequate for high-quality fine art prints.

Traditional offset printers, as well as digital offset printers are quite fast. HP, for example, gives a printing rate of about 4,000 A4 pages per hour for its HP Indigo press 5000. The speed of traditional offset printing presses may exceed 100,000 pages per hour.

The costs of digital offset printers starts at about $50,000 US and up. The price of a traditional offset press may easily exceed one million dollars.

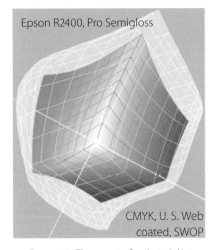

Epson R2400, Pro Semigloss

CMYK, U. S. Web coated, SWOP

Figure 1-6: The gamut of a photo inkjet printer (gray cover) is larger than the gamut with traditional analog offset printing (colored form).

1.3   Laser printers

Laser printers are well established, reasonably fast (from four pages per minute up to 100 pages per minute) and reasonably inexpensive for the cost per page (typically about 4–6 cents per A4/Letter page in black-and-white at an ink coverage of 5% per page and about 16–20 cents at an ink coverage of 90% per page). While color laser printers were quite expensive formerly, in 2004 and 2005 their price dropped dramatically. You can buy a color laser printer for less than $500 US currently. With low-priced color laser printers, manufacturers use a business model similar to low-cost inkjet printers: they sell inexpensive printers and earn their return via rather expensive toner units. A color toner set – lasting for about 3,000–5,000 pages at 5% medium ink page coverage – costs about the same as the basic laser printer unit ($300–$400 US), resulting in a cost per page (A4/letter) of roughly $0.1 US with a 5% medium ink coverage per page and about $1.6 US when printing full page size colored images. Nevertheless, printing of text and graphic pages with a color laser printer is much faster and somewhat cheaper than using an inkjet printer.

Laser printers use very much the same technique (see Figure 1-7) used by modern photocopy systems (some models even combine both functions: scanning and printing).

A photo drum ① is charged positively by a charging unit ②. The image of the print is rasterized by the printer's RIP (*Raster Image Processor*), and this raster is applied onto a drum using a laser beam and rotating mirror ③ (or alternatively by an array of LEDs). Where the light hits the drum, the positive charge is erased or the surface is charged negatively. Then, the drum passes the toner unit ④. Those parts that saw light pick up the positively charged toner, while those parts that bear a positive charge reject the toner. Further on, the toner is transfused onto the paper and burned in by a heated roller (fuser) ⑤. Instead of a laser and a rotating mirror, some printers use an array of LEDs for discharging the drum.

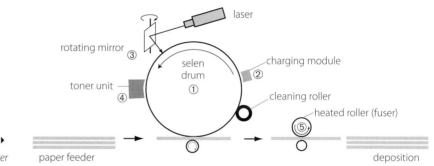

Figure 1-7: ▶
Functional model of a laser printer

Color laser printers use four inks – cyan, magenta, yellow, and black (CMYK). They either use four drums or a transfer belt that picks up toner from four separate drum rotations and four toner units and transfers the complete color image onto the paper with one rotation.

As for image quality, the limiting factor of today's color laser printers is the resolution used (600–2,400 dpi, usually just 600 or 1,200 dpi) and the number of colors they use – which is only four (CMYK). A further limitation stems from the size of the toner particles, much larger than those of dye-based or even pigment-based inks on inkjet printers.

Most laser printers have problems producing homogeneously colored areas or fine tonal gradients (you usually see smaller blotches of unevenly printed colors). With several of the color laser printers, the image shows a gloss, which may impair viewing with some images. You cannot avoid the gloss even when using matte papers. This is especially true for solid inks used by some XEROX color laser printers.

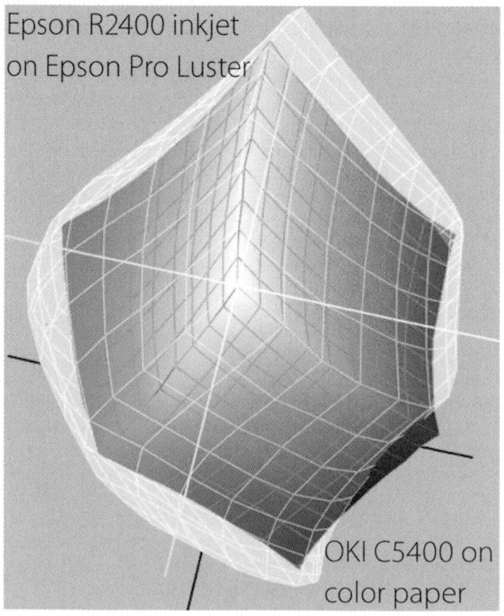

For this reason, image quality with color laser printers is clearly inferior to all other printing methods described here and can't touch that of photo inkjet printers. If, however, you have a color laser printer, we recommend using it for fast index printing. The color and detail quality, in most cases, is good enough for a first, fast inspection.

Image longevity very much depends on the type of paper and inks (toner) used and ranges from about 10 to 20 years. The permanence of black-and-white prints is much better, and may be used for archiving documents (provided you use the appropriate paper).

Figure 1-8: Gamut comparison of a color laser printer (OKI C5400) (inner colored figure) and a photo inkjet printer (Epson R2400, using Epson Pro Luster paper, outer gray cover).

1.4 **Dye-sublimation printers**

Thermo-sublimation printers are frequently used for the fast and simple production of photographic prints, often directly from the digital camera via a USB cable using the DPOF (*Digital Print Order Format*) or PictBridge protocol supported by today's digital cameras – even the cheaper consumer models. Alternatively, you may plug your camera's memory card into a card-slot the printer provides.

With thermo-sublimation printing (also called *dye-sublimation* or *dye-sub* for short), color is transferred from a color-coated ribbon (foil) onto the paper. The transfer is done by an array of tiny heating elements (integrated into the print head). Where the ribbon is heated, the color on the foil evaporates (sublimates) and enters the paper where it cools down. CMY as well as CMYK ribbons are used. Three or four passes (or sections) of colored ribbons are needed to produce a complete image on the paper. Usually the ribbon consists of sections with the alternating basic colors (three for CMY or four for CMYK). The used portion of a ribbon becomes unusable, is rolled up and finally discarded. The paper must make three (CMY) or four (CMYK) passes under the print head. Individual color intensity is determined by the amount of heat. When the next primary color is added (to those colors previously composed of several primary colors), their colors merge into a combined color due to the heat. The three or four colors merge in the paper and form an (almost) continuously toned color.

With these systems, production costs are independent of the number and kinds of colors and the amount of color a printed page has, as a ribbon section is used only once and then discarded.

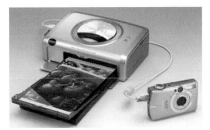

Figure 1-10: *Canon SELPHY CP600 dye-sublimation printer, 300 dpi, print-size up to 10 x 20 cm, (Courtesy Canon Germany)*

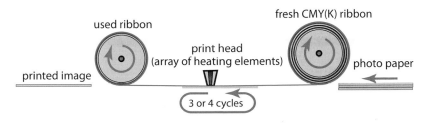

◀ Figure 1-9:
Working scheme of a thermo-sublimation printer

The typical resolution of dye-sublimation printers is 240–300 dpi, which sounds very low. However, keep in mind that dye-sub printers do not render a color via dithering, but do it by merging their basic colors by sublimation, thus achieving an (almost) continuous color tonal range for every dot and a highly photographic image at these resolutions.

Typical dye-sub printers today range from 4 × 6 inch to A4 in print size, the lower-cost models (partly portable) are mainly in the 4 × 6 inches (10 × 15 cm) range. A typical print speed is about 30–100 seconds for a 4 × 6 inch photo. Some printers are much faster (e.g. Kodak Photo Printer 6850, 300 dpi, 8 sec. for 4 × 6 inch).

The range of printing material used with dye-subs is very limited and highly restricted to papers provided by the manufacturer of the printer – one kind for glossy and another kind for matte paper, in most cases. The same is true for inks (color ribbons).

The lightfastness and longevity of dye-sub prints is about five to fifteen years (considerably more in dark storage).

Prices for small dye-sub printers start at about $ 120 US and go higher with print/printer size; about $ 500–$ 1,500 US for a letter/A4 size printer. The cost per print is about $0.20–$0.30 for a 4 × 6 inch print and about $ 1.5–$ 2.5 for an A4/letter-sized print.

1.5 Lightjet printing (digital photo print)

* LightJet is a trade name of Cymbolic Science, nowadays a subsidery of Océ.

There are various names for this technique: *digital photo print* or *lightjet printing** or *direct digital printing* or *direct photo printing*. Here, in essence, the image is imposed onto conventional photographic material by lasers. To produce an RGB print, three lasers are used. The material may be photographic paper also used for traditional color photos or may be photographic film for translucent prints. The exposed material is then developed in a traditional wet process. The resolution used by most printers is either 300 dpi (or ppi) or 400 dpi. Lower resolutions may be used, as well, and will be interpolated to the printers native resolution. This seems very low, compared to the resolution of inkjet printers or offset presses. With lightjet printing, however, no dithering is required to produce halftones, and every exposed dot on the paper combines red, green, and blue, thus resulting in (almost) continuous tone dots. For this reason, 400 dpi or even 300 dpi will produce a very fine image quality.

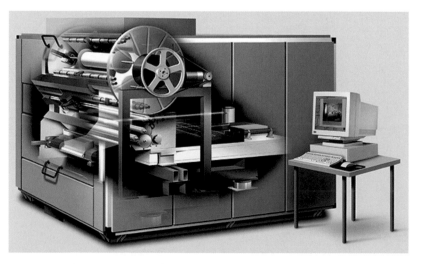

Figure 1-11: ▶
Durst Lambda® large-format photo laser
imager
(Courtesy Durst Phototechnik AG, Brixen, Italy)

There are a number of different makers and models of this type of digital photo printer (e.g. Fuji Frontier minlab, Agfa D-Lab, Lambda, Océ LightJet®,

Chromira). Print image size may vary from 4 × 6 inch up to 50 × 50 inches). With some digital photographic printers, you may even go much larger (e.g. the Durst Lambda photo laser imager may produced prints up to a width of 50 inches and a length of 262 feet).

As lightjet printers are quite expensive,* this technique is almost exclusively used by service shops – often the very largest ones.

* They start from about $ 100,000 US and may go up even higher.

There are two kinds of photographic print shops:

1. **Consumer-oriented photographic print shops**
   They produce a very large quantity of prints per day at very low prices (typically from 15 cents for a 4 × 7 inch print to about $5 US for a letter-sized print). The processing is done fully automatically and in large quantities. Special requests are usually not handled by these shops. In most cases, an automatic image optimization is performed. This may be disabled at most shops when you place an order, which you should do if you have done your own optimization.

   The quality of their prints is usually quite reasonable and uniform, in most cases.

   Currently, ICC profiles are ignored by these printers; all images are assumed to be in sRGB. If you send an image to them for processing, you should convert it to sRGB (if not already in this format).

   Most of these shops offer only standard image formats. If your image format differs from those supported, you have the option of using either the full width with some parts of the image being trimmed off or receive an image with white borders – which, for fine art prints, may be what you want, anyway. In most cases, it is preferable to set your image to one of their standard formats and decide where and what kind of white frame (or other colored frame) you wish to use.

2. **Professional photographic service bureaus**
   They specialize in high quality prints (usually in smaller quantities), also accommodating special requests. They may even offer to optimize your image for printing, which may or may not be appropriate. These bureaus should provide you with a printer's ICC profile (often, you may download this from their Web home-page). These profiles may be used for two purposes:

   A) Use as soft-proofing to assess how your image will appear when printed.

   For soft-proofing see Chapter 3.10.

   B) To convert your image to another profile. When you send your images to a service bureau, the image should be converted to the correct profile as other embedded profiles are ignored by the printing process. This hopefully will change in the future!

Print permanence of digital photographic prints is the same as that of photographic paper (silver-halide color prints), which typically range from

17 years (e.g., Konica Minolta QA Paper Impressa) to 40 years (e.g., Fuji Crystal Archive paper), depending on the kind of paper used. All these data assume that all the chemical residues are removed from the photographic papers. If not, its lifetime will be substantially reduced.

Most shops offer three to four kinds of paper (glossy, semigloss, pearl, and matte). As standard photographic papers may be used for printing, there is sometimes a choice of several papers from different suppliers. For higher quality, often Fuji Crystal Archive paper is used due to its high print permanence.

Some digital photo printers allow printing on transparent and translucent photographic film.

Print speed is quite fast – at least compared to inkjet printers. The Océ LightJet 5000, for example, prints a 50" × 50" print at 405 dpi in about 12 minutes.

The Color gamut of modern lightjet printers is about that of Adobe RGB (1998) (slightly larger).

If you want to produce many prints of the same image with the papers offered and their lightfastness (print permanence) sufficient for your purpose, lightjet prints ordered via the Internet may be an easy and cost-effective way to go.

It is best to start with a test order, and only order more if the results are satisfactory. While you may have your pictures the next day with consumer photographic print shops (at least in Europe, where even snail mail is reasonably fast), prints from a professional service bureau usually take three to five days, plus delivery time.

While most photo services will even print black-and-white prints on C4 paper (photo paper designed for color prints), there are a few pure black-and-white papers available nowadays for lightjet printing. They will probably result in better neutral prints. If your service provider only offers C4 paper, make sure that the system is well (neutral) calibrated – otherwise you may get an undesired color cast in your black-and-white prints. It is best to try the service with a small black-and-white print first.

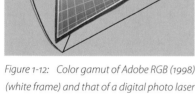

Figure 1-12: Color gamut of Adobe RGB (1998) (white frame) and that of a digital photo laser printer (Océ LightJet 5000) (colored frame)

1.6   Inkjet printing

Having taken a glance at other printing techniques, we want to dig deeper into inkjet printing. While some techniques mentioned are rather old, inkjet printing is rather young. The first color inkjet printers came to the market in about 1985. Compared to today's inkjet printers, they were very slow and showed extremely poor image quality. They were used largely to render simple color plots and production of transparencies for presentations. Print permanence of that first generation of color inkjet printers was quite poor.

Soon, however, some specialized high-end printers came on the market. The IRIS printer – made by IRIS Graphics of Bedford, Massachusetts (later acquired by Scitex) – was one such machine. The IRIS printer, at an early stage of inkjet history, provided a reasonably high print speed and considerable resolution and image quality, while print permanence and maintenance were problems. Prints produced by IRIS printers are sometimes called *Giclée prints.*

A very nice page of Harold Johnson on Giclée prints may be found on www.dpandi.com/giclee/.

Along with the growth of the PC and Macintosh markets, the need for inkjet printers grew, and today you scarcely find a home PC without an inkjet printer, their cost dropping from several thousands of dollars US to about 150–800 dollars (depending on the maximum print size) for quite acceptable desktop photo inkjet printers. For large-format inkjet printers (those beyond a print size of A3+/Super B), you will have to spend several thousand dollars.

Inkjet technology

There are a number of different inkjet technologies in use. The basis of all of them is that tiny ink droplets are ejected from a printhead and projected onto a paper. To increase print speed, a printhead now consists of many nozzles – up to about 180–500 per color on contemporary printers.

The technique making the ink droplets eject differs with various printers and printer makers (most printer manufacturers use a single technique in all machines).

The main techniques are:

▸ Continuous flow inkjet printers

The following methods are also called *drop-on-demand*, as they eject a droplet only when needed on the paper:

▸ Thermal inkjet printers (e.g., used by most HP and Canon printers). Canon calls this technique *bubble-jet.*

▸ Piezoelectric inkjet printers (e.g., used by most Epson printers)

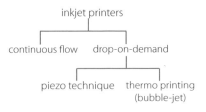

Classification of inkjet printer techniques

Continuous flow inkjet

This technique was developed by IBM in the 1970s. With continuous ink flow systems, a continuous stream of charged ink droplets is produced. Those droplets intended to print fly straight onto the paper, while charged droplets are electronically deflected into a gutter for recirculation. This is the oldest inkjet technology and is used for high-speed production lines. The complex ink-circulation system makes these printers costly in maintenance. They can be very fast compared with the typical drop-on-demand type printers.

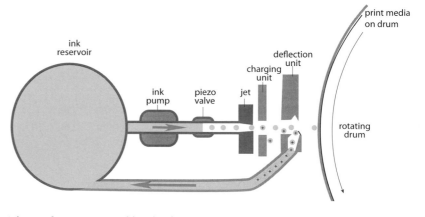

Figure 1-13: ▶

Principle ink flow in a continuous flow inkjet printer

This technique is used by the famous IRIS inkjet printer, where the paper is mounted on a rotating drum. These systems are quite expensive and not suited for desktop usage or smaller installations. Usually solvent-based inks are used with these printers.

Piezo inkjet

Certain kinds of crystals expand or contract when subjected to an electrical charge. This piezoelectric effect is used in certain inkjet printers. To eject a droplet, a voltage is applied to the crystal in the print head, the crystal deflects inward, forcing a droplet out of the nozzle. The returning deflection pulls fresh ink from the reservoir, and the cycle repeats. A print head consists of many of these miniature jets (nozzles), and the system allows variations in the size of droplets to produce a finer pattern and smoother color gradients.

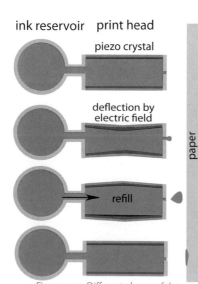

Figure 1-14: Different phases of the ejection of a droplet with a piezo print head

Thermal inkjet

With thermal inkjet printing – also called bubble-jet printing – there is a resistor in the print head chamber. When it is heated by a short pulse of electrical current, a vapor bubble forms in the chamber increasing pressure. This pressure forces an ink droplet out of the nozzle. Then the bubble collapses and draws in more ink from the reservoir. For the next droplet, the cycle repeats. This technique is used by some HP printers (e.g. HP Designjet 30), as well as by most Canon printers (e.g. Canon i9900, W6200). Also some wide-format printers like the HP Designjet 130 and the ENCAD Novajet 1000i use thermal print heads. The technique may be used with dye-based, as well as pigment-based inks, however, it does require an ink suited for thermal inkjet printing (with a low boiling point). The life-cycle of these printers is a bit shorter than that of piezo-based print heads, but the production cost is lower.

Droplet size

Along with increasing printer resolution, the size of the individual ink droplets has decreased. A smaller droplet allows production of a finer raster of dots on the paper. Today, photo printers use a droplet size down to 1–5 picoliter (1 picoliter is 0.000 000 000 001 liter or 1×10^{-12} liter), thus allowing a single pixel (a raster cell) of the image to be built by many tiny dots, achieving a fine raster (e.g. 360 ppi or even 600 ppi) with a broad range of tonal values.

With some photo inkjet printers (e.g., with piezo-based ones) the droplet size can vary. For dark colors – especially colors of a primary ink color – larger droplet sizes are used. This allows increasing print speed. For light colors, a smaller droplet size and wider droplet spacing is used.

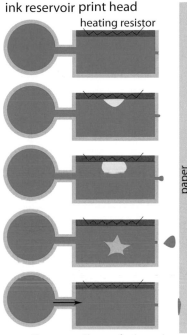

ink reservoir print head

heating resistor

paper

Figure 1-15: Phases of a thermal inkjet printer

Printer resolution

When inkjet printers first arrived, a resolution of 150 dots per inch was considered good. Today, resolutions of 2,400 dpi, 4,800 dpi, 5,800 dpi, and even 9,600 dpi are normal for photo printers. Please do not be mislead by these advertising claims, as they refer to resolution only in one direction, e.g., horizontal. Canon's i9950 photo printer has a maximum resolution of 4,800 x 2,400 dpi, where the higher resolution is seen in the horizontal direction (achieved by the horizontally moving print head) and the lower resolution in the vertical direction. Here, the increments are determined by the step motor that moves the paper. The same is true for most inkjet printers.

Before you invest your money in one of these high-resolution printers, consider carefully whether you actually need the maximum resolution advertised by these printers. To take advantage of a manufacturer's maximum resolution, you need a paper or other printing medium that can accommodate the fine pattern of ink droplets, so the ink will not bleed noticeably into the open area. The paper (or its coating) must absorb ink very quickly to keep it localized. Ensure your paper can accommodate the resolution you wish to use.

We have found that a horizontal resolution of 1,400 dpi or 2,800 dpi, both of which are typical for Epson printers, is sufficient, even for fine art

➜ *Please do not confuse the 'printer resolution' – given in 'dots per inch' (dpi) – and the resolution of the image sent to the printer (the latter given in pixel per inch – ppi). The printing resolution has to be much higher as inkjet printers produce halftones using a pattern of single dots and need several of these dots to simulate the halftone of a single image pixel in paper.*

prints. For higher resolutions, the print speed decreases dramatically and ink usage increases, neither of which result in noticeably better image quality. Of course, print speed and ink usage can vary among different printers, even from the same manufacturer.

Number of inks

"light cyan" and "light magenta" are also called "photo cyan" and "photo magenta".

While inkjet printers originally used a single black ink, three more inks (CMY) were added to produce what we now take for granted as the norm: CMYK. All of today's photo inkjet printers use at least six inks: CcMmYK (c = light cyan, m = light magenta).

To enhance the color gamut of these printers, more inks are often used. Epson's Stylus Photo R1800, for instance, uses Red and Blue (and, optionally, a gloss optimizer) but has no Light Cyan nor Light Magenta. Epson's R2400 uses three shades of black inks: a Photo Black (or alternatively Matte Black), a *Light Black,* as well as a *Light Light Black,* in addition to the CcMmYK, thus adding up to eight inks. This latter collection of inks produces neutral black-and-white prints with very fine tonal gradients.

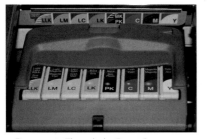

Figure 1-16: Though the Epson R2400 may use 9 different inks, only 8 cartridges may be in place at any point of time. You may either have 'Photo Black' (OK) or 'Matte Black' (MK) in place.

The color gamut and print permanence of today's professional and semi-professional inkjet prints now surpasses that of traditional silver-halide photographic prints, although there are some weak spots: e.g., saturated blue and red. For this reason, the number of different inks used in a fine art printer will likely increase to 11, with the addition of R, B and a gloss optimizer.

In 2006, Canon announced its "PIXMA Prograf iPF 5000". This printer accommodates 12 single inks: CcMmYK plus RGB plus *Light Black* and *Light Light Black.* For Black there is a *Photo Black* and a *Matte Black* (all in the printer at the same time). This 17" printer uses pigment inks.

Practically, though, the number of inks that may be used is limited by the size and weight of the print heads, and the cost of the numerous ink cartridges.

Type of inks

Two different types of inks are mainly used in today's normal inkjet printers:

For more details on dye-based and pigment-based inks, see Chapter 2.

▸ dye-based
▸ pigment-based

There are, however, several other types of inks on the market, e.g., inks with an oil base that are primarily for large-scale printing and weatherized and/ or ruggedized prints for outdoor use. Other inks are formulated for printing on fabric, and are usually solvent based. Some printers use hybrid inks: dye-based for colors, and pigment-based for black to achieve a dark, deep black, a technique used by some Canon printers.

1.7   Other printing techniques

Other printing techniques available for fine art printing include: screen printing or silk-screen printing. Solid-ink printing (used by some Xerox Phaser printers), thermoautochrome printing, and various other techniques. Unfortunately, these methods are not practical for home-based printing, because they are expensive, involve large equipment, and are time consuming. Rather they are better suited to a service bureau, especially when producing a large number of prints of the same image or producing very large prints. In these cases, you should ask the service bureau for specific details on how to prepare your images for printing.

1.8   How to pick your fine art printer

The inkjet printer market continues to grow. With so many viable choices, how do you pick a suitable printer for your needs?

Though it may appear trivial, the first question is: what do you intend to do with your printer? We assume it's for fine art printing or high-quality printing.

First, let's define the requirements for fine art printing:

- ▸ High to very high image quality
- ▸ Rich color gamut
- ▸ Reasonable print permanence (more than 25 years)
- ▸ Two or more tints of black inks for optimal black-and-white prints
- ▸ Adequate print size and print performance
- ▸ Costs

Image quality

When photos are printed, you should achieve a clearly photographic image, provided you use the proper paper, e.g. Glossy. Tonal gradients should be smooth and should show no banding or posterization. The individual pixel (raster cell) should not be visible at a proper viewing distance. Almost all of today's photo inkjet printers with print resolutions greater than 1,200 dpi and having more than the four basic inks (CMYK) achieve this goal.

Rich color gamut

A color gamut is the spectrum of colors a particular printer can produce. Dye-based inks tend to provide a larger range than do those which are pigment based. The manufacturers of pigment-based inkjet printers try to compensate for this by employing new ink formulas. Epson, for example, in 2005, with its K3 inks, reached its third generation of UltraChrome ink. Additionally, colors beyond the basic CMYK sets are often used to expand the color palette. Most of them use at least six inks: CMYK, c (light cyan) and m (light magenta). Some add red and blue, others add several shades of black. As stated earlier, we will probably see printers using both CcMmYKRB and two to four black variations. In fact, the race appears to have started in February 2006, when Canon announced their new printer model PROGRAF iPF 5000 would come with 12 inks: C c M m Y, R G B, Photo Black, Matte Black, Gray and Photo Gray.

With new ink formulas and more colors in use, the gamut difference between dye-based and pigment-based inks virtually vanishes. You may enhance the achievable gamut by using bright white glossy papers, which produces the maximum gamut. These papers are available for both kinds of printers and most, if not all, available inks.

It's very difficult to interpret gamut size from the technical specification of a printer. If the last bit of gamut size really matters, you will have to compare ICC profiles provided by the printer manufacturer.[*] There are also hundreds of custom profiles available from fine art printing professionals like Bill Atkinson and Joseph Holmes, both pioneers in the relatively new field of fine art printing using inkjet printers.

In almost all cases, you can download profiles from each manufacturer's Web site. However, these profiles only cover the manufacturers own ink and papers.

Black-and-white printing

To produce good black-and-white or monochrome images, look for a printer with at least two shades of black ink, or use a good RIP like The QuadTone RIP or ImagePrint, both of which allow you to compensate somewhat for fewer black inks. For some printers, there are also multi-tone black-ink sets. For the Epson 2100/2200, for one example, a number of multi-tone black-ink sets are on the market.[**] Before switching from color to black inks for monochrome printing, you must carefully clean your print heads. Ideally, a printer using multiple black inks in its original set would be preferred. The Epson R2400, using three different black inks (Black, Light Black and Light Light Black) or the HP 8450 and 8750, also using three black/gray inks, are examples of printers well suited for black-and-white printing.

With the introduction of printers using several shades of black ink, the use of third-party, multi-tone ink sets decreases. If the printer uses two or three toned black inks, its printer driver provided by the OEM usually has special settings for black-and-white printing.

You will find more on RIPs in Chapter 6 and more on black-and-white printing in Chapter 7.

** e.g., MIS Ultra Tone family of inks [59] and Piezography Neutral K7 inks [45] or Luminos [47]

Canon too offers several inkjet printers using three black inks – e.g., the 'Pixma Pro 9500 Photo' and the 'imagePROGRAF 5000'.

Print permanence

A print should last for a reasonable time without noticeable degradation of color or density. So, what is reasonable? This answer may vary greatly depending on your own expectations and what you hope to do with the print.

According to our definition, the print should have, at a minimum, a print permanence of at least 25 years, depending on how it will be used and displayed. If you intend to sell your prints, especially to serious collectors,

20 years may not be long enough. Fifty years or even 100 years is considered the minimum time for museum-quality prints, so perhaps you should consider this metric. You must define your own expectations, however.

You will find more on print permanence in Chapter 2.1.

Adequate print size and print performance

To create the most striking and lasting impression, a print must be displayed at an optimum size. While most desktop printers offer a maximum size of A4/Letter, fine art printing demands a minimum size of A3/Ledger. For some prints, especially for exhibitions, larger formats may be needed. Since larger-format printers tend to be a bit pricey, you might consider something in between, say, a printer that produces prints up to 13" or 17" wide. These are relatively affordable, even for many home-based printing aficionados, and may save you countless trips to the neighborhood print shop. If larger prints are, in fact, your bent, then perhaps the print shop is your best bet. Before choosing, though, analyze your true needs and wishes, then decide whether to purchase your own printer or have someone else do the printing for you.

Types of papers supported

Not every printer can adequately accommodate every type of paper. You must carefully match the paper to the printer, considering the following items: size, ink, and paper thickness. While size is obvious, the other two factors may not be. Most printers can only accommodate paper up to a maximum thickness and flexibility. You can find this information in the technical specifications. Maximum media thickness is largely influenced by the path through the printer the paper will travel. The Epson R2400, for example, provides three different paper paths: the normal one, from the top; a second one, using rear-feeding; and a third one, where the paper is pulled in from the front and pushed out at the front again. This last method allows a paper thickness of up to 0.06 inch (1.6 mm). HP's Designjet 30, in comparison, allows only a maximum thickness of 0.02 inch (0.4 mm).

Using these two printers as examples, let's take a further look at paper compatibility. With the HP solution, you are restricted only to HP specialty papers, according to the technical specifications. Lightfastness of HP papers is about 65–130 years for black-and-white prints. Using different papers, print longevity may be shorter. For the dye-based inks of the HP DJ 30, you must use a special swellable paper when print permanence is an issue.* For fine art printing, this is always an issue. This may not be a severe restriction, as HP offers a number of different and reasonably priced papers for this line of printers.

* *For more on swellable paper see Chapter 2.3, page 41.*

With the Epson R2400 (and printers of the same line), using pigmented inks, your choice of papers is greater. Apart from many Epson papers, there is a variety of other third-party papers to use with this printer and its inks. Using pigment-based inks, you do have greater freedom when choosing papers.

Some printers also accommodate roll paper, which reduces paper cost, and may become more important when you want to print panoramas or long flyers. When using roll paper, an automatic cutter is a necessary advantage, although these are primarily available for larger-scale printers.

A printer's ink set also must be correctly matched to the desired paper. There are inks better suited for glossy and semigloss, while other inks work better for matte paper. To accommodate these differences, some modern photo printers allow switching some inks on the fly, however, it is usually only the black ink cartridges. Perhaps in the future all printers will simply have more cartridges preinstalled, instead of having to switch them physically for different paper types.

So, for example, the Epson R800/R1800 using UltraChrome Hi-Gloss inks and an additional gloss optimizer targets gloss, semigloss and luster papers, and is less suited for matte papers or canvas. You may, however, use either Photo Black (on gloss or semigloss) or Matte Black, depending on the type of paper used. If you print matte, velvet or watercolor papers, the Epson R2400 is the better choice, although you may use either Photo Black for gloss or semigloss, or Matte Black on matte papers.

See Chapter 2-2 for more on this.

In general, dye-based inks are better suited for glossy paper, while pigment-based inks print better on matte papers.[*]

Costs

There are three categories of costs to consider:

▸ The price of the printer
▸ Paper costs
▸ Operational costs, e.g., for inks, print heads, etc.

In printing, the price of the printer is often a minor cost. Paper costs vary greatly depending on the size, type and brand of paper used and the quantity you buy. Generally, the price of an A4/letter size page will be $1–$2 and for an A3/leger size page will be $2–$4 for good-quality fine art paper.

In Chapter 2.3, page 49/50 we name a few papers we tested and liked. Some papers that give a fine print for black-and-white printing are listed in Chapter 7.4, page 190/191.

It's possible to find a cheaper, third-party, in-house paper at Staples or Office Max, but you must consider whether they provide profiles for their papers, or if they offer a lightfastness statement. Probably not. With papers for fine art printing it's best to use inkjet papers from suppliers with a proven track record.

The most expensive part of fine art printing is the ink set . This is true for most desktop printers, while large-format printers have large ink cartridges that are less expensive per print of a given size. Ink costs per print depend on:

Some newer printer drivers no longer give the printing resolution in dpi but via quality settings like "Photo", "Best Photo" or "Maximum dpi".

▸ The size of your print
▸ The type of printer used
▸ The resolution used for printing
  The higher the resolution chosen, the more ink is consumed. Therefore, ensure that the maximum resolution actually achieves a visible improve-

ment. In our experience, resolution beyond 2,400 dpi uses up more inks without noticeably better image quality. Using some printers and papers, you may even reduce resolution to 1,400 dpi.

▸ The kind of paper used. Some papers, to improve image quality, soak up more ink than other papers.

You may slightly reduce ink consumption by avoiding unnecessarily turning the printer on and off. Each time you power up the printer, some ink is used for nozzle cleaning. However, you should activate the printer from time to time, say, once a week, and should clean the nozzles periodically to prevent clogging. If you use your printer infrequently, you may even have to replace a clogged print head or two, clogged by dried ink.

If you print often, it may be cost-effective to buy a larger printer (beyond the A3+ size), since larger printers often use larger ink cartridges, which are less expensive relative to volume; for example, with the Epson R2400 you pay about $1/ml. With the R4800, you only pay about $ 0.5/ml ($54/110 ml), or only $ 0.38/ml when using 220-ml cartridges.

Another way to reduce ink costs is to use third-party inks. For consumer A4/Letter-sized printers, there are many brands. Most of them will result in poorer lightfastness, but this is not true for all of them. Here, you may have a look at tests published by some PC and photo magazines. For A3 and larger professional printers, there are fewer offerings, however, some inks do offer reasonable quality.

A potential problem using third-party inks is that you may void your printer's warranty. You should clean the print heads thoroughly before changing ink brands. For this, there are special cleaning cartridges available. For the printers we discuss, there are OEM-compatible replacement cartridges that come rebranded. Some are original OEM cartridges refilled (ink counters reset). While a few of them are unsuitable for fine art printing, some companies like Phantone ([61]) or Lyson ([82]) claim high quality, good lightfastness, and lower prices.

For more ink suppliers, see [43] – [46], [51], [52] and [57].

A technique offered for many large-scale printers that also may be used for some A4/Letter-sized printers are *Continuous Flow Ink Systems* (CIS or CFS), also called *bulk-ink systems*. This technique should not be confused with the continuous-flow printing technique described on page 16). Here, the OEM ink cartridge is replaced by a different cartridge that gets ink via a tube from a bulk-ink bottle. These systems have two major advantages:

1. The ink per print or per milliliter is much cheaper than using OEM cartridges. For our previous example for the R2400, this is about $0.17/ml with the Mediastreet Niagara II system, 4-ounce (118 ml) or 8-ounce (236 ml) ink bottles. With larger printers and larger bottles, it may be even cheaper.

2. You may print much longer before replacing ink cartridges.

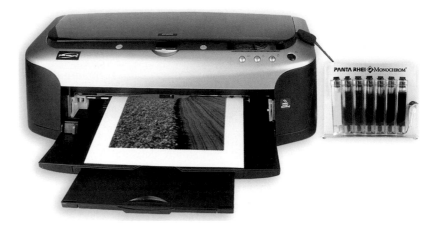

Figure 1-17: ▶
Panta Rhei continuous flow ink system
(Courtesy Monochrom Germany)

* *A microchip inside the ink cartridge*
controls the ink usage. When the normal
amount of ink is used up the printer will tell
you to change the ink cartridge. When you
refill the cartridge, you have to reset the ink
usage counter of the controlling chip. The
same is true if you use a bulk ink system
(continuous ink system).

A disadvantage is that you make a pre-investment: for the R2400, it would be about $ 335 for the Mediastreet system (with filled bottles). If you switch inks, e.g., Photo Black to Matte Black, you waste a lot of ink to clean out the tubes. Additionally, you must use auto-reset chips to fool the printer or cartridge.* Also, you can't use the OEM original ICC profiles, and will need profiles for the new ink. If you print a lot, this could be a minor problem. Some ink suppliers offer ICC profiles for their ink and various common fine art papers.

Now, how about lightfastness? Here again, you will find some ink manufacturers (e.g. Lyson), that refer to tests done by WIR ([44]).

More points to consider

There are a few other points you may want to consider when selecting an inkjet printer:

Printer interface

Some years ago, the standard interface for PC printers was the parallel port (Centronics or IEEE 1284) or serial format for Macs. This, fortunately, was replaced by USB 1.1 and more recently by USB 2.0 for most desktop printers. Some printers include an additional Firewire (IEEE 1394) interface. This could be an advantage when connecting the printer to two systems. Most large-scale printers also have a local area network (LAN) interface. The LAN is useful if you want to print from several systems in a local network. A small, low-cost print-server with a USB interface to the printer will achieve the same end and may be cheaper than an optional printer LAN interface.

PostScript RIP

Most desktop inkjet printers use their own proprietary printer language, and most printers additionally support HP's HPCL. In some cases, it is an advantage if the printer also supports PostScript, e.g. to print DTP documents. Most fine art printer manufacturers, however, do not consider this necessary, at least not for printing raster images like photos. With inkjet printers, an integrated PostScript RIP will add about $150 to the basic printer price. If you need PostScript printing only occasionally, you may use a software PostScript RIP in your PC. With Mac OS X, a software-based PostScript RIP comes with GIMP Print, and also with OS 10.4 preinstalled. With Windows, you may use the free public domain version of GostScript.

Exchangeable print heads

In some printers, usually consumer inkjet printers (e.g., by HP), the print head is part of the ink cartridge. This makes cartridges somewhat more expensive. When the nozzles of a head are clogged beyond repair, simply replace the cartridge and the problem is solved. With most Epson printers, you can't easily replace the print head, but must send the printer out for repair.* With some HP printers, e.g., the Designjet 130, the ink cartridge and print head are separate, and you may easily replace a print head with a new one. It's definitely an advantage when you can easily pull out the print head and clean it outside the printer, using a hot damp cloth or even some alcohol.

For A4/Letter-sized printers, it is cheaper to buy a new printer.

Cutters

On large-scale printers, a paper roll feeder is standard. For these printers, it is an advantage when the printer has an automatic paper cutter. Many of the default cutters on large-format printers, however, are not suited for heavy paper. For heavy paper you may have to replace them with cutters available as optional accessories.

Densiometers

Some printers have an integrated densiometer that allows measurement of the density of color laid down on paper. This allows the firmware of the printer to recognize clogged nozzles, and may also help auto-calibrate the printer. HP uses this technique in some of its inkjet printers, e.g., HP Designjet 30/130. Be aware that this is not a substitute for a true profiling device.

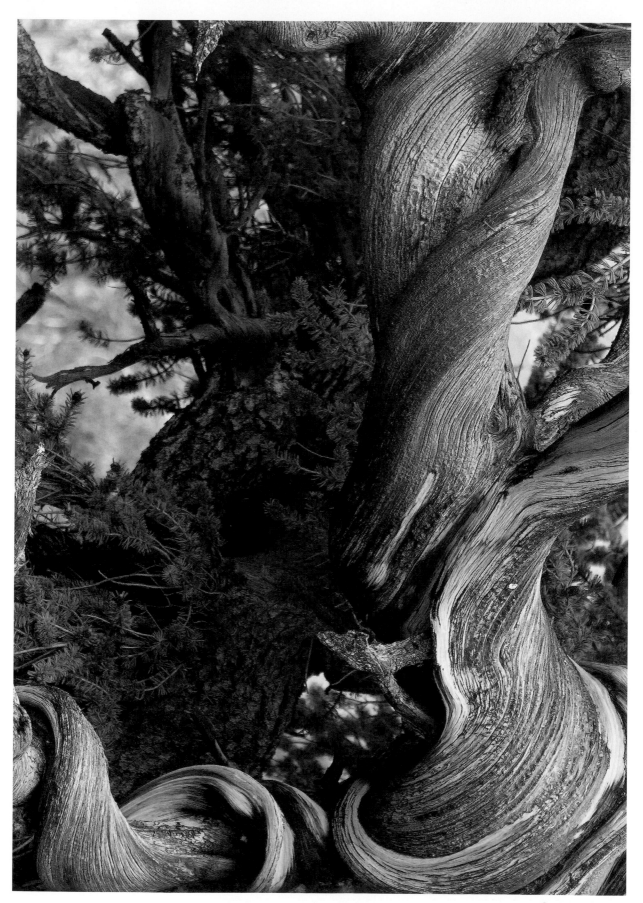

Inks, Papers, and Print Permanence

With photographic prints, paper, ink and the compatibility of these two materials are an important key to a good quality print – assuming you have a good image. You can't actually discuss fine art printing without discussing fine art papers and the right inks for them. For this reason, in this chapter we want to go deeper into inks (for inkjet printers) and papers, and what to watch for, so that these two important components match.

Fine art papers are indeed a hot discussion theme when fine art printers meet – and virtually endless. A fine art paper not only should work smoothly with the type of ink used, but also should accommodate for the photographic subject printed. A print of a landscape may ask for a different paper than a portrait and a product shoot may ask for yet another paper to achieve the optimal visual impression. Additionally, personal preferences have to be taken into account.

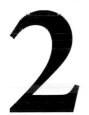

Another issue with inks and papers are the longevity of prints that can be achieved using a certain printer-ink-paper combination. This chapter should answer most questions on this.

2.1   Print permanence

Whether you sell or give away your prints, print permanence (print longevity) is important. It is determined by three major factors:

▸ Stability and permanence of the paper

▸ Permanence of the ink (its colorants). Additionally, ink and paper must match and work smoothly together.

▸ Environmental factors, such as light (especially UV), temperature, humidity, and gases (especially ozone)

The permanence of a digital image is limited only by the permanence of the digital storage media, whether hard disk, CD/DVD or tape. You may extend this range by making a copy of the data on newer media. You must still be cautious to ensure that your media may still be read by your computer hardware and operating system, and that your printing application still supports the data format used to produce your prints. In most cases, this will be years in the future. *Permanence,* in this case, means that you can read the data without unrecoverable errors, and can open the data for displaying, printing or modification.

When you make a print of an image, its permanence may range from four weeks to many years. Here, *permanence* means that the print will maintain its visual impact without noticeable deterioration, and that colors do not fade and the paper does not yellow.

This definition of *print permanence* has two soft factors:

▸ What is a "noticeable image deterioration"?
▸ What are the conditions under which the print is kept?

Until mid 2006, there was no ANSI or ISO standard for print permanence – at least not for the kinds of prints we are talking about. Most suppliers of printers, inks and papers state a "permanence" value for their materials, without actually defining how they calculate their "permanence." However, in the community of fine art printers, there is a quasi-standard currently defined by the *Wilhelm Imaging Research Institute* (WIR, [44]). This institute, founded by Henry Wilhelm and his wife Carol Brower Wilhelm, is one of the most highly recognized and established institutes for the testing of print permanence and lightfastness, and is highly regarded for being independent and unbiased. Most serious manufacturers of components for fine art printing (e. g., HP, Epson, and Canon) use WIR to obtain permanence tests.* You will find a large number of results for various papers and inks (and paper/ink-combinations) at their Web site.

They use a well-defined test procedure for their permanence tests of prints, and continually update their tests, considering additional factors that affect fading, e. g., air pollutants.

* Naturally, there are a number of other institutes that do the same and should be considered, e.g. the Rochester Imaging Permanence Institute [43]. However, it is widely accepted that Wilhelm Imaging Research defines the standard in the fine art printing industry.

"Display Permanence Ratings" are predictions

When we talk about the *display permanence ratings* (DPR) of digital fine art prints, we look for and talk of a *permanence* of at least 25 years. By using adequate fine art papers and inks, you may achieve a permanence of 60–100 years and perhaps even longer. For black-and-white prints, this figure may be 160 years or more. The difference lies in color-ink colorants being more prone to fading than those used for black inks.

To date, all data on permanence are based on accelerated lab tests and predictions. Prints are exposed to much brighter light (about 20,000 Lux) and at higher temperatures than found in a common exhibition or office environment. The results are then extrapolated, based on years of experience. Nonetheless, the true accuracy of these results will not be known for another hundred or so years.

For exhibition conditions, WIR assumes an average light level of 450 lux for 12 hours a day. They also assume that the print is displayed behind (normal) glass and displayed at 24° C (75° F) and 60% *relative humidity* (RH).

WIR = "Wilhelm Imaging Research", see [44].

Fine art printers should not necessarily rely on these conditions when looking at a data sheet, as not all suppliers use the test conditions specified by WRI. Read a manufacturer's claims carefully. Kodak, for one, seems to use two different types of tests: one for consumer materials, and another for professional materials, although there is no information about which papers Kodak rates as *consumer* or *professional*. The data resulting from these two tests differ by up to a factor of five, mostly because they use 120 lux/12 hours per day testing consumer material versus 450 lux testing professional material, and assume a UV filter will be used when displaying the print. The reality is that most tests use a standard glass filter, which absorbs much less UV light.

See Figure 2-1 on page 30 for some examples of WRI ratings.

Some of the permanence ratings Canon provides are for *darkroom* or *album storage*. The decrease in print quality in darkroom storage is much slower than that in a lighted office environment. Only the fine print describes a given permanence as *darkroom storage* permanence. What good is long darkroom permanence if you want to hang your prints in an office or studio environment?

We have seen fading in prints made with Canon dye-based inks and papers, specified to have a print permanence of about 100 years, in less than four weeks when presented in a well-lit office environment.

There are several environmental factors influencing the permanence of prints, and not all are yet fully understood or evaluated. Some of the well-known factors are:

▸ Ink
▸ Paper
▸ Paper-to-ink match
▸ Light, especially UV, which causes the most fading
▸ Temperature: the higher, the more damaging
▸ Relative humidity: the higher, the more damaging
▸ Gases: ozone is now considered one of the most degrading factors in an "office environment"; sulphur gases are also known to be destructive

WIR Display Permanence Ratings for Current Products in the 4x6-inch Photo Printer Category

Type of 4x6-inch Dye-Sub Photo Printer, Inkjet Printer/Inkjet Paper, And Digital Silver-Halide Color Paper/Digital Minilab Photo Printer[1]	WIR v3.0 Endpoints at Both 1.0 and 0.6 Densities With Cool White Fluorescent Illumination and Years of Display Based on 450 lux/12 hrs/day With Prints Framed Under Glass[2]

1. Epson PictureMate Personal Photo Lab (and new PictureMate Deluxe Viewer Edition) — **104 years**
    – Printed with Epson PictureMate Inks and Photo Paper (pigment-based inkjet prints)

2. HP Photosmart 325, 335, 375, 385, 422, and 475 Compact Photo Printers — **82 years**[3]
    – Printed with HP Vivera Inks (HP 95, 97, 343, or 344 Tri-color cartridges) (dye-based inkjet prints) With HP Premium Plus and HP Premium Photo Papers, High Gloss, Glossy, or Soft Gloss

3. Canon Selphy DS700 Compact Photo Printer (dye-based inkjet prints) — **41 years**
    – Printed with Canon BCI-16 tricolor ink cartridge and Canon Photo Paper Pro PR-101

4. Fujicolor Crystal Archive Type One Paper (silver-halide color prints) — **40 years**
    – Printed with Fuji Frontier 370 digital minilab and Fuji washless chemicals

5. Kodak EasyShare Printer Dock, Plus, Series 3, and 6000 Printers (dye-sub prints) — **26 years**

6. Dell Photo Printer 540 (dye-sub prints) — **26 years**

7. Agfacolor Sensatis and Agfacolor Splendix Papers (silver-halide color prints) — **22 years**[4]
    – Printed with Agfa d-lab.2plus/Select digital minilab and Agfa washless chemicals

8. Kodak Edge Generations and Royal Generations Papers (silver-halide color prints) — **19 years**[5]
    – Printed with Noritsu QSS-3011SM digital minilab and Kodak washless chemicals

9. HP Photosmart 145 and 245 Compact Photo Printers (dye-based inkjet prints) — **18 years**
    – Printed using HP No. 57 Tri-color cartridge with HP Premium Plus and HP Premium Photo Papers, High Gloss, Glossy, or Soft Gloss

    – Printed with HP No. 57 Tri-color cartridge and — **11 years**[6]
      Kodak Ultima Picture Paper, High Gloss (Ultima ColorLast "Lasts Over 100 Years" version)

10. Konica Minolta QA Paper Impresa and Centuria For Digital (silver-halide color prints) — **17 years**[7]
    – Printed with Konica Minolta R2 Super 1000 digital minilab and Konica washless chemicals

11. Lexmark SnapShot P315 Photo Jetprinter (dye-based inkjet prints) — **16 years**
    – Printed with Lexmark 33 or 35 color ink cartridges and Lexmark Premium Photo Paper

12. Olympus P-10 Digital Photo Printer (dye-sub prints) — **8 years**

13. Canon CP-200, CP-220, CP-330, CP400, and CP500 Printers (dye-sub prints) — **7 years**

14. Sony DPP-FP30 PictureStation Photo Printer (dye-sub prints) — **6 years**

15. Sony DPP-EX5, DPP-EX7, and DPP-EX50 Printers (dye-sub prints) — **4 years**

. . . . continues next page

This document originated at <www.wilhelm-research.com> File name: <WIR_4x6_Prints_2005_07_03.pdf>

Figure 2-1: Some permanence ratings by WIR (Courtesy of Wilhelm Research Inc, [44]). See [45] for the complete and original document.

Light as a factor of print permanence

Light is one of the most important factors in determining the permanence of prints.* The more light your prints absorb, the faster their colors (colorants) degenerate. More specifically, the quantity, duration, and wavelength of that light striking the print all determine the level of degradation of a print. Shorter wavelengths in the visible spectrum have a greater effect than longer wavelengths. UV light has a higher energy and higher destructive effect (see Figure 2-2). Direct unfiltered sun has a very high degree of UV in its spectrum. For this reason, fine art prints should never be exposed to direct sunlight.

* provided you use well-matched, reliable, stable inks and paper

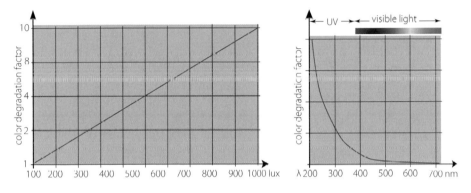
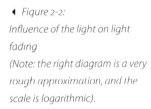

◀ Figure 2-2:
Influence of the light on light fading
(Note: the right diagram is a very rough approximation, and the scale is logarithmic).

Not all ink colors fade at the same rate. With most pigmented inks, yellow fades less and slower than other colors. This difference may lead to stronger color shifts and changes in contrast than if all colors faded at the same rate. Usually, there is a shift from red and green to yellow, and from neutral (built with CMYK) to a reddish hue.

Temperature influencing "dark fading"

When storing (archiving) prints for an extended time, temperature is a critical factor. Its influence is termed *thermal degradation* or *dark fade*, as this fading also occurs when prints are stored in the dark. From our chemistry classes, we may recall that higher temperature accelerates chemical processes, and image decay is mainly a chemical process. Figure 2-3 illustrates that temperature is a dominant factor in image degradation when stored in the dark.

Temperature also influences images in the light, but the light factor is dominant. Please note the linear X-axis (temperature) the logarithmic Y-axis (longevity factor).

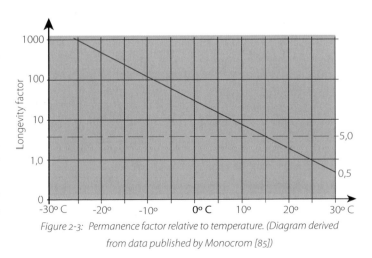

Figure 2-3: Permanence factor relative to temperature. (Diagram derived from data published by Monocrom [85])

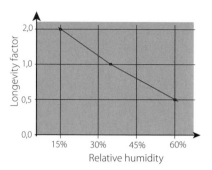

Figure 2-4: Permanence factor in relation to air humidity (diagram derived from data published by Monochrom [85])

Humidity

Relative humidity will influence the longevity of a print as well, though not as strongly as temperature. The higher the relative humidity, the shorter the life of a print (Figure 2-4).

Even if relative air humidity is not dominant, humidity above a certain level, around 80%, may lead to fungal decay which, in turn, may quickly and seriously damage your prints. Note that when the temperature in a room drops, relative humidity rises.

Gases and their influence on print permanence

Several atmospheric gases strongly affect print permanence. Ozone appears to have the strongest negative effect. Generated by unfiltered sun, as well as by some machines, ozone accelerates oxidation and, as such, the decay of colors. Ozone is also a bleaching agent.

Framing a print with glass, acrylic (e.g., Plexiglas), an UV-absorbing foil or other coating decreases air flow, and hence fresh ozone, over a print. The more UV light in your environment, the more ozone you will probably have, as UV light stimulates the production of ozone. Also, some electric engines like laser printers, photocopying machines, air-conditioners, and refrigerators produce ozone.

As ozone decreases in the upper atmosphere, especially near polar regions, the UV level at the earth's surface increases, generating even more ozone at the surface.

Other atmospheric gases also have a negative effect on the longevity of prints; for example, nitrogen dioxide (NO_2) and sulfur dioxide (SO_2) are suspected of yellowing paper. While their overall effect is not fully understood, it does appear to be less than that of ozone.

Paper additives

Additives to paper can also influence the light stability of a print; for example, optical brighteners, mainly used to make paper appear whiter, can have a negative effect on photo-fading, as their chemical half-life is rather short (a few years).

When optical brighteners break down, the paper loses its whiteness and the color of the print shifts a bit due to the more yellowish paper color.

These brighteners also may have a negative effect when doing ICC profiling, so we recommend avoiding papers with a high degree of optical brighteners.

How to improve the permanence of your prints

All things considered, the optimum recipe for maintaining your prints and their colorants as long as possible is very simple: keep them dark, cool, and dry. For most situations, none of these is practical when prints are to be displayed prominently. There are several ways to improve print permanence:

For more on framing, post-coating and lamination see Chapter 9.3.

▸ **Framing using a glass or acrylic cover**
A covering reduces gas flow and has a filtering effect on UV light. It also helps protect a print from dust and dirt, and may resist large changes in humidity.
   Standard glass or standard acrylic decreases the amount of UV light striking an image by reflecting or absorbing some of the light. Even normal window glass reduces UV light by up to 90 %. Using special glass, as some museums do, you can achieve a reduction of up to 99 % or more. There are also foils on the market, though quite expensive, that absorb about 99% of the UV light.

▸ **Spraying/coating**
Standard glass adds to reflections and is not always suitable for some types of presentations. To protect a print from UV light, ozone and soiling, you may apply protective material over a print, using either a spray or brush. There are many solutions available, but only a few carry a certificate from one of the well known institutes (e.g. WRI).

▸ **Reducing UV light**
Since UV light has the most damaging effect on print permanence, you can reduce it by using appropriate lighting that limits the amount of UV. Interestingly, unfiltered fluorescent light has a higher UV share than tungsten light. You also can cover the light source with special foil or glass, the latter of which can absorb about 99 % of UV light. These foils, properly applied, are hardly visible, but may change the surface appearance of the print slightly. Additionally, these foils are not cheap.

According to some reports, these foils tend to shrink over time (noticeable only after three to four years).

▸ **Laminating**
Lamination is similar to coating: protecting a print from UV light, ozone, dust, and other undesirable materials. An advantage of some lamination techniques over coating is that both sides of the print are protected, providing greater protection.

2.2   Inks

High-quality prints have two important items in common: good inks and good paper, both of which allow the longevity of your artwork. Inkjet printers have been around for about 15 years. Prints from the earliest printers showed noticeable degradation within a few weeks, or even within a few days when exposed to sunlight. In 2001, Epson became one of the first companies to address this problem, with reasonably priced inkjet printers and an acceptable image lightfastness, using UltraChrome® ink. In 2005, Epson and UltraChrome K3 introduced its third generation of this pigment-based type of ink.

Desktop and larger fine art inkjet printers use two types of inks:

▸ Dye based
▸ Pigment based

You may even see some hybrid inks, where dye-based ink is used for colors to achieve a large gamut, while pigment-based ink is used to create a dark, dense, saturated black and better longevity; Canon does this with some printers. Some publications use the term *pigmented inks* to refer to hybrid inks. In this book, the term describes true inks with solid pigment.

Each of these two types of inks has specific advantages and drawbacks. HP achieved a very respectable longevity of about 70–200 years with its dye-based Viveria® inks,* while Epson managed to achieve a rich color gamut with its third generation of pigment-based UltraBrite® and UltraChrome® inks. Pigment-based inks tend to provide a smaller gamut. In reality, with desktop printers, you normally have no choice between dye-based and pigment-based inks for a particular printer: they are either one or the other. With some higher-end, large-format printers, different types of inks may be used on the same printer.

* Dye-based inks tend to have general problems with lightfastness.

Dye-based inks

With dye-based inks, the colorants are water soluble and dissolved in the ink liquid. Thus, when hitting the paper, they sink into the paper or its coating, while a small portion remains on the surface. This makes dye-based inks well suited for glossy paper, but they are equally well-suited for matte papers. When the liquid dries, the colorants attach to the fibers of the paper or molecules of the coating. To prevent excessive bleeding and mixing with neighboring color points, in general, a coated paper may be used (see section 2-2). To give the print maximum vividness, its coating should be transparent. As the ink penetrates the paper surface or coating, dye-based inks deliver better scratch resistance than pigmented inks.

Compared to the colorants in pigmented ink, the molecules in dye ink are much finer, up to a factor of 1,000. As dye-based inks contain a higher percentage of liquid (mostly water), they dry more slowly. Also, such prints are more prone to smudging when coming in contact with moisture or when touched by a moist finger. A microporous coating (or other special sizing) can compensate for both of these effects.

The disadvantage of these tiny dye molecules is that they have a larger surface open to attack by light and air contamination, like ozone, NO_2, and SO_2, leading to faster fading. To reduce this effect, HP and other printer-makers recommend using swellable papers for optimum print permanence.[*]

See section 2-3 for more on this.

Most desktop inkjet printers and many large-format printers today use dye-based inks. Almost all HP and Canon printers use them.

Dye-based inks are cheaper to produce than pigment ink and are less prone to print-head clogging. Even if the print-head is clogged, it cleans more easily (with a moist Q-tip or a damp tissue) than the heads of pigmented-ink machines. Even if the colorants in the ink should settle down in the ink cartridge after some time, they will dilute when the ink cartridge is shaken.

Dye-based inks tend to provide a richer color gamut, more vivid colors and a darker black than pigmented inks, although newer formulations of pigment inks are gaining some ground.

Pigmented inks

In pigmented inks, the color stems from pigments, comparatively large colored material that consists of a tightly coupled conglomerate of colored molecules. A single pigment is about 1/1,000th the size of a molecule of dye used in dye-based inks, and thus produces several advantages over dye-based inks: the pigment has a relatively small surface and, thus, is more resistant to light, water/moisture, and air pollutants. Pigment inks resist damage from light, moisture, gases, and temperature.

The downside of pigments is their somewhat reduced color intensity, compared to dyes, and that they poorly dissolve in the solvent of the ink. Thus, there is a tendency to settle at the bottom of the ink cartridge, similar to sand in a very slow-moving river. You can stir them up but, after some time, they sink down once more.[*]

The cartridges of pigmented ink should consequently be thoroughly shaken (while closed and packed) before inserting a new ink cartridge into the printer. What's more, the ink should be used up within about six months, pigmented-ink cartridges are prone to clogging.

Also, pigment-based inks tend to show a stronger *bronzing* effect than dye-based inks. Here, dark or black areas show a slight color of bronze under some lighting. Similar pigment-based inks show a stronger tendency toward metamerism, where two colors look identical under one lighting situation, but look different viewed in a different lighting situation.

When used in an inkjet printer, most of the ink/pigment will settle on the surface of the paper and not penetrate the paper (or its coating) to the same degree as dye-based ink. As the pigment sits mainly on the surface of the paper, the print is more prone to abrasion than are dye-based inks. On the other hand, pigment ink dries faster than dye-based ink, since pigment ink uses less solvent. With pigment ink, your choice of paper is somewhat

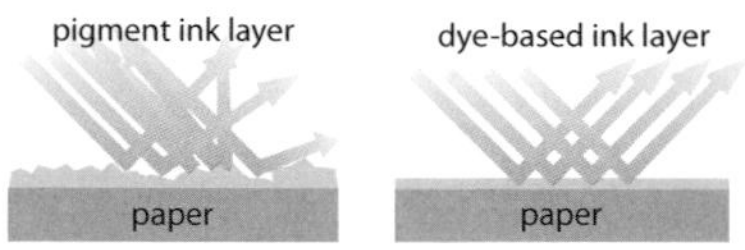

Figure 2-5: The dye molecules are much smaller than pigments. Pigments diffuse and scatter light more than dyes.

On the PMA 2006, HP introduced its "Photosmart Pro 9180" and Canon its "Pixma Pro9500" and its "PROGRAF iF 5000". These new inkjet printer target the fine art market and they use pigment inks.

expanded, as you may use coated or uncoated paper (uncoated paper is prone to ink bleeding and a large dot gain), and swellable or porous coatings.

Because pigments mainly reside on a paper's surface, the gloss of a color depends on the quantity of ink/pigment used in the various areas of the print, resulting potentially in an uneven gloss. Additionally, pigments give a more dispersed reflection (see Figure 2-5). For this reason, pigment ink is better suited for matte or semi-matte surfaces than to glossy paper. You might compensate for this by post-applying an additional gloss coating if gloss is desired. Epson offers this in its R800/R1800 printers by using a separate gloss optimizer cartridge.

Pigmented inks, when combined with the optimum paper, have a long lifespan, based on their better light stability, gas resistance, and temperature fastness. Additionally, there is less tendency of prints to smudge when touched with moist fingers or a high moisture content. Taken together, pigmented inks are excellent for stable, long-lasting fine art prints. With its new DuraBrite™ and UltraChrome K3™ inks, Epson shows that you now can produce a richer color gamut and achieve a higher maximum density (*Dmax*) in a print.

We assume that both HP and Canon will add pigmented inks to their list of fine art products, if they want to be competitive in the fine art and high-quality photo printing markets.

The overall quality of both types of ink has improved considerably over the past few years. The lightfastness of dye-based inks has improved considerably, and the color gamut of pigment inks also has increased. The tendency toward bronzing and metamerism with pigment-based ink has been considerably reduced, especially by Epson. The total color gamut achievable with inkjets is ultimately improved by better inks and the use of more primary colors.

2.3   Papers

Paper is an ancient, well-studied material. First produced in China, and mass-produced over the past 600 years in the western world, we inherited a long and rich tradition of paper making. There are several paper makers today, whose companies date back several centuries. Since 1584, Hahnemühle has been one of the best known German paper makers for fine art.

Most of the time, we are unaware of the stability or longevity of paper, but concentrate on its color, surface texture, and the color gamut we can achieve printing on it. For fine art printing, however, we must consider two other items:

▸ Longevity and lightfastness of the paper itself
   (it should neither disintegrate nor yellow within a certain time)

▸ Suitability of the paper for the ink used
(the paper must absorb ink without the ink bleeding excessively, drying too quickly or warping. With dye-based inks, it must protect the ink from ozone and other atmospheric pollutants)

The longevity of the paper is largely determined by the ingredients in the paper and how it's stored:

▸ The stability and constitution of the paper. Today, if you use chloride-free, acid-free papers, this is not an issue. The paper will remain stable for hundreds of years, if stored under appropriate conditions.

▸ The paper should not noticeably change color over the period of time considered, i.e., it should not yellow. One precondition for this is that it be lignin-free and not contain an overabundance of optical brighteners.

For fine art printing, in most cases, special fine art papers should be considered. Fine art paper for inkjet printing is almost always specially coated for printing (Figure 2-6).

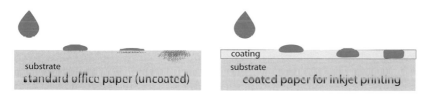

◂ Figure 2-6:
The coating prevents the ink from bleeding excessively.

Thus, paper consists of a base material (*substrate*) and a coating (and/or *sizing*) that ensures that the ink is properly absorbed by the paper and dries quickly. Additionally, the coating must prevent the ink from bleeding excessively (Figure 2-6). This permits higher-resolution printing and finer color gradients.

Paper characteristics

There are many characteristics of a good fine art paper:

▸ the raw material used to produce the paper
▸ coating (influencing absorbency): single or double sided
▸ color (whiteness and brightness) and opacity
▸ base weight and paper thickness
▸ surface texture (finish)
▸ size

The technical part of a technical data sheet might look like the following example, extracted from specifications of Hahnemühle Photo Rag:

Physical Characteristics (Hahnemuehle Photo Rag™, 308 g/m²)

	Unity	Valuation	Test Norm / Notes
Test Conditions		23° C / 50% RH	CSS19
Weight	g/m²	188	ISO536
Thickness	mm	0.30	EN 20534
Whiteness	%	97.5	ISO 11475 (W_{cie}/ D65,2°)
Opacity	%	92.5	DIN 53146
Media Color		white	not bleached
pH		7.9	DIN 53124
Water resistance		very high	
Cobb		70.0	EN 20535
Ink limit	%	245	
Special features	optical brighteners		

Data shown are average values.

Paper ingredients

The raw-material composition of a paper largely determines its overall quality, plus its behavior for printing, display and storage. With fine papers for inkjet printing, there are at least two layers: the paper base and a coating onto this base. The top layer is also called the *ink reception layer* or *inkjet receptive layer*. Both its layers and its raw materials are important in giving a paper its characteristics. Here, we specifically focus on papers excellent for fine art prints. There are two basic kinds of raw materials: cotton (rag) fibers and cellulose fibers, and any combination of the two. Thus you may have rag paper, half-rag paper, wood-free, and wood-containing paper. Today, only few real rags are used, mostly raw cotton, even if a paper's name implies otherwise.

There are many other ingredients in the paper to give it the desired color, surface feel, pH, absorbance and finish, yet cotton/rag or cellulose from wood remain the two basic ingredients.

Rag paper may contain up to 100 % cotton or linen fiber and is the most expensive paper. But one may mix cotton/rag with cellulose in almost any combination to reduce cost. For high quality, cotton/linen-based paper is the better paper, but some new formulations of cellulose-based paper can achieve about the same longevity as rag/cotton paper.

Cellulose is mainly produced from wood, but there are other plants, like hemp, also used for cellulose production. Wood pulp contains a lot of

➔ *Rag (or cotton) as well as wood is primarily build up of cellulose. These two base materials of paper, however, use different kinds of cellulose. The cellulose from wood and similar plants is called "alpha cellulose".*

lignin, which causes low-quality papers to yellow, and works as a kind of glue in the cellulose cell. For good-quality papers, lignin, or *lignen,* must be removed during the pulping process.

To differentiate between cotton paper and mainly cellulose-based paper, sometimes the term *alpha cellulose* paper is used for the latter. Also the term *sulphite* or *sulphite paper* is used for this paper, as the wood pulp is cooked in sodium sulphite or in calcium bisulphate.

Whatever the raw material may be, it is important that the paper is acid-free, meaning it has a pH-value of 7.0 or greater, up to a certain pH. Previously, 7.0–8.5 pH was considered optimal for archival papers. New findings now indicate a range of 7.0–10.0 pH. A pH of 7.5–9.0 seems ideal and provides a buffer for acids absorbed from acidic air pollutants. The latter are also referred to as *buffered* papers. This buffering is often achieved by addition of calcium carbonate.

Whiteness and brightness

The whiter a paper is, the higher the contrast of colors in your print and the richer the color gamut. For this reason, photographers prefer bright white papers. Since the base material for paper is not bright white, paper manufacturers must use some tricks to achieve proper whiteness. This is especially true when the coating is transparent. If you look at the numerous variations of fine art papers, you will find a very wide range of shades of white, from a bluish bright white to a "natural" white, i.e., a tint of yellow or beige, to ivory or creamy white.

There are several techniques to improve whiteness and brightness of paper, e.g., bleaching. Even white colorants are added to the paper base material. Additionally, optical brighteners may be added, partly to compensate for possible color variations in different paper batches. You will see optical brighteners even in well-known fine art papers like the Photo Rag by Hahnemüehle.

Technically, brightness is a percent of light reflection and ranges from 0 (or 1) to 100 %. While multipurpose bond paper, used for copying machines, has a brightness value in the 80s, the brightness of most fine art paper is 90–98.5 %.

Most papers look very white when viewed alone. The true color becomes visible when compared to other white surfaces, e.g., that of a matte or white frame.

When you choose a paper, you should consider the subject you want reproduced in your print. For most portraits, for example, bright white is not advisable. The same is true for most landscape subjects. So, if high brightness is not important or necessary, you may be able to use a paper free of optical brighteners.

Optical brighteners

Optical brighteners, or *optical brightening additives* (OBA) in paper are used to remove any yellow appearance of the raw materials. Additionally, optical brighteners increase the brightness of a paper, thus increasing the maximum contrast in a print, and enlarging the color gamut. They also increase the reflectivity of a (white) paper. Most optical brighteners are fluorescent brighteners. They absorb light in the UV range and re-emit white light in the visible range, tending slightly toward blue.

There are some disadvantages to optical brighteners: a spectrophotometer may give inaccurate results when measuring colors for ICC profiling, leading to incorrect ICC profiles. More importantly, brighteners deteriorate faster than (good) ink colors. This may lead to a gradual color shift in the print. Usually a paper manufacturer will provide a note when an optical brightener is contained in a digital fine art paper, unfortunately, the amount may vary somewhat among batches of paper. There are different-quality brighteners: better ones deteriorate more slowly. Papers using fluorescent-based optical brighteners can lose some of their brightness and whiteness when the light source has little or no UV light, or when UV filters are used.

For these reasons, if long-term image permanence is an important issue, fluorescent brighteners should be minimized or avoided altogether.

You may test a paper for optical brighteners by viewing the paper in the dark using a UV light source. If brighteners are present, the OBAs will glow under UV.

➡ *There are two ways to handle the influence of brighteners in ICC profiling packages. They either use a UV filter attached in front of the spectrophotometer or they recognize the brightener effect in software and deal with it in software (the latter e.g., is done in ProfileMaker by GretagMacbeth).*

Paper weight and paper thickness

The weight of a paper is given in either *grams per square meter* (gsm or g/m²) or in pounds per 500 sheets (ream) of a specific size (lbs.). We consider gsm better for comparison as it is independent of the paper size. For fine art printing, a heavier paper usually is preferred, as it gives your print rigidity and a more substantial feel. While a standard office copy paper measures about 80–120 gsm, a traditional low-cost photo paper is about 120–150 gsm. We prefer papers of 230 gsm or heavier.

A second measurement to look for is actual paper thickness, or *caliper,* as not all paper has the same weight per square meter. This measurement is either given in millimeters (mm) or in *mils* (a thousandth of an inch). Photo paper is usually 7–10 mils (approximately 0.18–0.25 mm), typical fine art papers 10–35 mils (0.25–0.90 mm).

1 mils = 0.0254 mm
1 mm ≈ 39.4 mil

Using thick papers, you may have to manually assist the printer in feeding the paper, or perhaps use a straight paper path and set special options in the printer driver (e.g., see page 137). Using lighter papers, on the other hand, you may have to reduce the amount of ink to prevent warping (e.g. see page 133).

Paper coating

For inkjet printing, paper may be *uncoated*, like bond paper used for laser printers and photocopying machines, or *coated*. Traditionally, many fine art papers used for painting or drawing are uncoated, and thus have a very fine surface. Though you may use these papers also for inkjet printing, as mentioned before, for true fine art prints you should use coated paper. The coating may also affect the surface finish of the paper, e.g., to be more matte, satin or glossy. There are several different types of coatings:

▸ microporous
▸ swellable
▸ resin coated (RC)

Microporous coating ▸ Here, the coating consists of a fine layer of ceramic (inorganic, inert particles) material ground to fine powder. The ink sinks into the cavities of this layer and is thus absorbed quickly with minimal spread. Ink printed on this kind of paper dries very quickly. This coating provides good water resistance. Unfortunately, the open areas of the coating allow dye-based colorants of the ink to come in contact with air-contaminants and thus these gases accelerate deterioration processes of the ink (Figure 2-7). For this reason, microporous papers are not the best choice for dye-based inks when print longevity is essential.

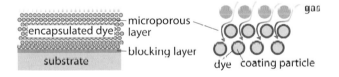

◂ *Figure 2-7:*
Structure of a microporous paper
(Source: HP, [35])

With pigmented inks, it is best to use microporous papers. They dry very quickly and produce sharp images. Pigmented inks do not sink in like dye-based inks, leaving the pigments on the surface.

Swellable papers ▸ As their name implies, the coating is made of material (polymers) that swell in the presence of moisture, i.e., when the inks hits the paper. The coating absorbs the ink and allows the colorants to penetrate the top layer of the coating. The encapsulating layer below encloses the colorants (dyes), leaving only minor parts of the dye on top of the paper (where it is exposed to light and gases). With swellable papers, you usually have a four-layer paper:

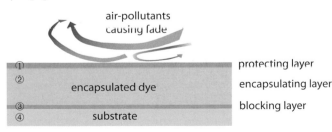

◂ *Figure 2-8:*
Layers of a swellable inkjet paper
(Source: HP, [35])

These papers, primarily intended for dye-based inks, produce a very fine and crisp print, but are sensitive to high humidity and water contact. You may find swellable papers from Epson, Fujifilm (e.g., Premium Plus), HP (e.g., HP Premium Plus Photo Paper), Ilford, Kodak, and others. Most of these papers are either glossy or luster/satin.

Swellable papers take a bit longer to dry, as the swelling caused by the inks has to release its moisture and return to a smaller size. Keep this in mind when handling prints on swellable paper. Wait even longer if you intend to frame a print, laminate or coat it. Colors also take a bit longer to stabilize and establish their final values. These unique factors are important when you do your own printer profiling.

When printing with the HP printers mentioned in Chapter 5.8 (using dye-based inks), we recommend using only swellable paper if print permanence is an issue.

Resin coated (RC) papers ▶ This is not actually a real coating but a kind of paper well known in the photographic world for simple consumer prints from the wet darkroom. Classic, good quality, wet prints still use fiber-based paper. This kind of paper is also now used for digital inkjet printing. With RC papers, the base substrate is made of resin (plastic, rather than paper) and usually sandwiched between two thin polyethylene layers. To make it suitable for inkjet printing, either a swellable or a microporous coating is applied on top. This coating determines the printing behavior of the paper.

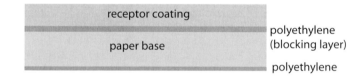

Figure 2-9: ▶
Layers of an RC paper

With some inkjet papers, a distinction is made between "Fine Art Papers" and "Photographic Papers," the latter meaning RC papers. Most RC papers provide a glossy or satin surface and are closer to the feeling of traditional consumer photo material. For many artists, this feeling is too similar to plastic and it lacks the feel and look of real paper.

Do your own coating Finally, you may use uncoated paper and do your own precoating (before you print). Here, you must differentiate between *topcoats*, or *overcoats*, which are intended to protect the finished print against UV light, abrasion and soiling. Basic paper is also coated to make it suitable for inkjet printing. Here, we describe the latter. There are several coatings for inkjet printing on the market, but we do not have personal experience with them. These coatings may be applied with a brush or roller. You may also use low-pressure sprayers. inkAID offers several different precoatings, from White Matte to Clear Gloss.

We have had positive reports from photographers using PixelTrust [88]. Another recommended coating is inkAID [76].

Sizing The term *sizing* or *internal sizing* describes the application of substances to reduce overall absorbency and to keep the ink from coming in direct contact with the fibers that make up the support. With different substances, absorbency of coatings is controlled. The term (*surface*) *sizing* is also used for the creation of special paper surfaces.

Paper surface – paper finish

As with silver-halide-based prints, there are papers with different surface structures. For inkjet printing, the choice is even larger, and a paper's surface type is another way to classify papers, from shiny to dull:

▸ Glossy
▸ Semigloss, Luster, Satin
▸ Matte, Watercolor

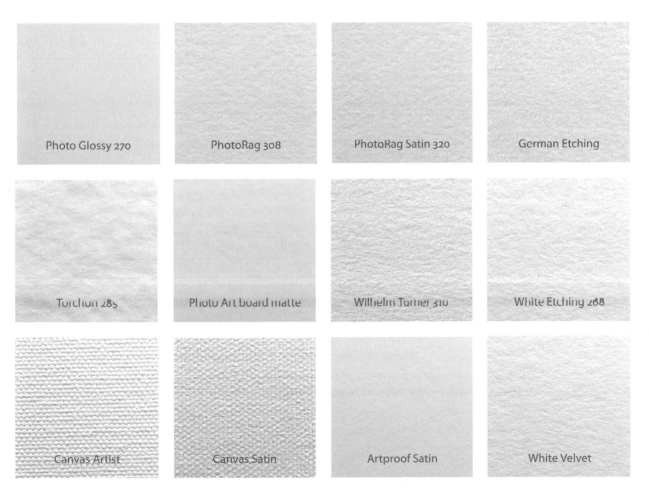

Figure 2-10: A small collection of paper surfaces and colors. The images show some papers from Hahnemühle (courtesy of Hahnemühle Germany).

While these names or attributes mainly describe surface glossiness, the surface may have an additional structure, most obvious when using canvas.

While glossy paper is usually very smooth, all less glossy papers may have different degrees of surface structure.

The smoother the paper surface, the sharper a photo appears, provided you have sufficient contrast in the subject. For optimum brilliance, glossy and semigloss papers are best, while matte and velvet papers provide some more abstraction, especially when used for black-and-white prints.

The surface not only has an influence on the visual appearance of the paper and the print, but may also affect the suitability of the paper for certain inks and, thus, printers. Typically, glossy papers are not optimal for pigmented inks, as pigments mainly reside on the surface and may interfere with the gloss of the surface. To offer a printer for a broad range of suitable applications, the printer manufacturers of pigment-based inkjets must compensate for this effect, e.g., by including a gloss optimizer for glossy prints or by selecting an ink formulation that results in a glossy ink.

If you want to apply your own additional finish to a print, e.g., by doing a post-coating or embellishing, ensure that your coating material is not only compatible with your ink but also with your paper surface. Often, however, at least two versions of a post-coating material are available: one for glossy and one for matte surfaces. This, for example, is the case for the Eco Print Shield product from PremierArt ([90]).

Paper size

Not all papers are available in all sizes. When we discuss fine art printing, usually we talk about prints at least the size of Letter or A4. Since most images require a minimal size for optimum viewing, A3, A3+ and even larger are favorite sizes.* Another option is to use roll paper, which you may either cut down to your preferred size (you must flatten the paper afterward) or may use with a roll feeder on your printer if you have one. Some papers may be less expensive when ordered in larger sizes, and cut down to more usable sizes.

See page 51 for more standard paper sizes.

Matching inkjet technology, subject paper, and ink

In general, it is recommended to use a paper that:

▸ matches the type of printing method used
▸ works smoothly together with the ink and final print resolution
▸ suits the image subject
▸ suits your personal preferences

For a print with many fine details, such as a photo of a fashion model, a glossy bright white paper may give the best result, considering resolution, sharpness, detail, and wide color gamut. A print of a landscape with picturesque scenery may look better on a watercolor paper. Likewise a black-and-white print of a portrait may not want a bright white paper, but may gain from a paper with a slightly off-white tint, or "natural white." Here, Hahnemühle "German Etching" may be appropriate.

While there are many technical specifications to note when choosing a suitable fine art paper, it is still a subjective decision. There is no single right or wrong choice, and you may even select different papers for different subjects in different print sizes. The larger the print, the thicker the paper, up to a certain size. For very large fine art prints, you may have to return to a thinner paper, as you will likely mount them to a separate backboard. When paper bonding is required, thinner papers are easier to handle.

Some more characteristics

There are other characteristics to consider when selecting a paper. For example, the pH value of the paper. This value tells how acidic or alkaline a paper is. "Neutral" would be a pH of 7.0. When the paper is more acidic, it will destroy itself after a length of time. As paper may pick up acid components from the environment, other papers, a wooden frame or the air itself, most fine art papers have a native pH of 7.5–10. This provides a buffer when picking up acid. Fine art materials with a prescribed amount of added alkaline are called *buffered*.

Cobb number   The *cobb-number*, mentioned in the table on page 38, gives an indication how much water can be absorbed by a paper over a certain period of time. This number is rarely given by paper manufacturers, and we have found no recommendation for *good* cobb values for fine art papers.

Ink limit   The *ink limit* is an important factor in offset printing. Darker colors are built up by overlaying primary colors (in offset printing, usually C, M, Y and K),[*] theoretically, up to 400% to be applied using four inks. This is, in many cases, more than a paper can absorb. When too much ink is applied, the color will break or smear, or the paper may warp. Thus the ink limit specifies how much ink may be overlaid at a particular point. The higher this value, the higher density may be achieved in dark or black areas of the print. Values beyond 230–240 are considered quite good using fine art papers.

> *   Using C, M and Y in addition to Black can achieve a darker, deeper Black.

    With some RIPs, you may explicitly control the maximum amount of ink laid down.

Print maximum density (Dmax)   According to Norman Koren [71] Dmax = $-\log_{10}$ (minimum print reflectivity), and is a measure of the deepest black tone a printer/ink/paper combination can reproduce. This is an extremely important print-quality factor. Prints with poor Dmax look pale and weak. A Dmax of 1.7 is a good value for matte prints; 2.0 is good for glossy, semi-gloss and luster prints. There have been reports that the new Epson

UltraChrome K3 printers have a Dmax as high as 2.3 with Premium Luster paper.

You only rarely find this value in a paper-manufacturer's data sheet, as it also depends on the type of ink used and on some driver settings. These values become especially interesting when printing black-and-white. Dmax is measured using a densiometer, but may also be measured using a good flatbed scanner and a spectrophotometer.*

Opacity Opacity determines to what degree elements on the back of a sheet (or elements behind the paper surface) are visible. This is important when intending to print on both sides of the paper. This value may range from zero (complete transparency) to 100 (completely opaque). The thicker the paper and the more dense the paper and coating, the higher the opacity value will be. For fine art papers, opacity values of more than 85 are reasonable and greater than 90 is considered good.

Other materials

For fine art prints, there are several other materials available on which to print, e.g., printable canvas. Hahnemühle offers a fine "Canvas Artist Matte" (340 gsm, natural white), although you also may use conventional canvas, after preparing it with a coating described earlier.

Traditional film, either clear or white, may be used for backlit prints, or as a digital negative to produce contact prints in a wet darkroom, using papers for Baryt or platinum prints. For backlit film, Kodak offers a "Reverse Print Backlit Film, 6 mil" that may be used with pigmented Epson Ultrachrome inks and dye-based inks. Pictorico [86] offers "Photo Gallery Hi-Gloss Inkjet-White-Film" that has received positive comments in several publications. The film is also available in A4. This material may be used to produce large-format negatives for contact proofs. While browsing the Pictorico Web site, check out "OHP Transparency Film," which is excellent for general display transparencies and for making platinum/palladium prints.

A problem with film is that it is difficult to locate ICC profiles for these media. Even though standard profiling software suggests that it's relatively easy to generate your own profiles, it's no simple task when using reflective white paper as the print medium.

Fabric has become a popular print medium for the fine art community. Here, however, you will need specialized inks. Also, fabric needs special treatment before printing. Most desktop inkjets are poorly designed for printing on fabric. Moreover, this type of printing is usually done on large-format printers. The intrepid fine art printer should also look into sign-maker and craft supplies, which offer unique papers, e.g., rice paper, and other supplies to enhance the look and feel of fine art prints.

Paper handling

Handling before printing Printing paper should be kept dry, clean and dark. The manufacturer's box is a suitable, short-term storage solution. Check the expiration date to ensure you use the paper well before it "expires." Also, ensure the humidity is kept at about 50–60 % to prevent excess drying or swelling.

Digital fine art printing paper is quite sensitive to oils and perspiration (which is acidic), so you should wear thin cotton gloves when handling it. This practice is standard when handling photographs, as well.*

* The sweat of your hand is acidic.

Preparing for printing Often there are loose, tiny paper particles attached to paper. These particles may clog your printer's print heads and rollers. If they remain on the paper while printing and fall off later, you could have tiny white (or paper-colored) spots on your print. For that reason, we advise wiping the paper using a very soft brush, or blowing off the particles using low-pressure compressed air immediately before printing.

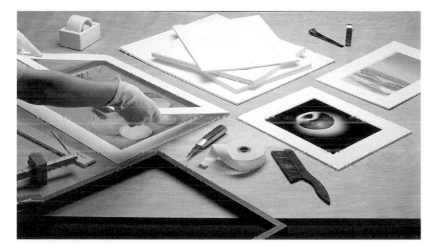

◀ Figure 2-11:
Use cotton gloves to handle your fine art papers, and brush or air-spray your paper before inserting it into the printer (Courtesy Monochrom Germany [85])

Handling for printing Make certain you print on the coated side of a paper. Usually, you can see or feel the coating on the paper surface. On glossy and semigloss papers, the coated surface is most obvious: the shiny side. With matte and similar papers, it usually is the side showing the more prominent matte texture. If in doubt, test the paper lightly with a thumbnail. On the coated side, the nail will leave a clearly visible trace as you lightly crease the paper.

If you intend to use thick or heavy paper, first check to learn if your printer is capable of printing that paper thickness (see technical specification of the printer). Even if suitable, it may be necessary to manually guide the paper in the feeder. We recommend feeding any paper a single sheet at a time when printing fine art, and always remember to handle paper only by its edges, or use cotton gloves.

→ *For further information, please see:*
"A–Z of Paper: Interesting Facts on Paper"
by Hahnemühle [75].

After printing   When retrieving a print after printing, avoid contact with the freshly printed surface until it is completely dry. Place the fresh print on a clean, flat surface, avoiding bright light and direct sunlight, and let it dry sufficiently. Drying time depends on the kind of inks used and on properties of the media. Most dye-based inks take a bit longer to dry, but for most inks and papers, one hour is reasonable. Try to keep the print in a dust-free environment while drying.

If you intend to frame the print or do further protective coating, we recommend waiting at least 24 hours after printing. With RC papers (see page 42), you should wait longer, perhaps a week, to give the paper and ink adequate time to off-gas.

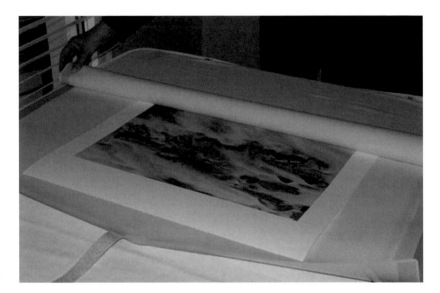

Figure 2-12: ▶
Using a D-Roller to remove paper curl

If you use roll paper, you will have to flatten the paper to remove the curl from the paper roll. When the paper is dry, you may have to run it with a slight pressure over a table edge (the back of the print toward the table) to help remove curl.

D-Roller (Fig. 2-12), produced by Glastonbury Design ([73]), allows you to take the curl out of fine art papers that come from a roll. Papers may be D-Rolled prior to or after printing with no drying time needed for the inks. (See Uwe's short note on the D-Roller*).

* *See Uwe's paper "Printing Insights #27:*
The D-Roller":
www.outbackphoto.com/printinginsights/
pio27/essay.html

Storing your prints Storing digital prints is the same as storing silver-halide-based photos. Keep them clean, dry and, when not on display, in the dark. When stored for archiving, be sure their container is acid free. It is recommended to isolate prints from each other using sheet separators with acid-free paper. There are special buffered tissue papers expressly for this purpose, meaning they have a pH of about 8, so they can absorb/neutralize acidic components from contact chemicals and air pollution.

Suitable digital fine art papers

There are many different types of fine art papers available. Here, we only list papers that we have some experience with. Papers are classified according to their surface and make:

▸ Matte papers
▸ Matte fine art papers
▸ Satin/glossy coated rag papers (new, emerging category)
▸ Satin papers with a very soft gloss finish
▸ Luster/pearl papers
▸ High-gloss papers
▸ Specialty papers and canvas

Matte papers

▸ **Epson Enhanced Matte:** Very nice, smooth paper that is also relatively inexpensive. Be aware, though, that the strong brighteners used in this paper may cause yellowing. This paper is also very thin, and may warp more easily than thicker papers.

Matte Fine Art Papers

▸ **Hahnemühle Photo Rag / (Satin):** Very popular, but expensive. Both papers are available in different weights (from 188 gsm to 460 gsm. Photo Rag is also well suited for black-and-white prints. You have to watch for scuffing and cotton dust and should gently clean the paper with a soft brush or compressed air before printing.

▸ **Somerset Velvet Photo Enhanced:** Very nice paper. One of our favorites.

▸ **Moab Entrada Natural:** Excellent, reasonably priced paper.

▸ **Epson Ultra Smooth:** Top paper that is also archival. Watch for cotton dust, however.

▸ **Crane Museo II:** Very fine paper.

▸ **Arches:** Expensive paper with a very good reputation. We have not had a chance to test it ourselves, though.

Satin/glossy coated rag papers (new emerging category)

▸ **Crane Museo Silver Rag:** Very new paper.

▸ We expect that many papers will follow in this category.

Satin or soft gloss papers

Most of these papers have a slightly plastic feel. This is more an issue in open portfolios than when displayed behind glass.

▸ **Epson Premium Semimatte**: Nice surface for a satin paper.

▸ **HP Premium Plus Satin**: Very nice satin surface.

▸ **Epson Premium Semigloss**: Comes close to the Epson Premium Semimatte paper, but maybe not quite as nice.

We expect new papers in this category to show up in the very near future, as the demand for fine art inkjet papers increases.

Luster/pearl papers

▸ **Epson Premium Luster:** popular paper with good Dmax. Some people don't like the surface texture, which is somewhat alleviated when displayed behind glass.

▸ **Ilford Galerie Classic Pearl**: a popular alternative to Epson Premium Luster

High-Gloss papers

▸ **Epson Premium Glossy:** Some bronzing can show. The bronzing may largely be reduced using the new Epson K3 inks.

▸ **HP Premium Plus Gloss**: Very nice glossy paper surface.

▸ **Pictorico Photo Gallery Hi-Gloss White Film**: Very special paper, that has an ultra-smooth surface and also a lot of contrast and depth. It is rated to be very archival.

Specialty papers and canvas

▸ All sorts of canvas
▸ Rice paper
▸ Many more variations

A new generation of fine art papers

* A good review of these Papers may be found at:
www.booksmartstudio.com/
services.php?section=8&SID=33

Since 2006, there has been a new generation of very fine Fine Art Papers coming to the market. Innova FibaPrint Gloss, Museo Silver Rag, Premiere Art Platinum Rag, and Hahnemühle FineArt Pearl are examples of these new fine art papers. All these papers are semi-matte or matte and have a very fine smooth surface.* They are suitable for color as well as black-and-white prints, have a rich color gamut and a very good Dmax.

Table 2-2: Standard paper sizes

Format/Name	Metric size	U.S. equivalent
Metric names		
A6	10.5 × 14.8 cm	4.13 × 5.82 inches
A5	14.8 × 21.0 cm	5.82 × 8.27 inches
A4	21.0 × 29.7 cm	8.27 × 11.69 inches
A4 Plus	21.0 × 33.0 cm	8.27 × 13.00 inches
A3	29.7 × 42.0 cm	11.69 × 16.53 inches
A3+	32.9 × 48.3 cm	13.00 × 19.00 inches
A2	42.0 × 59.4 cm	16.53 × 23.38 inches
A2+	48.0 × 62.8 cm	19.90 × 27.72 inches
A1	59.4 × 84.1 cm	23.38 × 33.11 inches
A1+	62.5 × 91.4 cm	24.60 × 39.98 inches
A0	84.1 × 118.9 cm	33.11 × 46.81 inches
A0++	91.4 × 125.0 cm	35.98 × 49.21 inches
U.S. names		
Executive	18.4 × 118.9 cm	7.1 × 10.5 inches
A (US Letter)	21.6 × 27.9 cm	8.5 × 11.0 inches
Legal	21.6 × 35.6 cm	8.5 × 14.0 inches
B (Leger, Tabloid)	43.2 × 27.9 cm	11.0 × 17.0 inches
Super B/Super A3	33.0 × 48.3 cm	13.0 × 19.0 inches
C (Broadsheet)	43.2 × 55.9 cm	17.0 × 22.0 inches
D	55.9 × 86.4 cm	22.0 × 34.0 inches
E	86.4 × 111.8 cm	34.0 × 44.0 inches

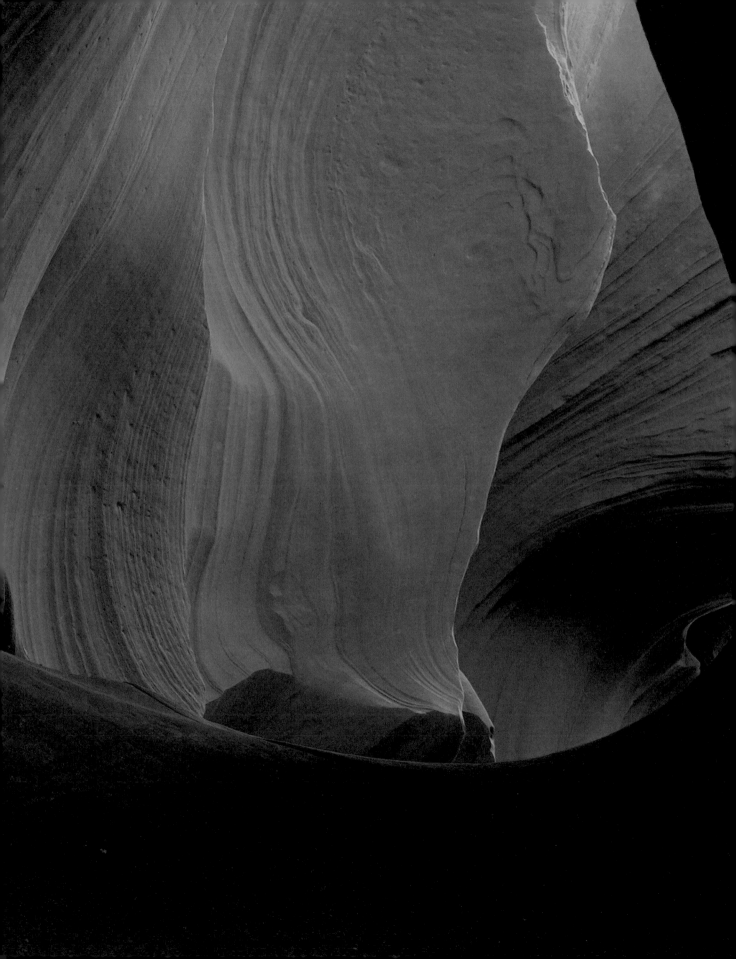

CMS Management for Printing

With photographic prints, we usually work in color, so it is essential that the color on our monitor is correctly calibrated. It should closely match that seen by the various input devices, e.g., camera and scanner.

After balancing white and black values, adjusting color saturation, or performing other color corrections or contrast enhancements, the color we see on a monitor should accurately represent the color values of our image. Most importantly, when we finally print the image, after optimizing and enhancing, the colors in our print will closely match those we view on our monitor. This is what color management is all about. Of course, to do efficient color work, it is essential to understand the basics of color and color management.

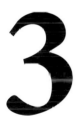

Color management is one of the most demanding subjects in digital photography, and has been the subject of entire books. Because of the extensive information available elsewhere, we provide only a short introduction to color management, with a focus on those parts important to a workflow for fine art printing.

3.1 Understanding different color models

→ *There are several good books on color management: "Color Confidence" by Tim Grey ([1]) and "Real World Color Management" by Bruce Fraser ([2]).*

Let us start with some easy stuff – with the different color models Photoshop supports. We will meet these color modes (or models) again and again – at least some of them. A *color model* defines the way colors are described, in a technical, mathematical way – e.g., from what basic components a color is built up – these components are called *primary colors* or **primaries** – how the numbers of those components are interpreted and are arranged in the color data and – as an extension to this – how much data is used for each component.

Photoshop supports several different color models. A color model defines mathematically how colors in an image are described. The main color models for photographers are:

▸ RGB
▸ LAB
▸ CMYK
▸ Grayscale

Photoshop provides additional color models, but these are rarely used by photographers, so a discussion of them is beyond the scope of this book. These include *Bitmap* for pure black-and-white (bitonality) images, and *Index mode*, used primarily for Web graphics (if you can live with fewer than 256 different color values). *Duotone* is used with grayscale images and allows the addition of a second color, giving a print more depth and feel.

* Some formats even allow for 32 bit per primary color. This, for example, is used with HDR (high dynamic range) images.

Color depth: In a color model, you may use either 8-bit (one byte) to specify the amount (or percentage) of a single value (e.g., red) or 16-bit (2 bytes).* Thus, you may have your image in 8-bit or 16-bit mode. A different bit depth is possible, but not supported by most applications. Using 16-bit doubles the space needed to store values, but gives you more headroom when it comes to differentiating color values, and allows for more precise calculations with less rounding errors. Using 8-bit, the value of a single component may vary from 0 to 255 (using integers).** Using 16-bit, the range runs from 0 to 65,536 (actually only 15-bits are used in Photoshop, so the range becomes 0 to 32,768). Though we recommend using 16-bit whenever possible and reasonable, it is common practice to use 8-bit values (0–255).

** For the technicians among us: integer values are used for 8-bit as well as for 16-bit data (per color channel). With some 32-bit formats, floating point numbers are used.

For most issues in color management, it doesn't matter which mode you use. When producing final output, e.g., printing, you will be required to reduce your image to 8-bit mode, since nearly all real devices can not actually produce more than 256 different shades of a color. Considering the various combinations of the three primary colors of RGB, this adds up to 16,777,216 different colors (256 × 256 × 256). Our eyes can only differentiate about 120–200 different hues of a particular color, depending on illumination, contrast, viewing distance, etc. During actual color optimization, however, where color shifting, transformation, and calculation of color values is done, 16-bit is the preferred mode.

Starting with Photoshop CS2, Photoshop also supports 32-bit (per channel) color data. There are different file formats for this (e.g., PSD, PSB, Radiance, PFM, OpenEXR and TIFF).

RGB color model

All colors in the RGB color model are created from three primary colors: red, green, and blue. RGB is the color model most commonly used today in digital photography, and we will perform our workflow mainly in this mode. RGB is an *additive color model*, meaning that the sum (addition) of all three basic colors at full strength (100 percent) will add up to pure white.

"0, 0, 0" defines black while "255, 255, 255" is bright white. Pure white should hardly occur in any photo.

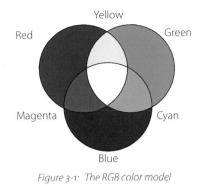

Figure 3-1: The RGB color model

LAB color model

The *CIE-LAB color model* (often spelled Lab, LAB or L*a*b*) separates colors (chroma, A+B) from the detail and brightness (luminance, L) in images. As in RGB, Lab uses three basic components to build or describe a color: L (for Luminance), ranging from black (0 = no light) to white (100), and two color axes: *a* and *b*. The a-axis is Green to Red (actually more Magenta) and the b-axis, Blue to Yellow.

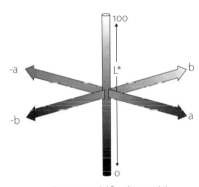

Figure 3-2: LAB color model

CMYK color model

The CMYK color model uses four primary colors to define a color: cyan (C), magenta (M), yellow (Y), and black (K). CMYK was designed for printing, where incoming light is reflected by the print.

CMYK is a *subtractive color model*, as each of these colored inks absorbs (subtracts) a certain spectrum of light. Figure 3-3 shows that mixing cyan and magenta gives you blue, and when you add magenta to yellow you get red. In theory, the combination of the colors C, M, and Y alone should be sufficient to produce black, but due to certain impurities in inks, they produce a dark muddy brown instead. To solve this problem, a fourth color, black, is added, and is called the *key color* (K for short).

Although CMYK is an important color model for a printing press, it is not used much in digital photography. Though inkjet printers are technically CMYK printers (most are even CcMmYK with additional light Cyan and Magenta inks), they provide an RGB interface to the user. Transformation from RGB to CMYK is done by the printer driver in the background.

We rarely use the CMYK color model in our workflow. Even when preparing images for printing that requires CMYK, you should stick with RGB-mode images whenever possible and resort to an RGB-to-CMYK conversion as the very last step. After conversion, some additional sharpening and some slight increasing of saturation may be required afterward. Working on photos in CMYK mode has these disadvantages:

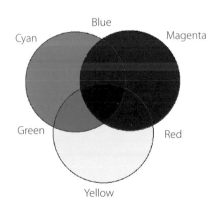

Figure 3-3: CMYK color model

▸ CMYK images are larger than RGB (with four color values per pixel instead of three with RGB).

➜ *If you have to convert a photo from RGB to CMYK, you should do the conversion on a copy of your photo.*

▶ Some photo filters do not work in CMYK mode.

▶ The CMYK color space usually contains fewer colors than most RGB color spaces. Thus, when you convert from RGB to CMYK, you may lose some colors, and there is no way to retrieve them should you want to later use your image for something such as Lightjet printing, which is used by photo services to output your image on photographic paper, or a digital presentation using an RGB monitor.

Grayscale mode

How to convert a color image to a greyscale or monochrom image is described in Chapter 7.

Photoshop also works with images in pure black-and-white (B&W) – also called *bitonal* – or in grayscale. However, when working in grayscale, the color of a pixel only describes a single (gray) value. Consequently, even when intending to produce a black-and-white photo (grayscale photo), we use RGB mode to preserve color information. This gives the black-and-white print some tint.

When using Photoshop's bitmap mode, a picture has only two possible color values: black or white; no gray. Bitmap mode is rarely used with photographs, and most imaging techniques and filters do not support Bitmap mode.

HSB/HSL color model

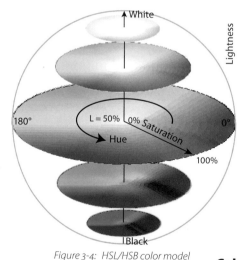

Figure 3-4: HSL/HSB color model

The HSB (*Hue, Saturation and Brightness*) or HSL (*Hue, Saturation and Lightness*) models are not explicitly supported by Photoshop, but are used in quite a few places like the Photoshop color picker (see Figure 3-31) or the Hue/Saturation tool. Here, the hue is given using an angle from 0° to 360°. 0° (as well as 360°) corresponds to red, 90° to green, 180° to cyan and 210° to blue. Saturation has a range from 0% (white) to 100% while Brightness runs from 0% (black) to 100 % (white).

In some dialog boxes, i.e. those changed from the current saturation like the Hue/Saturation dialog, Saturation may also run from -100 to +100. The same is true for Lightness slider.

Color spaces

* *e.g. represented by the sRGB color space*

A *color space* is the total range of colors that real devices like monitors or printers, or virtual devices like *theoretical average monitor** can record or reproduce. This range defines the *gamut* of the device.

Every real device has a unique color space, and even identical devices (same make and model) have slightly different color spaces, e.g. due to different age and production tolerances. These differences increase with variations in user-selected hardware or software settings: different monitor resolution, different printer inks or paper, or even a different brightness setting on a monitor.

To improve the ability to work with color, the International Color Consortium (ICC) and some other companies (e.g., Adobe, Kodak, Apple) have defined *virtual color spaces* representing the gamut of a virtual, rather than a real, device. Later, we discuss the advantages of these virtual, standardized color spaces.

For ICC see www.color.org. There, you will find a lot of information on color management.

3.2 Understanding color management

Color correction and *color management (CM)* are two of the most important yet difficult areas to master in digital photography. As stated earlier, the goal of color management is to ensure that the photo you view on your monitor accurately matches the print produced by your printer or Lightjet print from a photo service. Color management helps reproduce colors as faithfully as possible across a broad range of different devices. While an identical reproduction is often impossible, because of the different ways various devices produce color, you should at least be able to predict the printed color from the color you view on your monitor.

For an in-depth introduction to color management, we recommend [1], [2], [4] and [5].

The ability of a color-managed application to display on your monitor the colors and the impression that an image will have when printed on a specific printer or other output device is called *soft proofing*. *Hard proofing* is when you actually print using the same inks and the same paper used for final output. Some printers now use less-expensive paper and printing techniques for their proofs, unless the client specifies otherwise.

On "soft-proofing" see section 3.10 at page 82.

Why you need to understand color management

If you post a photo on the Web and ask different people to discuss its color quality, without color management the resulting image will display colors at least slightly differently on all monitors. In fact, some monitors may not even render some RGB values at all. It is the domain of color management to significantly reduce the problem described here.

The challenge Your challenge is to have a monitor display the correct impression of how a certain photo would print on a color printer. The latest inkjet printers produce amazing results, but without proper color management, color printing largely remains trial and error. You end up changing the printer's color settings for every print; hardly a satisfactory solution.

The solution The solution to this color problem is to determine the color characteristics of a device, and to incorporate them when reading colors from an input device, or when sending color to an output device. Essentially, you put a "tag" on color images that defines how the color values of the image are to be interpreted most accurately.

ICC profiles

The ICC color profile describes a device's color characteristics, e.g., the colors the device can record or reproduce, the values recorded for a perceived color (input device), or the values you must send to an output device to produce a certain color. These profiles are available from the device manufacturer (usually called *canned profiles*), or you produce your own using special profiling hardware and software. A profile produced for your specific device is called a *custom profile*. Almost all color management systems today use ICC profiles. With the help of such a profile, the color values required to produce a specific color on device A, e.g., a monitor, can be translated to values that will reproduce that specific color on device B, e.g., a printer, as accurately as possible. The profile also describes the gamut of the device.

> **Note:** Because most people use their monitor as their soft-proofing device, the first step toward complete color management is to profile your monitor.

> **Note:** A raw RGB value does not define color in an absolute way, as the color produced by a certain RGB value is very much dependent on the device used or on the device that recorded that value. An RGB value in the context of a color space, defined by the ICC profile of the color space, however, does define an absolute color.

What do you do when you get an image that, without color management, displays different colors on different monitors? With the help of the input profile, a color management system may correctly interpret the RGB values of the (input) image and, with the aid of an ICC profile for your monitor, will accurately transfer them to color values that produce a similar color on your output device. The next section describes this in detail.

What is a color management system?

A color management system (CMS) is a set of program modules that mediate color translation among different devices. These modules are often part of a computer's operating system, and also are usually provided by software companies (e.g., Adobe). If an application is used to display, edit or print a color image, it initiates the proper function(s), e.g., displaying a particular image, generates the correct ICC profile information, and then tells the CMS what function should be performed. The central part of the CMS is a color management module,[*] which performs the calculations needed to translate (transform) a color from color space A to color space B. Here's how it works:

CMM = "color management modul". This is also called "color matching module".

1. First, the *color management module (CMM)* translates the device-dependent color values of the image to a device-independent color space, using the description of the source ICC profile. Now the color values of the image are in Lab color space, which is device-independent.

This intermediate space is called *transfer color space* or *profile connection space* (PCS).

2. Next, these LAB values are translated to color values that will produce a color on the output device that is as close to the original color impression as possible. If the output device cannot produce the very same color, the CMM will try to find the closest match. Finding the best match is determined by the translation intent (explained at page 52/53), also called *rendering intent.*

The ICC profiles used in this scheme are actually simple translation tables. They support translation from device-dependent color values to device-independent color values, and vice-versa.

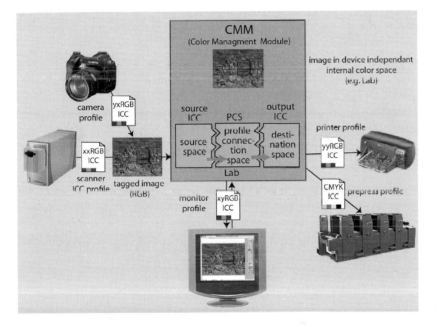

◀ *Figure 3-5:*
How color profiles function within a color management system

Photoshop and other applications that support color management embed the ICC profile data within the image file; this new file is called a *tagged file* or *tagged image.* When you pass the tagged image along, the profile information is passed along, as well. You should be aware that not all image file formats can include ICC profiles. While TIFFs and JPEGs can, GIFs cannot. As you have probably noticed, a GIF image has an unacceptable color depth anyway.

Color working spaces

It is often a challenge to work with a large number of different device-dependent color spaces, which is how virtual, standardized color spaces were defined. Rather than describe the gamut of a real device, they define the gamut for an abstract or virtual device. There are several different spaces for each of the color models (RGB, Lab, CMYK), and range from a narrow

Note: Avoid applications that do not use or create these embedded profiles, or that do not support use of monitor profiles. The color of the image they display on the monitor or print may or may not be correct or even close to the true colors. Some applications may even remove the profiles from your image when editing without alerting you.

➜ *Avoid color space conversions (explicit ones) whenever possible, as every conversion will result in some rounding errors and – more seriously – in some color compression or color clipping in many cases.*

* *e.g. inkjet printer, LightJet printer, monitor, etc.*

** *With 8-bit there are only 256 discrete values available.*

to a broad gamut: for the RGB color model, we have sRGB, Apple RGB, Adobe RGB (1998), ECI-RGB and Pro Photo RGB (and several others).

To eliminate a specific working space (including its ICC profile) of your input device, you usually convert an image from the original input color space to a standardized color space and continue to work on this image using this working space. With digital photos, you may accomplish this conversion using the RAW converter.

Why define several working spaces for a color model? These spaces differ mainly in the color range (their gamut) they cover. In some work-flows, it is advantageous to use a narrow color space, while in others, a wide space is better. If your input device, say, a digital camera, has a wide gamut, you should use a work space with a wide gamut if you are intending to produce output for several different methods.* If you convert your image to a working space with a narrow gamut, you may lose some colors that could be reproduced by some output devices. If, however, you use a work-ing space with a very wide gamut, the numbers (bits) representing color values may not be sufficient to differentiate the many different colors your gamut allows.** Many of these discrete values may be lost because your image may never have colors that extend to the outer edge of the theoretical gamut of the space. This may become worse if you must do a lot of correcting, rounding, and perform transformations. For this reason, we recommend using 16-bit mode, when you intend to use a color space with a wide gamut.

The following list shows some of the most important color spaces for pho-tographers:

▸ **sRGB**: This color space was designed to be used with monitors, and is probably a good one for photos to be presented on the Web. It defines a gamut that can be displayed by the average monitor, a relatively narrow color space. Though many DSLRs allow you to produce images using this color space, sRGB color space is much narrower than the color space cameras can see and record.

▸ **Adobe RGB (1998)**: A very popular color space among Photoshop users. It has a larger gamut than sRGB and covers most printable colors. This is the color space we prefer for digital photos.

▸ **Pro Photo RGB**: This color space was defined and is supported by Kodak. It provides a very large gamut and should only be used when working with a color depth of 16-bit. Of the RGB working spaces men-tioned here, it is the only one that can hold the full camera gamut. It is also the internal working space for Adobe Camera Raw.

Another color space often mentioned is "Apple RGB". But Apple RGB is outdated and should no longer be used today! It was defined by the gamut of a certain line of Apple monitors.

▸ **ECI-RGB**: This color space was defined by ECI, the European Color Initiative, a group of companies attempting to define color-production standards in Europe. The ECI-RGB color space was designed to include all colors that may be reproduced by printers. Its gamut is somewhat wider than that of Adobe RGB and includes some green colors that can be reproduced by many printers (inkjet and offset, as well as gravure), but that are not part of either sRGB or Adobe RGB (1998). ECI-RGB is the standard RGB color space within the European prepress industry and serves as the European alternative to Adobe RGB for prepress work.

Since the ECI-RGB profile is not part of Adobe's Photoshop distribution, you have to download this profile from ECI's Web site (www.eci.org).

Visualization of color spaces

Color spaces are actually three-dimensional (L-, A-, B-axis). The profile shown in Figure 3-6 is that of sRGB, using the ColorSync utility of Mac OS X. For Windows XP, there is a similar utility, *MS Color Control Panel*, that you may download [58]. In Figure 3-5, the gray outer space shows the gamut of Adobe RGB (1998) and allows comparison of these two color spaces.

The industry also uses some form of 2D charts to display color spaces. The color space plot shown in Figure 3-7 was generated with the GretagMacbeth Profile Maker Pro 4.1 Profile Editor.

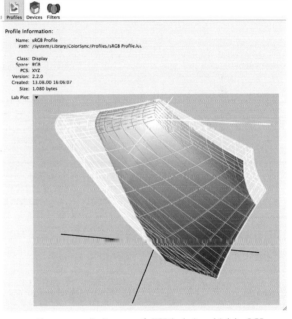

▲ *Figure 3-6: 3D diagram of sRGB (color) and Adobe RGB (1998) (gray shape)*

→ *Even a free demo-version of ProfileMaker will allow visualization of color gamuts – restricted to two gamuts.*
Other useful tools for this are BableColor [30] and ColorThink [31]. All these programs support different display modes.

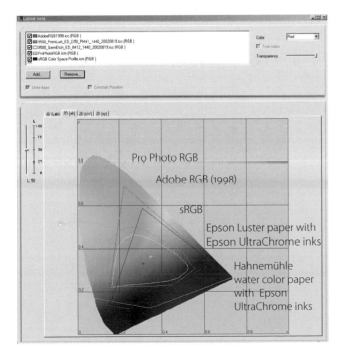

◀ *Figure 3-7:*
Gamut Display (using ProfileMaker Pro)

In Figure 3-7, Pro Photo RGB is extremely wide, while Adobe RGB (1998) is much smaller and sRGB is very narrow.

We often use "Hahnemühle German Etching watercolor paper" when printing with our inkjet printers. This paper's gamut, using Epson's Ultra-Chrome inks, exceeds sRGB's but fits well into Adobe RGB's gamut. The color space of the "Epson Lustre paper" has a much wider range than that of "Hahnemühle watercolor paper," and exceeds both sRGB and Adobe RGB (in some blues and greens). If you have ICC profiles describing different printing sets, i.e., combinations of printer + ink + paper, a display like the ones shown in Figure 3-6 allows you to compare the gamut and thus the color richness you may achieve using different papers.

Color-space mapping

When images need to be converted from one color space to another, e.g., when displaying an image on a monitor, the image is transformed from its source color space (device color space or working color space) to that of the output device, in this case, your monitor. In most cases, the gamut of the source and the destination are different, so some color mapping has to take place. This transformation is performed by the color-management module (also called the color-management engine).

The main challenge is what to do with those colors of the source space that are not present in the destination space. Because there are several ways to handle this problem, ICC has defined four different ways of mapping, called *intents*:

Perceptual (also called *Photographic*): If the gamut of the source space is wider than that of the destination space, all colors are compressed to fit into the destination space (Figure 3-8). If the gamut of the source space is smaller than the destination space, i.e., all colors of the source are present at the destination space, a one-to-one mapping takes place: all colors keep their original appearance.

When mapping from a wider space to a smaller space, perceptual mapping usually shifts colors to a bit less saturated and somewhat lighter colors, but the overall impression of the image is preserved, i.e., different colors keep their relative color distance. When the white point of the color spaces are different, a white point mapping takes place. Perceptual and *Relative colorimetric* mapping are the two intents used when converting photographs.

Relative colorimetric: When mapping from a wider color space to a smaller color space, a color in the source space that is not present at the destination space is mapped to the closest color at the destination space, usually at the border of the destination space (Figure 3-9).

With this type of mapping, two colors, both different in the source space and not present in the destination space, may be mapped to the same color in the destination space, but usually at the edge of the envelope. This could result in some color clipping or banding. The white point of the source space is mapped to the white point of the destination (if they differ), and all colors are adapted relative to the destination white point.

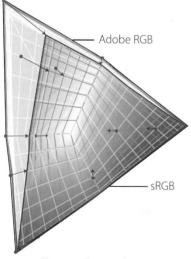

Figure 3-8: Perceptual gamut mapping from Adobe RGB to sRGB

Adobe RGB

sRGB

Here, the "white point" is the color temperature (or color spectrum) of the color 'white' of the corresponding color space. Adobe RGB (1998), for example, has a white point at 6 500 K while ECI-RGB has its white point at 5 000 K.

This intent is useful for photographs and should be used when the source and destination spaces have a similar gamut with lots of overlap. It is also useful if most of the colors in your image, which may not use the full gamut of the source space, have an identical color in the destination space. In this case, most colors remain unmodified when transformed. This intent also is used when colors in an image are translated to colors on your monitor.

Absolute colorimetric: This intent is like a relative colorimetric, where colors present in both color spaces are mapped 1:1, and colors that are *out of the gamut*, i.e., when a color of the source space is not present in the destination space, are mapped to the border of the destination space. This mapping is particularly useful when using your output device (e.g., monitor) to simulate the behavior of another device, e.g., for soft proofing. In this case, the monitor simulates the white color of the paper. Note that there is no mapping for the white point.

Saturation: This intent tries to map an out-of-gamut color to a color of the destination space with the same level of saturation, even if the color has to be shifted significantly. Use this intent when converting logos and colored diagrams from a larger color space to smaller one. It is not useful for photographs, as it discards information for hue and lightness, and does not preserve color realism. Some third-party profiles adapt this intent for a special color mapping that retains the saturation as best as possible, without a noticeable color shift; it may be used for some photos.

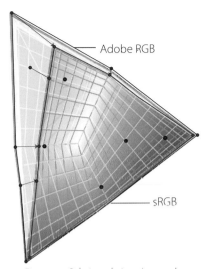

Figure 3-9: Relative colorimetric mapping (Adobe RGB to sRGB)

➜ *Some profiling packages – and accordingly some profiles – misuse the "Saturation" rendering for a modified version of "Perceptual", which will result in less color shifting than regular "Perceptual".*

3.3   **Creating device profiles**

Since most of our digital work is done using a monitor, when setting up a color managed workflow, we need to consider monitor profiling as our most important task. In this section, we turn our attention to building a device profile. Normally, there are two steps:

1. **Calibration**
    The aim of calibration is to define a highly accurate, *standardized state* for the device; for example, when calibrating a monitor, you manually set the controls of your monitor to achieve a certain *luminance* (brightness of your monitor's white) that is known to be good for color work. Also, you set a *white point* that conforms to an industry standard, such as D50 or D65 (color temperatures of 5,000 or 6,500 Kelvin, respectively). The *white point* of your monitor is a mix of R, G, and B that will represent *white*.

2. **Characterization**
    When characterizing a device, a *target* is recorded by the input device, or sent to an output device. A target (test chart) is a pattern of color

patches with known color values. By comparing the color values recorded by the device (such as a scanner) to the known color values of the target, the profiling program calculates a device's *color profile*. The profile is essentially a translation table of device-dependant color values to device-independent color values (with input devices), or vice-versa (with output devices); for example, if the profile is for an input device, it translates device-dependant colors seen by the device into the device-independent profile connection space (PCS, which is CIE-LAB space). If, on the other hand, it is for a profile of an output device, the table provides translation from the profile connection space to the device-dependant colors of the output device.

To perform either step, especially when calibrating a monitor, it is advisable to use a hardware device like a colorimeter or a spectrophotometer to measure color.

We discuss profiling only briefly in this book, focusing mainly on profiling your monitor and your printer(s).

Camera profiles

There are two types of camera profiles: *generic camera* and *custom camera profiles*; the latter are for specific cameras. All RAW converters come with quite good generic profiles. Some of them also support custom profiles.* For some RAW converters, you may also buy good third-party camera profiles.

* e. g., Raw Shooter and Capture One

Creating your own camera profiles can be very tricky since targets must be shot under highly controlled lighting conditions. Additionally, individual cameras of the same model can vary significantly: certain cameras vary more than others within type and brand. For more details on camera profiling, see one of our RAW conversion books ([9]).

Printer profiles

There is no single profile for a printer. A printer profile is always specific to that printer using a specific paper, ink set, and a specific driver and its settings.** Profiles for different types of printing paper also vary significantly.

** such as the same dpi or quality settings

When profiling a printer, a target is printed using precisely the printer settings, ink, and paper specified by the profile. Once the print has dried (from one to 24 hours), the color values of the print are measured using either a spectrophotometer or a profiled scanner (less accurate). By comparing known values of the color patches of the target to those of the measured patches of the print, the profiling software produces the printer profile.

Fortunately, you don't need to invest in a costly spectrophotometer and profiling software; you can use several profiling services that do this job for you. Look up "printer profiling service" in your favorite search engine. For more details on printer profiling, see section 3.6.

3.4   **Profiling your monitor**

As stated earlier, an accurate monitor profile is the basis for highly accurate color-managed workflow. When calibrating your monitor, you have a choice of doing so by eye or with specialized hardware.

When profiling your monitor, begin by turning it on and leaving it on at least 30 minutes before beginning any calibration. To perform the calibration, follow the instructions provided by your choice of tool, whether calibrating by eye or using hardware-based tools as those discussed below.

Be aware that room lightning, the color of your walls and desktop, and even your clothing, can influence precise calibration.

Calibration by eye

Photoshop for Windows comes with a utility called *Adobe Gamma* that lets you calibrate your monitor. With Mac OS X there is a similar utility called *ColorSync Calibrator*. Both utilities use your eyes as their measuring instrument, which is better than nothing at all but not as good as a hardware-based calibration.

➜ *With hardware-based calibration packages such as huey™ [61] or Spyder2 Express ([48]) for about USD $ 90, there is hardly an excuse for not using one of these hardware-based monitor profiling packages devices If you care for color confidence in your work!*

Hardware-based calibration

Although calibrating your monitor by eye is better than doing no calibration at all, if accuracy and precision are important to you, you should use a hardware-based, color-measuring device, e.g., a spectrophotometer or colorimeter, to achieve much more precise results. There are several reasonably priced packages currently available: $100–$300 for a complete kit.[*]

We use and recommend GretagMacbeth Eye-One Display 2 and Monaco Optix .

The entire calibration and profiling process will take you about ten minutes. Once a good initial calibration is achieved, the next calibration will be much faster.

* *Your choices include: GretagMacbeth Eye-One Display 2 [55], ColorVision Spyder and Spyder Pro products [48], MonacoOPTIX from Monaco Systems [59] and the entry level device huey, that is sold by Pantone [61] as well as by GretagMacbeth [55].*

Calibration settings

We recommend using the following values when calibrating and profiling a monitor:

White point $6500°$ K (D65)
Gamma   2.2
Luminance   100 150 cd/m^2

We recommend these values even for prepress work (where a white point of 5,000° K is the standard) and even if you work on a Mac where a gamma of 1.8 is traditional.

➜ *Before starting to calibrate and profile your monitor, make sure you have set a display color depth of at least 24 bits. Additionally, the monitor should have warmed up for at least 30 minutes.*

Calibrating and profiling using Eye-One Display 2

The Eye-One Display package from GretagMacbeth ([55]) includes software (Eye-One Match) for calibrating and profiling monitors, as well as a sensor (colorimeter). It supports both Mac and Windows, and allows the calibration of CRTs as well as LCDs and laptop displays. To use it to calibrate your monitor:

1. Launch Eye-One Match (EOM) and select the monitor from the list of devices you can profile. We recommend using Advanced mode.

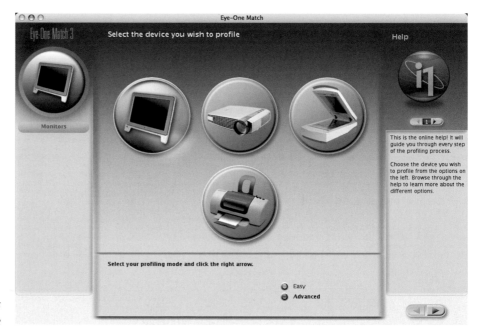

Figure 3-10: ▶
Startup screen of Eye-One Match:
Select the monitor to profile

2. Select the type of monitor you intend to calibrate (CRT, LCD or Laptop), then Click ▷ to continue.

3. The first task is to calibrate the sensor (not your monitor). Follow the instructions given on the screen. (Help will provide you with additional information.)

4. Select your target calibration settings. We recommend these values: ▷ will take you to the next step.

5. Attach the sensor to your monitor, using either the suction-cup (if calibrating a CRT), or by attaching the lead weights to your sensor cable and letting them dangle on the backside of the monitor. If calibrating an LCD, you may have to tilt the monitor backward a bit, so that the sensor lies flat on the screen.

White point:	Medium White (6500)	⬍
Gamma:	2.2 – Recommended	⬍
Luminance:	140 – LCD recommenda...	⬍

Figure 3-11: Recommended settings
for your monitor calibration

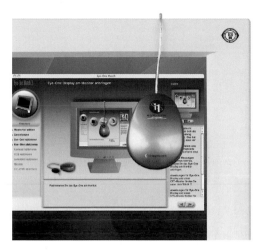

◀ *Figure 3-12:*
Eye-One Display colorimeter

6. Begin the calibration phase using the controls on your monitor, if it has them. (Skip this step if you are calibrating a laptop or LCD without controls, and continue with step 9).

   You will set the contrast control to maximum, and then slowly reduce it until the green arrow is inside the green area and close to 0. Don't worry: Eye-One Match will guide you through this calibration.

   If possible, place your OSD menu somewhat off the middle of your display. It should not interfere with your Eye-One Match screen.

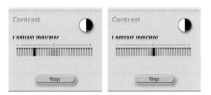

Figure 3-13: Use your monitor dial to bring the contrast marker near the zero value.

7. Press Start to have EOM begin measuring the contrast values, then Stop and ▶ to begin calibration of the RGB controls. This step will set the control dials so that the monitor's white point is set close to the intended color temperature (6,500° K or 5,000° K).

   This may be achieved either by adjusting an Online Screen Display (OSD) setting on the monitor choosing a color temperature of 6,500° K, or by setting the monitor's R-, G- and B-controls, if any. In this step, all three colored bars should be in the green area for optimum calibration. The Eye-One Match screen will provide useful feedback.

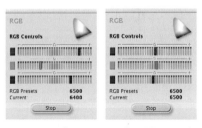

Figure 3-14: If your monitor has RGB controls, set your target white point.

8. Next, set luminance using your monitor's brightness controls. A luminance of 140 cd/m² is recommended for LCD monitors. If your calibrate a laptop display, you may have to reduce the value to 120 cd/m². For CRT monitors, providing less brightness, you will probably have to chose 120 cd/m².

9. This finishes the calibration phase. Eye-One Match now will start the actual characterization: it will display a number of color patches and measure their values. You won't need to do anything during this approximately five-minute process.

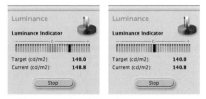

Figure 3-15: Set the luminance using your brightness control of the monitor to a target value of 120–150 cd/m².

10. Once the characterization is finished, Eye-One Match will display the values used and then display a diagram of the resulting color space (Figure 3-16).

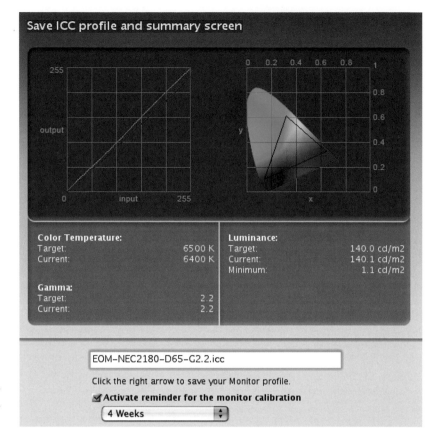

Figure 3-16: ▶
EOM shows the profiling values and the
monitor color space. Enter a descriptive
profile name.

EOM will also prompt you for a profile name. Choose a descriptive name reflecting the tool used, the make of the monitor, as well as the values used; for example, if your are using EOM to calibrate an NEC 2180 monitor with X values, a suggested name might be "EOM-NEC2180-D65-G2.2." You may also want to include the date.

Eye-One Match will save the ICC profile to the appropriate folder, depending on your operating system, and will immediately make it the active and default monitor profile. In Windows and with Adobe Gamma installed, you should move Adobe Gamma out of your start folder to prevent it interfering with the correct loading of the new monitor profile when Windows starts up.

Once you have completed these profiling steps, do not change any monitor settings without re-calibrating. You should plan to re-calibrate your monitor about once a month.

For LCD monitors, we recommend that you re-calibrate and re-profile about every four weeks. With CRTs, every second week would be preferable.

3.5   Photoshop color-management settings

Before beginning to work with Photoshop, set up the program with your personal color-management preferences. The way color settings are made is similar among all Adobe applications since Adobe Creative Suite 1 (CS1). When using CS2, you may use centralized color settings. These settings will be used (by default) by all other CS2 applications, as well. With CS2, the settings may be done in Bridge.

Photoshop probably offers the most advanced color-management support of any application. For that reason, its color settings offer many different options and parameters.

To begin setting your color-management preferences, select Edit ▸ Color Settings to open the color-setting dialog. Figure 3-17 shows how we set the Color Settings in Photoshop.

With Mac OS and CS1 (or previous versions), you will find this 'Color Settings' dialog in your Photoshop Preferences.

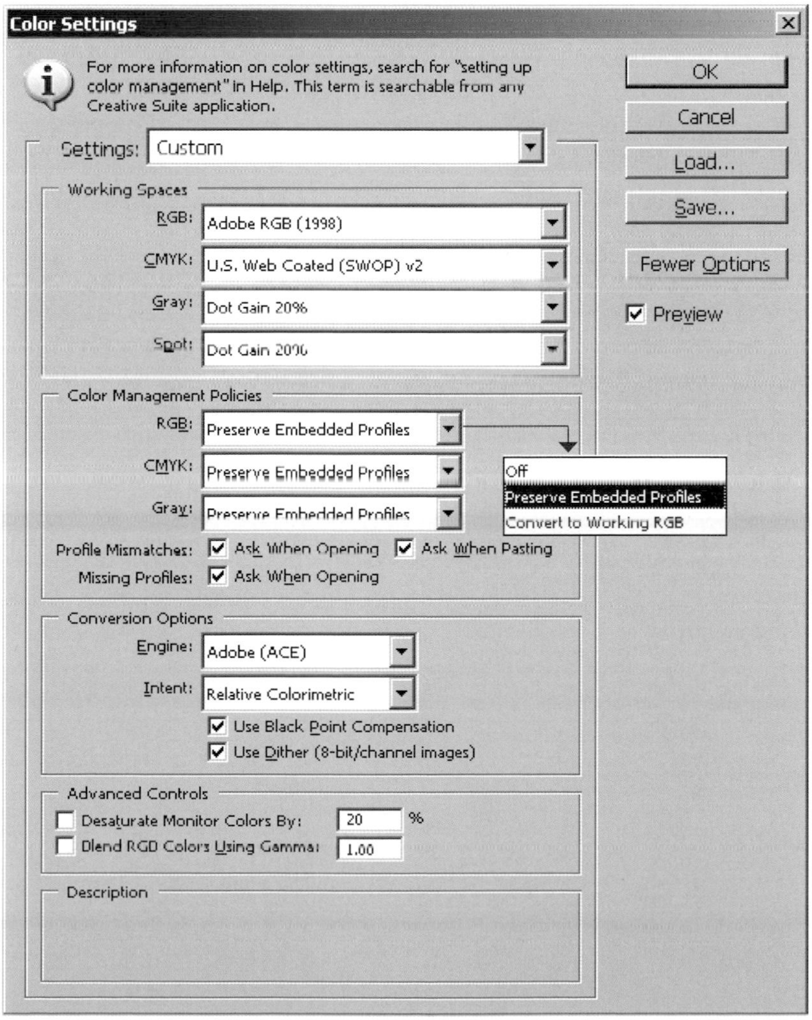

◀ *Figure 3-17:*
Photoshop color settings

Working Spaces

Here, you define your default working spaces for the various color modes (RGB, CMYK, Grayscale and Spot Color). The RGB working space is the most important for photographers.*

The CMYK working space is important only when converting RGB images to CMYK. The profile selected here is used as the destination color space.* In the United States, U.S. Web-Coated (SWAP) v2 is the best choice for CYMK, if your print shop does not provide you with different instructions.

* We use either Adobe RGB (1998) or Pro Photo RGB.

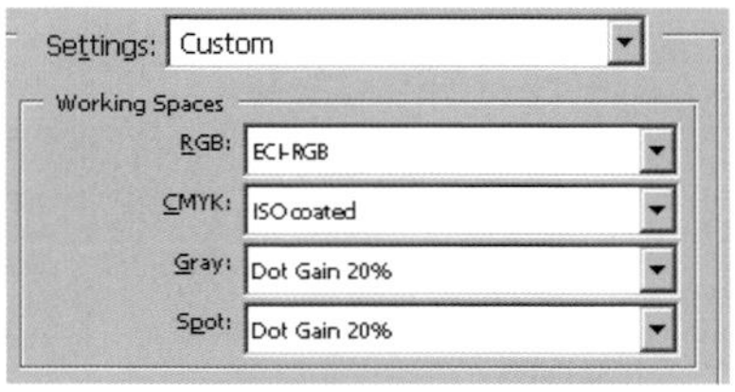

> **Note:** We ignore settings for CMYK and Gray here, as we only cover RGB color setup in our workflow. If you live in Europe, your CMYK setting should either be *Euroscale Coated* or *ISO Coated*. If you are mainly preparing your images for prepress, use ECI-RGB as your default RGB color space, in which case your settings might look like that in Figure 3-18.

Figure 3-18: Recommended working spaces for prepress work in Europe

Dot Gain 20, Photoshop's default value, is usually appropriate when you work with grayscale images. If your print shop gives you different values, use them. The same is true for spot color.

Color Management Policies

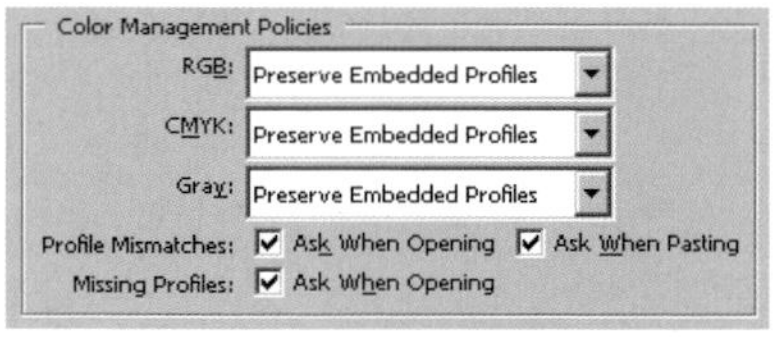

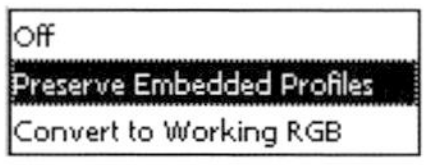

With Color-Management Policies, you define the default action that Photoshop takes when you open an image or paste pixels into your opened image, and when no profile is embedded or the color space of the image is not the same as your current working space. Again, you can set this for RGB, CMYK, and grayscale images.

In most cases, Preserve Embedded Profiles is the best choice. The only reasonable alternative is to choose Convert to Working. Selecting Off rarely makes sense in a color-managed workflow. If you choose Off, color management will still take place. With off, the colors of the image will be treated as if the image is the current working space. When the image is saved, no profile will be embedded. The check boxes allow you to define Photoshop default actions when a mismatch is found. If a box is not checked, Photoshop will execute the action selected for the particular color mode. When a box is checked, Photoshop will prompt you about what action it should take.

Conversion Options

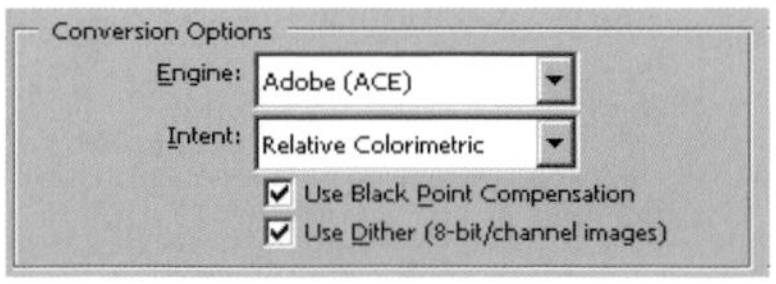

Using the Engine drop-down menu, you can select the color engine (color-management module) you want to use. We prefer Adobe (ACE) because it is probably better than ICM (Microsoft Windows) or ColorSync (Mac OS) and it will be the same on Mac and Windows.

As for Intent, you should choose Relative Colorimetric or Perceptual for photos (see "Color Space Mapping").

The Use Black Point Compensation option should always be checked. It helps when you are converting images from one profile to another by adapting the black point of the image to that of the destination space, thereby ensuring that the full tonal range of your destination is used.**

*   *e. g. a printer*

The Use Dither (8-bit/channel images) setting is effective only when converting 8-bit images from one color space to another. If the source color is not present in the destination space, Photoshop will try to simulate the source color using dithering. This may improve the color visual accuracy, but at the same time it will introduce some random noise (due to dithering) into your image.

You should experiment on your own to find the optimum setting for "Use Dithering"

Advanced Controls

Leave these settings at their defaults, as shown in Figure 3-17 page 69.

Photoshop is not particularly intuitive when it comes to finding the monitor profile in use. So use this method to find out which monitor profile is currently active:

Windows: Right-click on some free space of your desktop. Select Properties. A Display Properties dialog box will pop up. Select the Settings tag and click button Advanced. Select tab Color Management. This will show a dialog box with all monitor profiles installed. The profile currently active is highlighted (see Figure 3-19).

Here, you may add further monitor profiles, delete installed ones, and make another of the existing profiles your default monitor profile. You may have to restart RawShooter or Photoshop to activate or apply this change.

If you are running Windows XP and have MS Color Control Panel installed ([58]), you may also use *WinColor*. Go to tab Devices and select *Displays* to see the profile associated with your display.

Mac OS X: Call up System Preferences (you may find [apple icon] in your dock). Select Displays and activate tab Color. The dialog will list all monitor profiles installed and highlight the one currently active (Figure 3–20).

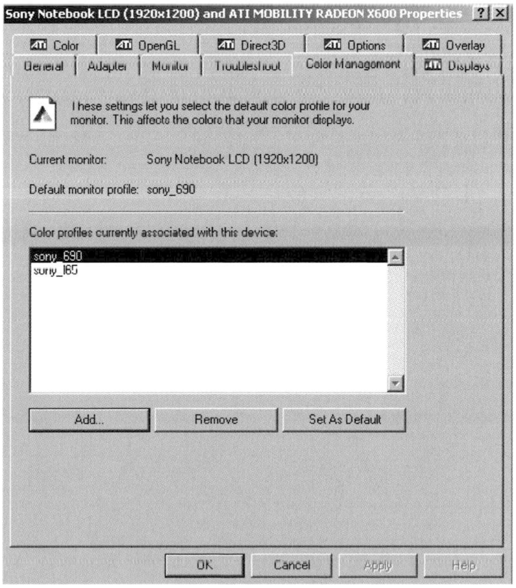

▲ *Figure 3-19: Finding the System Monitor Profile*

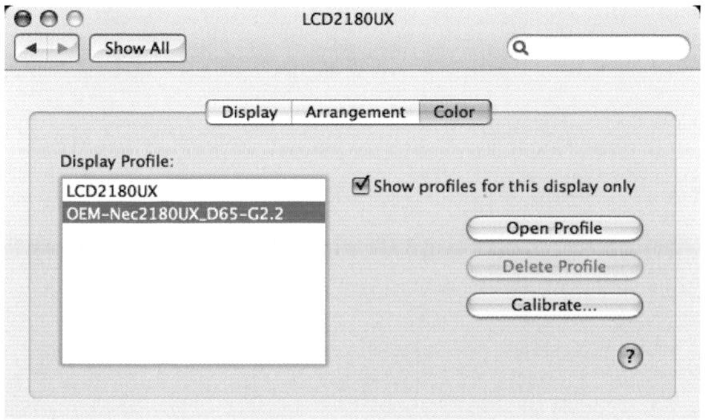

◀ *Figure 3-20:*
Current monitor profile in
Mac OS X

→ *Photoshop and most modern color-managed applications get their monitor profiles from the OS system settings.*

3.6   Profiles for your printer

Having set up your CMS settings in Photoshop and calibrated and profiled your monitor, it's time to think about profiling your printers. You must perform a profile for each combination of printer + printer-quality settings + paper + ink. Let us assume we deal with just one printer, e. g., an Epson R2400, and only use standard Epson inks for that printer. In this case, we still have a separate ICC profile for each type of paper and for each quality or resolution-setting of the printer. If you want to use glossy, semigloss and matte, we will need three different profiles, as each paper has a different gamut. Even if you want to use two different types of matte paper, e.g., "Epson Archival Matte" or "Hahnemühle PhotoRag", you will need two different profiles.

There are several ways to get a profile for your printer+ink+paper set:

1. **The profile may be part of your printer kit or may be downloaded from the Web site of the printer maker.**
    These profiles will only cover the original maker's inks and some papers the printer's manufacturer sells. These are "canned profiles" that do not consider individual derivations of your specific printer. They are a good start, depending on the manufacturer, the printer and the variations of the printer line. For the Epson R2400 or the HP Designjet 30/130 these manufacturers profiles will give up to 95% of the maximum quality a customer profile could provide.

2. When using a third-party paper, the manufacturer may provide profiles for their papers and some well-known fine art printers: Epson P2100/ 2200 with Epson Ultrachrome inks and other manufacturer's papers.[*] If a new printer hits the market, it usually takes a few months until the profiles for it are uploaded to their Web site.

    * e. g., Hahnemühle [38], Moab [39] or Tetanal [40]

3. Some suppliers of third-party inks provide generic profiles for their own inks that are profiled with often-used papers for some well-established printers: Lyson [81] offers profiles for several Epson and HP printers for their inks and their papers. You should also have a look at the Web site of Bill Atkinson [64] and his high-quality profile effort.

4. There are several companies out there that sell profiles for different printers and inks, e.g., Digital Domain, Inc. ([50]).

5. There are several services that produce a special profile for you:

    A) You download a print target from the service's Web site.

    B) You print the target using your specific printer, ink and paper (and other printer settings), and send the print to the service by regular mail.

C) The service will measure your target print, generate the profile and e-mail it to you.

D) You then install the profile.

The cost of this service varies from $30–$80 per RGB profile,* and is often lower if you order several profiles at once.

This is definitely not a bad choice for customer profiles. It avoids the cost of expensive printer-profiling software and hardware, plus the profiling is done by experienced personnel. Some companies restrict their services to specific printers or makers. You will find a list of profile services in Appendix C.

6. **Build your own customer profile.**
The next section describes this in detail.

* Ordering CMYK profiles, needed for press work, is somewhat more expensive. However, photographers only rarely need CMYK profiles – at least when printing with inkjet or lightjet printers.

Profiling your printer

Profiling a printer follows a basic scheme:

1. You select an appropriate target with well-known color patches, and print that target on the printer to be profiled. When printing, use the paper and ink set you intend to use.

    You should use the same printer driver settings for print resolution, paper-type and other settings that you will use later on. It is strongly recommended that you save these settings using a descriptive name; most printer drivers allow this. Avoid any color-correction settings at this point.

    Also, avoid any further color correction in the application you print from, e.g., Photoshop.

2. Let the print dry for at least one hour; 24 hours is better.

3. Now the colors of the print must be measured (there are several ways to do it) and profiling software will calculate the resulting ICC printer profile. Usually, it installs the profile immediately. Otherwise, you have to install it, using a method that is appropriate for your operating system (see section 3.7).

Most printer profiling packages offer several different print targets. The more color patches a target provides, the more precise your profile can be. But for more patches, the effort to measure them increases. There are profiling devices, that will read these printed targets with their patches automatically (e.g., DTP 41 or DTP 70 by X-Rite or Eye-One iO by Gretag Macbeth), but for most photographers, their price is prohibitive.

There are several ways to measure the colors of your target print:

A) Spectrophotometer.
This is the most accurate way to do this job, although a good photo-spectrometer is about $800–$1000. We recommend Eye-One Photo (or Eye-One Proof) by Gretag Macbeth or PULSE ColorElite by x.rite. We also saw some favorable reports on *PrintFix **Pro*** by Color Vision ([48]), priced at about $550, but we have no experiences of your own with this newer package.

*   Instead of buying PrintFix, we recommend
    that you spend some more money and
    buy PrintFix Pro, which comes with a
    spectrocolorimeter and will give much better
    results (profiles).

B) Dedicated patch-reader.
    The patch-reader is a small, dedicated scanner that reads the patches of
    the target print (e. g., as part of the *PrintFIX* kit by Color Vision [48]).*
    It is much cheaper than a spectrophotometer, but not as accurate. We
    have found it to be the least-accurate method of A-D.

C) Standard flatbed scanner for acquiring the patch values.
    This is probably the cheapest way to do the scanning. The accuracy of
    the method depends very much on the (color) quality of the scanner.
    The scanner itself should first be profiled. Some profiling packages, e.g.,
    MonacoEZcolor, scan a scanner target together with the printed target
    and (internally) do the profiling of the scanner first. Based on this "pro-
    file-enabled scanner," it interprets the color values of the patches of the
    printed target.

    This is a rather inexpensive and easy way for measuring the printed
    target, but for several reasons is less accurate than version A. Its accu-
    racy should be about the same as standard canned printer profiles and
    may be a cheap source of profiles, if using a third-party ink set or paper,
    where no generic profile is available.

D) You may send your printed target image to a profiling service. In this
    case, you should use the target the service provides on their Web site,
    and should accurately follow the instructions provided.

    The accuracy of theses profiles should be as good as version A, and
    may even be better, as the service personnel probably have more experi-
    ence than you do. The processing usually takes about two to three days
    plus the time it takes to send the print via regular mail. The cost per
    profile is $35–$80.

You may improve and optimize your profile using a profile editor, which is
part of some of the printer profiling packages (e.g., *Eye-One Proof* * or *Profile
Maker Pro* by Gretag Macbeth or *DoctorPro* by Color Vision). This, however,
should only be done when having gained some experience with profiling.

*   Since version 3.3, you may also edit profiles
    using Eye-One Match which is part of all
    One-One packages (e.g. Eye-One Photo).

Printer profiling using Eye-One Photo

Eye-One Photo is a profiling kit by Gretag Macbeth that consists of the
software Eye-One Match (EOM), a spectrophotometer Eye-One Pro, a scanner target (reflective) and a Mini-ColorChecker. It may be used to profile
displays, scanners, printers, and cameras, costs about $1,500, and runs on
Mac OS X and Windows. For profiling a printer, use the follow steps:

1. Launch Eye-One Match (EOM) and select the printer for profiling (see
    Figure 3-21).

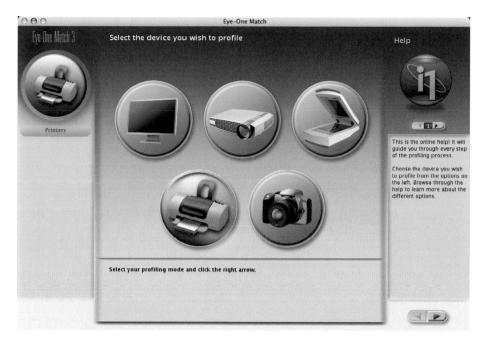

◀ Figure 3–21:
Eye-One match with "Printer"
selected for profiling

2. Select the type of target you want to print (Figure 3-22). EOM offers 3 types: a very simple one (i1 Easy RGB 1.x.txt), the standard target with 288 patches* and a TC9.18 target for best quality (i1 RGB 1.5.txt). The TC9.18 target should only be used if you use a device that scans the printed patches automacially. If you profile a PostScript printer, your choices may be reduced to just 1 or 2 targets. For inkjets, we recommend RGB 1.x.txt. Now click Print to print the target.

* i1 RGB 1.x.txt, which we recommend for inkjet printers

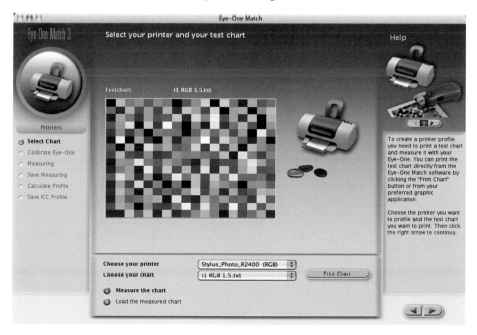

◀ Figure 3–22:
Select the printer to profile and
the target type

3. The print dialog of the operating system will display and should already be configured correctly. However, check that all driver color management is disabled, and that all other driver settings are appropriately set for your target:

➜ *We strongly recommend that you make notes about your printer driver settings and additionally save these settings in the printer driver using a descriptive name.*

A) correct paper type is selected
B) print resolution or quality settings are those you intend to use later on with that paper
C) all other settings, e.g., ink-set, ink-density, etc., are correctly set to those values you intend to use in your profile.

This setup is dependent on your operating system, your printer (and printer driver), and may even depend on optional installed components, or paper and ink-set used.

It may well be worth writing down and saving these settings for later use. When everything is set correctly, click on Print.

4. Let the print dry for at least 1 hour. We prefer to wait for about a day before we proceed (finishing EOM first).

5. Restart Eye-One-Match; again select the printer for profiling and the target type used before. Activate the option Measure the chart and click
   ▶.

6. EOM will ask you to calibrate your spectrometer by placing it on its profiling base. Press the calibration button at the site of the spectrometer. When EOM informs you that the calibration was successful, continue with ▶.

7. Select strip-mode for measuring. Put your target print on your desktop and put a white paper underneath (if your paper is not reasonably opaque) to prevent the color of your desktop from distorting the colors of the patches. Use the transparent plastic ruler to guide the spectrometer along the patches, as shown in Figure 3-23.

   To make sure that your measurements are not falsified by the color of your desktop shining through the paper of your target, you should put one or two sheets of the same paper below the target you scan.

➜ *If you scan a lot using Eye-One Pro, it may well be worth it to buy Eye-One iO, which will do the scanning in an automated way. This will allow you to use targets with more patches resulting in better (more precise) profiles.*

   Now scan, line by line, and release the button of the spectrometer at the end of your sweep. EOM will indicate if the measurement sequence for the row was not OK. In that case, repeat the last sweep. Repeat this step for each row of patches. Click ▶ when all rows are scanned.

   The first time you scan the patches, it will take some time to get the right feeling and the right speed for scanning. Scanning several targets will, however, provide experience and scanning will become smooth.

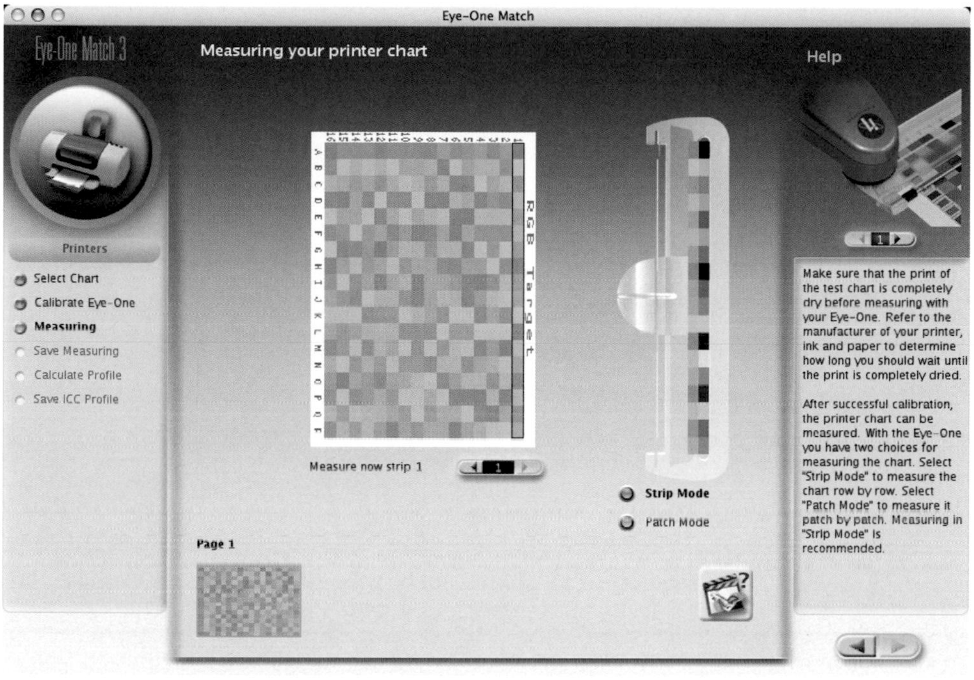

◀ *Figure 3-23:*
Select the printer to
profile and the target type

8. You may save the measurements. Continue with ▣.

9. Now EOM will automatically calculate the printer profile and ask for a profile name when finished. Use a descriptive name that includes the printer name, the paper used and, optionally, special settings used. Clicking Save As will save the new profile and install it.

Please keep in mind that this profile is only valid for the specific printer, the paper used for profiling, the ink set, and the specific driver settings used. If any of these parameters change, you should do a new profiling. This may happen when an ink supplier changes its ink recipe, without informing the customer; this happens from time to time. If your prints do not look as expected (after replacing ink), profile again.

You may use the same printer profile for Mac OS and Windows, provided the drivers work the same and offer the same settings. This should be true if you use the original manufacturer drivers of companies like HP, Canon or Epson. With third-party drivers, e.g., with Linux or Unix, or RIPs, you will have to profile again.

3.7   Installing and uninstalling profiles

Profiling software, in most cases, automatically installs freshly generated profiles. If you download profiles, you may be lucky getting executable files that also install the profiles. In some cases, though, you will have to install manually:

*   However, you may use Windows "icm" profiles as well.

[1] These profiles are accessible to all users of the system, however, you need to have administrator-level permission to set, add or delete them.

[2] These profiles are accessible only to the specific user and may be added or delete by the user.

[3] These profiles are those managed by Mac OS X and should be left alone.

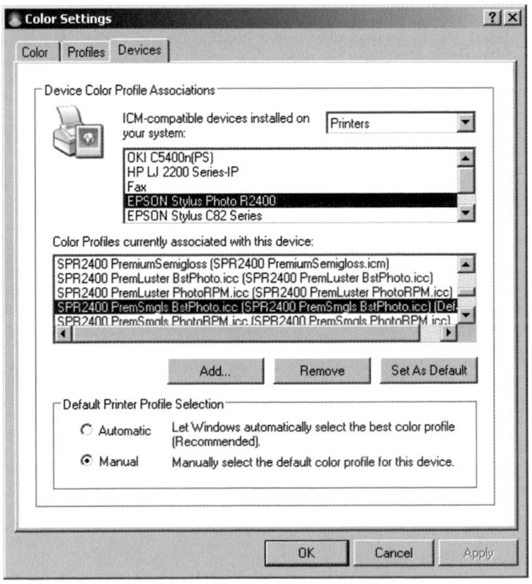

Mac OS X   Profiles use the file name extension "icc".* Simply move or copy the profile to one (or several) locations given below:

Mac OS X   System/Library/ColorSync/Profiles/[1]
                   ~*user*/Library/ColorSync/Profiles/ [2]
                   Library/ColorSync/Profiles/   [3]

Mac OS 9   System Folder/ColorSnyc Profile/

Adobe applications use an additional location: *Library/Application Support/ Adobe/Color/Profiles/* for some profiles. This location is for general use of Adobe applications. They should not be used for device-specific profiles, but only for new profiles for working spaces (e. g. to add ECI-RGB as a general work space).

To uninstall a profile, simply delete it or move it to another location.

Windows   With Windows, profiles use either the file name extension ".icm" or ".icc" (both types may be used). Right-click at the profile file. A popup menu will appear. Select Install Profile and Windows will install the profile for you. The profiles are stored in the following locations:

Windows XP	c:\windows\system32\spool\drivers\color\
Window 2K	c:\winnt\system32\spool\drivers\color\
Window NT	c:\windows\system32\color\
Windows 95/Me	c:\windows\system\color\

You should use the same method to uninstall the profile (this time selecting Uninstall Profile).

Avoid keeping too many profiles, especially with older Windows versions. For this reason, un-install those profiles not needed, yet do keep a copy of them somewhere.

In Windows XP, the Microsoft utility *Color Control Panel* or *WinColor* may be downloaded from [58]. It facilitates color management administration for Windows XP by installing and uninstalling ICC profiles. The utility also allows displaying the color gamut of a color space or profile, and compares the gamuts of two color spaces.

Figure 3-24:   Color Control Panel for Win XP

3.8 **Finding a printer's black point and white point**

You will need to print a white and black ramp to find out where your printer starts, to differentiate tonal values, especially when optimizing an image for printing to a specific printer.

Print the B&W-Ramp (a free version is here: [20]), using your standard printing method. Using your printer profile selected in Photoshop.* Let the print dry thoroughly. Inspect the print to find out at what black and what white values you can differentiate in the black/gray patch field from the enclosed black area and from the previous patch field. Use a bright white light source for inspection (preferably, a D50 light source or diffuse daylight). Write down this value. Do the same for the white or almost-white patches.

See Chapter 5.3, page 132.

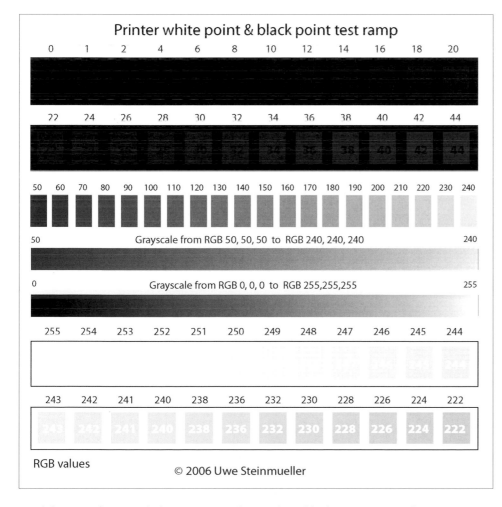

◄ *Figure 3-25:*
Image to find your printer's
black- and white-point

Don't become frustrated if your printer shows a long black ramp, especially when printing to a laser printer. This is usually not adequate for fine art printing. The undistinguished black ramp will probably go up to about

40–44, and the white ramp down to 251. With a good fine art printer, however, those values should be much tighter (about 10–20 for black; 252–253 for white). Remember, you have to repeat this test for each type of paper used.

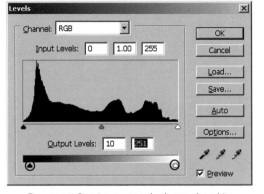

Figure 3-26: Restrict your tonal values to the white point and black point of your printer.

These are the values to which you should restrict your tonal values, using Levels in Photoshop when preparing your image for printing (Figure 3-26).

Don't use original images, but rather a copy made for printing, or use adjustment layers. This might look like reducing the tonality of an image, but as you see in the print of the B&W-Ramp, all pixel values beyond the black-point will be printed with the darkest black the printer can produce, and will not be distinguishable from black.

All pixel values lighter than this white point will not be distinguishable from the white of the paper.

With some pictures, however, you may not want differentiated structures in your shadows, which may even show some noise. Have them quite dark or black. In this case, use a lower value for your black point.

If you intend to use your image for a publication as part of a DTP project, and your image shows much white (or almost white) at the borders, it is often better to increase the white point a bit more into a light gray so that the white of an image will be set slightly apart from the white of the paper or the display.

3.9   Sanity-check

After profiling, wether it's your monitor or printer, some sanity check should be done. There are some good images available on the Web that include different colors, grayscale ramps and so-called *natural colors* or *memory colors* like skin and face colors that are critical in an image.

➔ *Bill Atkin's image is stored in CIELab mode. While this is no problem with Photoshop, some applications can't properly handle this image mode. For those, convert the image to a standard RGB mode (e.g. for printing using Qimage or Apple Aperture).*

You may find the image of Figure 3-27 on Bill Atkinson's Web site [63]. You may find some more useful images and test targets at Hutcheson Consulting [56]. Use one of those images to verify your profile and settings. If the displayed image on your monitor is off, or the print on your printer using your profile is off, search for the source of the problem. With the monitor, you have to redo calibration and profiling. With a print, ensure you did not perform the color-management steps twice, e.g., in Photoshop **and** again in your printer driver.

> **Note:** When doing profiling, you should take your time and work very carefully and thoroughly. Take notes on what you are doing step by step. This will be of help when reconstructing what went wrong (or right).

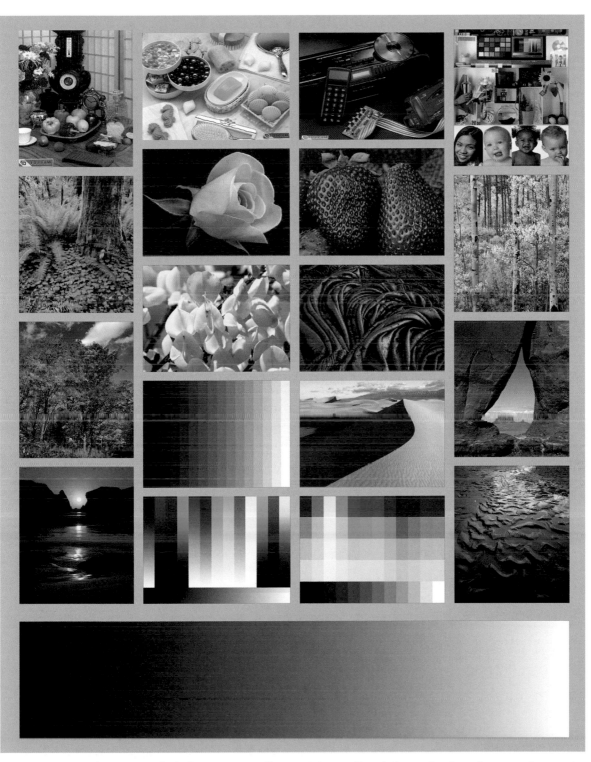

Figure 3-27: Image for your sanity check of your monitor profile or your printer profile and printer settings (www.jirvana.com/resources/

printing/bills_lab_test_image.zip, designed by Bill Atkinson)

3.10 Soft-proofing and gamut warning

As stated previously, a printer may not be able to reproduce all the colors of an image accurately: the printer may have a smaller gamut than the gamut of the image. All color management can do, is to prepare the printer to be as close as possible to the impression of the digital image. Before printing, it is often useful to view what a printed image will look like on your monitor. For this type of soft-proofing, the image is implicitly converted to a printer's color space,[*] and the result is displayed on the monitor. This is useful with inkjets to avoid costly and perhaps disappointing prints. It is still more important with commercial print runs, like offset prints, as those runs are much more expensive. Imagine a print run of 2,000 books with poor-quality photos. To achieve an optimum or accurate proofing, your proofing device, e.g., your monitor, should be able to reproduce all colors that the other proofing device (the printer) may reproduce. As we saw in Chapter 1, this may not be completely true if you soft-proof modern photo inkjet printers on your monitor, since modern photo inkjet printers have a gamut exceeding that of most current monitors, at least in some color areas.

You need the printer's ICC profile for this.

To set up soft-proofing in Photoshop, call up View ▸ Proof Setup ▸ Custom. The dialog box of Figure 3-28 will appear:

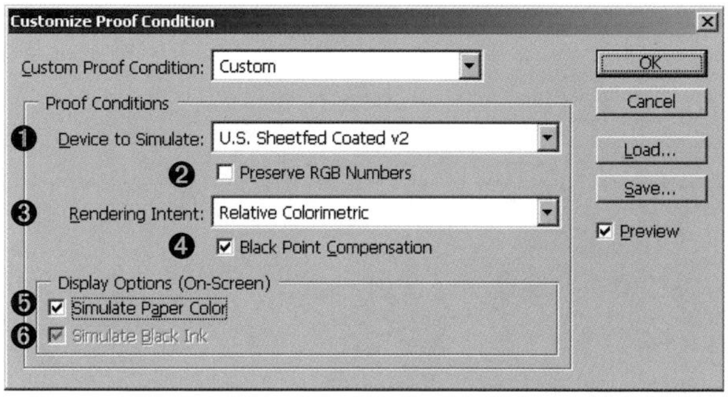

Figure 3-28: ▸
Proof setup in Photoshop

Select the profile of the printer you want to simulate with your proof ①. As with standard printing, ensure you use the printer profile that reflects the printer,[*] the type of paper used, the type of inks used and the proper printer settings. Leave Preserve RGB numbers ② **unchecked**! Select your rendering intent ③. As stated in section 3.2, page 52/53, select the rendering intent you will use later for printing or profile conversion. For photos, this should either be *Perceptive* or *Relative Colorimetric*.

or printing technique, in the case of offset or rotogravure printing

You should activate Black Point Compensation ④ and Simulate Paper Color ⑤. The latter will also activate Simulate Black Ink ⑥.

If you want to do soft-proofing regularly, you should save these proofing settings and give them a descriptive name, including the printer simulated, as well as the paper and printer settings.

To activate soft-proofing, select View ▸ Proof Colors (or just enter Ctrl - Y (Mac: ⌘ - Y)). Using Ctrl - Y you may toggle proofing on and off (in most cases, for image optimization, it should be off).

Gamut Warning

After setting up soft-proofing, you may also activate *Gamut Warning* (View ▸ Gamut Warning or ⇧-Ctrl-Y (Mac: ⇧-⌘-Y).

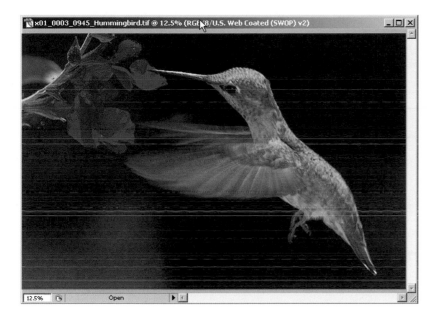

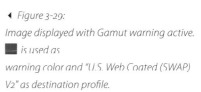

◀ *Figure 3-29:*
Image displayed with Gamut warning active.
■ *is used as*
warning color and "U.S. Web Coated (SWAP)
V2" as destination profile.

When Gamut Warning is active, Photoshop will mark all areas of your image that use colors that are out of gamut of your target color space. Default marking color is gray. Since gray is a color easily overlooked, we recommend selecting a different warning color, e.g. a loud and saturated magenta, which rarely occurs in photographic images.

To set a new gamut warning color, select Edit ▸ Preferences ▸ Transparency & Gamut. Click on the Color field to display the color picker.

If you did not do a custom proof setup in Photoshop and activate Gamut Warning or Proof Colors, the CMYK setting of your Working Spaces setting is used as a default (section 3.5).

Again, you may toggle Gamut Warning on and off using either ⇧-Ctrl-Y (Mac: ⇧-⌘-Y) or going via the View menu.

What is Gamut Warning really good for? First, you will get an impression of which colors in your image may not be reproduced accurately, but will have to be remapped to different colors. This usually involves mapping highly saturated colors to less-saturated ones. It may also help to modify these colors (colored areas of the image), so that they fit well into the destination color space (usually the printer's gamut). Decreasing their satu-

Figure 3-30: Setup for the color for Gamut Warning in Photoshop

ration, or otherwise tuning these colors, may be done in a more controlled way than is done by automatic gamut mapping, which may only be controlled by the selection of the rendering intent (see section 3.2, page 52/53).

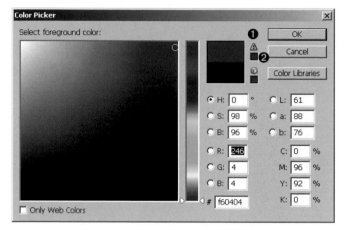

Figure 3-31: Gamut Warning in Color Picker

Even if Gamut Warning is not active, you will get a warning in the Color Picker dialog when you pick a color that is out of gamut of your target device (either selected explicitly by a proof setup or by default by your Photoshop Color Settings for CMYK). If you pick a color that is out of gamut, a triangle ⚠ will show up beside the selected color (Figure 3-31, ①). If you click into the field ②, the selected color will be replaced by a color as close as possible and fit into the destination color space.

3.11 Metamerism and bronzing

Metamerism usually refers to a problem that may occur using some inks in prints, i.e., it occurs when colors look different under different lighting. It is very natural and well known to us. When there is almost no light, all cats look gray. When there is very low light, colors may look bleached out because too much light is reflected. Similarly, printed colors are absorbing part of the light spectrum hitting the paper and reflecting other parts. When the lighting changes, the color spectrum and the intensity of the different wavelength of the incoming light changes. This will lead to a different pattern of absorbed and reflected light waves.

Under normal light, the metamerism effect may become a problem, when two colors built up of different primary colors create the same (or similar) color perception under one light (say, a halogen-based lamp) but create a different color perception under another lighting (say, tungsten lamps). The metamerism phenomenon may create a problem when two colors change their visual color distance with changed lighting. To achieve a sound basis for color judgment in practically any color management system, D50 (daylight at 5,000° K) is defined as the standard lighting for inspection of printed colors. Some printer-profiling packages and some RIPs allow compensation for a different lighting target.[*]

* *e.g., ImagePrint by ColorByte Software, as described in Chapter 6.3 at page 172.*

The intensity of the metamerism with two colors may depend on the kind of inks used, the combination of primary inks with which the colors are built up, and the dithering method used by the printer driver or RIP. Some pigment inks are more prone to produce problematic metamerism. This was a problem with the second-generation Epson UltraChrome inks, but was reduced by its third-generation K3 inks. The effect may be reduced somewhat by different mixing of primary inks to achieve certain colors, and it may be reduced further by using different dithering patterns. This is why some RIPs reduced metamerism using second-generation Epson Ultra-Chrome inks, e.g., using the Epson P2100/P2200 printer line.

Bronzing is a phenomenon occurring with some inks, mostly black, due to their reflective properties. Under certain lighting conditions, correct inks or build-up color samples take on a slightly bronze appearance. On prints, this is usually disturbing and undesirable. Bronzing is an effect attributed to some Epson pigment inks of the first-generation printers, e.g., the Epson P2000, and to a lesser extent of the second-generation printers like the Epson P2100/2200. The ink formulation of the third-generation of Ultra-Chrome inks eliminated this problem almost completely.

When a print shows disturbing bronzing, this effect may often be reduced or eliminated by framing the print under glass.

Fine Art Printing Workflow

So far, we have discussed some printing techniques, papers, inks, and basic color management. We now introduce how to prepare an image for printing. Of course, you may simply open a master image in Photoshop, call up the print dialog and leave the adaptation to Photoshop and the printer driver. This, however, may not lead to the most desirable results. With almost all images, some tuning of tonality and color will improve your image and result in better prints.

When an image is optimized and almost ready for printing, the final steps are scaling and sharpening. Both steps depend on your image size and your output method. So, they may have to be done for every print with a different size and for every different output method – wether that is inkjet or direct photo printing.

At this time, we want to describe our own workflow for printing, which you may adapt to your own preferences and requirements.

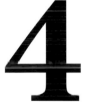

Camera: Canon 1Ds Mk. II

4.1   Basic printing workflow

Printing workflow begins when you have converted a file from RAW to TIFF or JPEG, or imported your camera JPEG or scanned image. Next, you edit your file: correct tilt, correct any problems with perspective, and crop your image (if necessary). Corrections of lens deficiencies may also be necessary: e.g., correcting lens distortions, vignetting, and chromatic aberrations. If there are dust patches, other blemishes or unwanted objects in your image, remove them now or as early as possible in your workflow. If you need to remove blemishes later, before you print, use the same techniques described in our e-books DOP2000 [8] and DOP3002 [9]).

> → Keep contrast on the softer side, as you can add contrast during fine tuning, but it is very hard to get soft gradations from harsh, contrasty images.

You have already done some initial sharpening, but final sharpening should be left until the end of optimization. In fact, you might leave this step to your RIP, if it offers good output-specific sharpening.

For this, your "first master" draft, you have made basic color corrections, and the image is now "correct," but still may not be satisfactory.

The next step is to optimize the image, until it appears similar to what you had in mind when the picture was taken or the scan was made. This often requires tonal optimizations, including contrast enhancements and selective color correction. We address this in sections 4.2 and 4.3.

Most of these corrections can be applied, first globally, and then both selectively and locally. The result is an image (an image file), we refer to as our *master image*.

The real printing workflow actually begins here (section 4.4). This implies that your image is pretty close to producing a good print, but you still need to fine-tune the result. It is also assumed that you are using a good printer profile. But a printing workflow is also about correcting imperfections in your profiles and/or printers.

4.2   Tuning tonality

Obtaining correct tonality is key in every good print. There are no hard-and-fast rules about what range or level of tonality is good and not so good. It very much depends on your image and on what you want to express.

* Take for examples the zebras at page xvi.

Take, for example, a photo of a foggy scene.* On one hand, you can make the image so soft that it looks like a hazy mess; on the other you can turn up the contrast so much that you lose all soft characteristics of fog.

It is important to remember that we are discussing the tonality you create on a print. It is not possible to produce the same high contrast on paper as can be viewed on screen. Keep in mind that matte papers produce consistently lower contrast prints than the same image on semi-gloss or gloss papers.

Tonality includes:*

▸ Brightness
▸ Contrast in:
  – Midtones
  – Shadows
  – Highlights
▸ Smoothness

*   Unfortunately, all these elements are related
    and must be tuned in careful steps.

As always, begin by adjusting the global tonality as best as possible, and then continue working on local areas to improve tonality there. The core tools used to adjust tonality are Photoshop Levels and Curves.

Brightness

Brightness seems to be a basic property. But again, it always depends upon what you want to show in your print. Both very dark and very bright images can be beautiful. Equally important is where you display your images. This is the reason you should try to judge images under controlled light, carefully considering both brightness and light spectrum.*

*   See Chapter 8: "Image Judgment".

First, let's take a look at the different tonality ranges of an image.

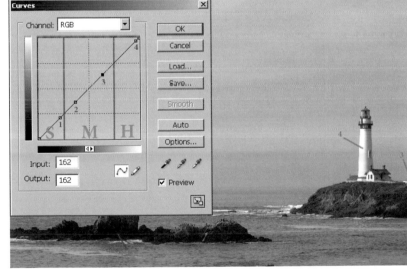

◀ Figure 4-1:
Tonality regions

We use the Curves tool (black on the left, white on the right). The standard grid setting displays four segments. Roughly, the first quarter makes up *shadows*; the next, two *midtones;* and the last, *highlights.* Three regions must be treated carefully but play a different role for the viewer.

▸ S = Shadow area
▸ M = Midtones
▸ H = Highlights

If you Alt -click the diagram, Photoshop will
switch the resolution of the raster lines from
five lines to ten lines and back.
In all our Curves examples, we will have black
to the left and white to the right!

Midtones

The primary content of any image is in its midtones. You must be very careful to achieve good midtone contrast. Otherwise, you end up with a flat image. We show the following test (Figure 4-2) to demonstrate that you do not lose content in an image by making the shadow range only black and the highlights white.

In Figure 4-2, we cut-off all data in shadows and highlights and stretched the midtones over the full range, from 0–255. As you can see, the entire content remains, but the image looks ugly and quite unrefined.

One might conclude that highlights and shadows are "the icing on the cake."

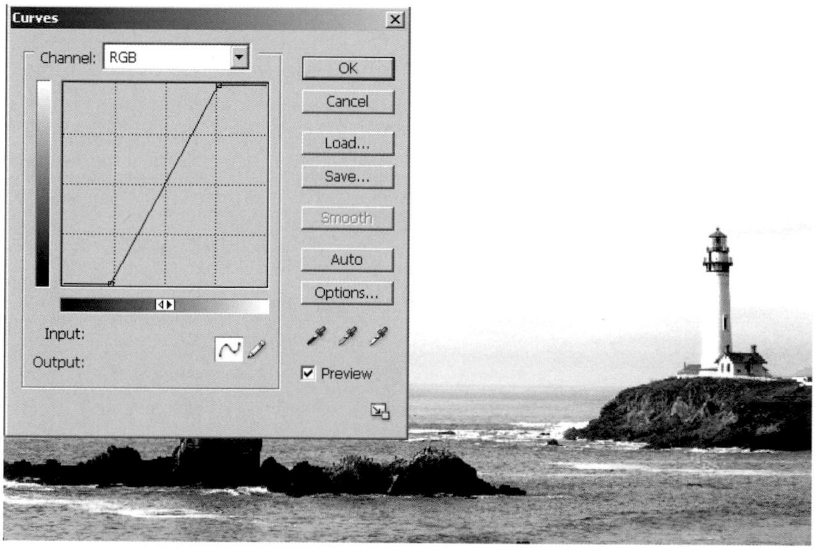

Figure 4-2: ▶
Showing only the midtones data

Without solid highlights and shadows, you cannot create a quality print. Both shadows and highlights are, in general, the more important parts.

Shadows

Shadows can be open or close to black. There are cases where complete black is not only acceptable but beautiful, as may be seen in the photo of Figure 4-3.

A solid black background works here, because the photo has a strong graphic character, and background details would be distracting. The rocks in our lighthouse photo cannot be only black. You must balance open shadows with overall contrast. You will realize that opening up shadows lowers the overall impression of contrast.

There is an additional challenge in the shadow portion of digital images: most noise is hidden in the shadows. This implies that you may find it necessary to remove noise when you open up shadows substantially (see later in this chapter).

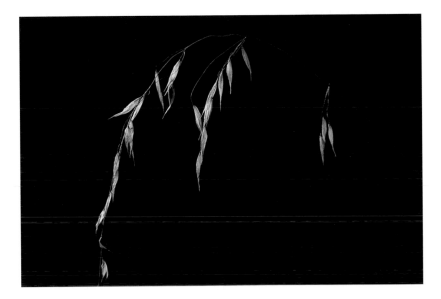

◀ *Figure 4-3:*
Grass – giving a very graphic image. This image consists almost completely of dark shadows and some highlights.

Highlights

Highlights are largely a challenge during image capture. If you overexpose highlights, data are lost forever.* If you underexpose too much, you lose dynamic range and pictures tend to be noisy.

Correct highlights bring a proper sparkle to your images. If they are too strong, like in Figure 4-4, all the smoothness and beauty of the photo disappears.

* Traditional film is somewhat more forgiving due to its different sensitivity curve for light.

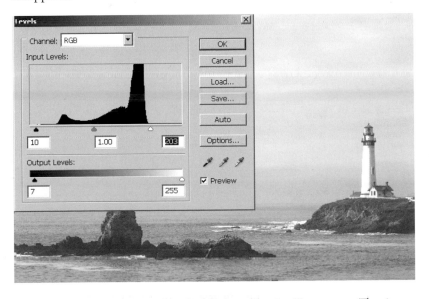

◀ *Figure 4-4:*
Overly strong and blown-out highlights

The other extreme is muddy highlights, like in Figure 4-5. The image looks dull and dark. We must find a balance between these two extremes. If your original photo resembles the first sample (Figure 4-4: blown-out highlights), there is little you can do to get a good, or even acceptable, print. The second example still permits getting a good print, if we correct tonality and live with some level of noise.

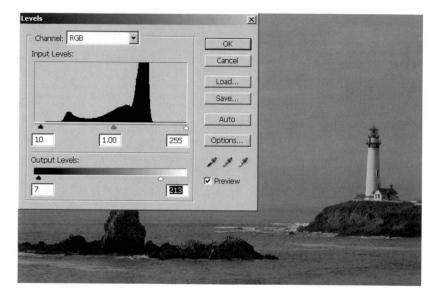

Figure 4-5: ▶
Muddy highlights

Contrast

The correct contrast is vital for any good print. With too little contrast, you end up with muddy, flat-looking prints, but with too much contrast, you get harsh tonality. There is no general rule here, as it depends on your images and what qualities you want them to depict. Be aware that paper cannot reproduce the contrast you see on screen. The same goes for brilliantly projected slides versus the same images on a print. Begin with slightly soft contrast, and tune the image for the balance you want.

Slides and a film negative may cover a contrast range of about 8–9 stops, digital still cameras about 7–8 stops and a print (using an inkjet printer) about 5–6 stops.

> **Note:** Comparing the same image with different contrast is quite tricky, as the more contrasty image nearly always grabs your attention. This does not suggest that a higher-contrast image is the better choice. Generally, it is good practice to view a photo at higher contrast, to discover whether you are missing an opportunity to improve your image. If the higher contrast is created at the expense of too highly compressed highlights and/or dark blocked shadows, then it is probably time to decrease it a bit.

Global tonality tuning

The first step in tonality tuning is to set global tonality as closely as possible to the final desired result. *Global* means that all pixels in an image are treated with the same transformation. What's more, this operation does not depend on other pixels (we cover this later in this chapter in the section "Local tonality tuning").

Tonality tuning using Photoshop "Levels"

Levels is a major tool for tuning tonality. It is easiest to understand its function by looking at a sample image:

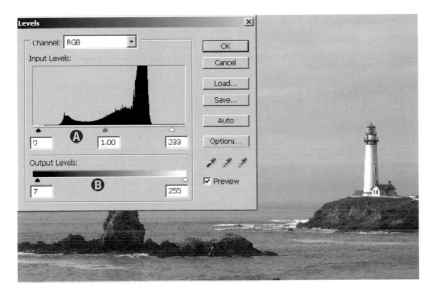

◀ Figure 4-6:
Levels in action (preview on)

We display the same image with preview "on" (Figure 4-6) and "off" (Figure 4-7). Levels in Photoshop has five sliders that are important to understand:

▸ Three for the Input Levels (Figure 4-6, **Ⓐ**) and
▸ Two for the Output Levels (Figure 4-6, **Ⓑ**)

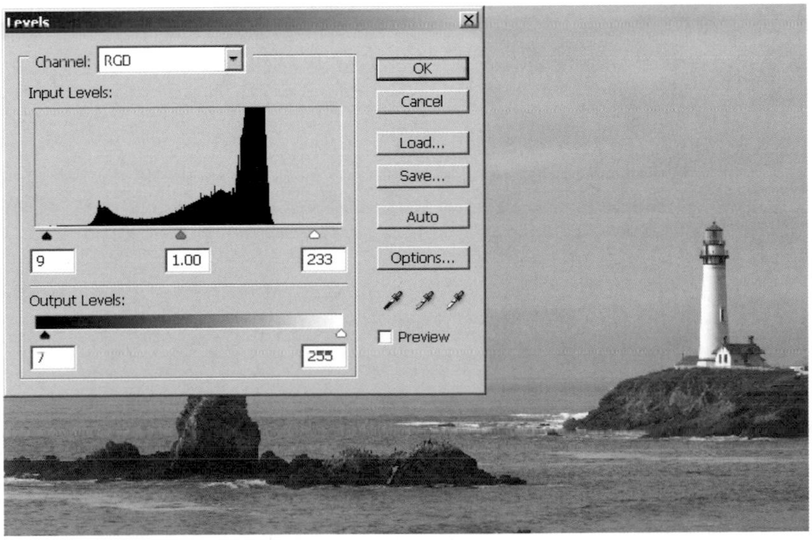

◀ Figure 4-7:
Levels in action (preview off)

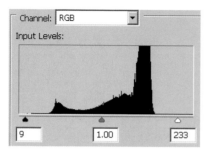

Figure 4-8: 3 basic sliders for Levels

Input Levels

Let's take a look at the **Input Levels:** We use Levels only in RGB mode. The histogram is some help in visualizing the distribution of different tones. It is not a good idea to correct by looking only at the histogram. We prefer to adjust Levels while viewing the full image. There are three triangles, each of which is a slider used to correct, from left to right:

 ‣ Black Point ◆
 ‣ Gamma (brightness) ◆
 ‣ White Point △

With this lighthouse photo, we use the Black Point slider (◆)to achieve a bit more black in the shadows. We have to be very careful not to block the shadows too severely in the rocks. If we set the value to 9, all pixels having a value of 9 or less will have a value of zero after this operation. All other values are linearly transformed, and receive some lower (darker) values. If we do not correct the white point, as well, the entire image becomes just a bit darker, with additional contrast.

The Gamma (Brightness) slider ◆ remains at a default value 1.00.

As said earlier, setting the White Point slider △ can be a balancing act. You want a slight sparkle, while maintaining a smoothness, in the highlights. If we set the value to 233, for example, all pixels at 233 will be now become 255. All the other values are linearly transformed, and will be set to some higher (brighter) values.

Output Levels

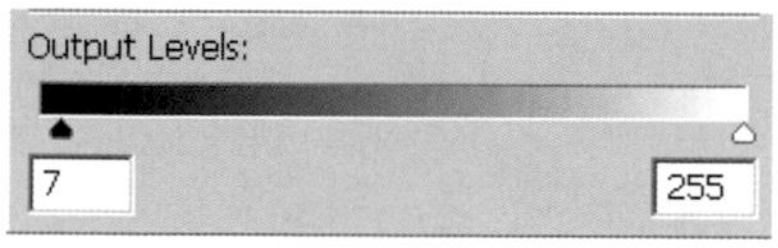

Output Levels becomes useful in a case where the printer (with its profile in use) cannot show a difference between lower black levels (0–x). Let's assume that the printer cannot show different black levels below 7. In such a case, we may push ◆ of *Output Levels* up to 7. This means that the black values of zero are now transformed to 7, and all other values above that are linearly transformed. See Chapter 3.8 page 79 for more on this topic.

Note that some images look perfectly fine with all black below a certain value, e.g., 7. For some of these images, we may need to make only very small corrections for the output white point △, as most well-made profiles compensate quite well.

Always correct by visually inspecting an image, and not trusting the histogram alone. On the other hand, try to avoid removing too much shadow detail, and always think twice before clipping off highlights.

We only perform Levels corrections using a new adjustment layer. By doing so, we "layer" corrections and still are able to fine-tune values later.

Figure 4-9: Output Levels

Note: When correcting tonality in black-and-white images, sometimes you can correct a bit more aggressively, gaining a higher contrast. Doing so can often help a black-and-white image.

Tonality tuning using Curves

Curves are more complex and also more powerful than Levels. In principle, you can do everything in Curves you can do in Levels, while the reverse is far from true. Our first example shows how you may simulate Levels using Curves:

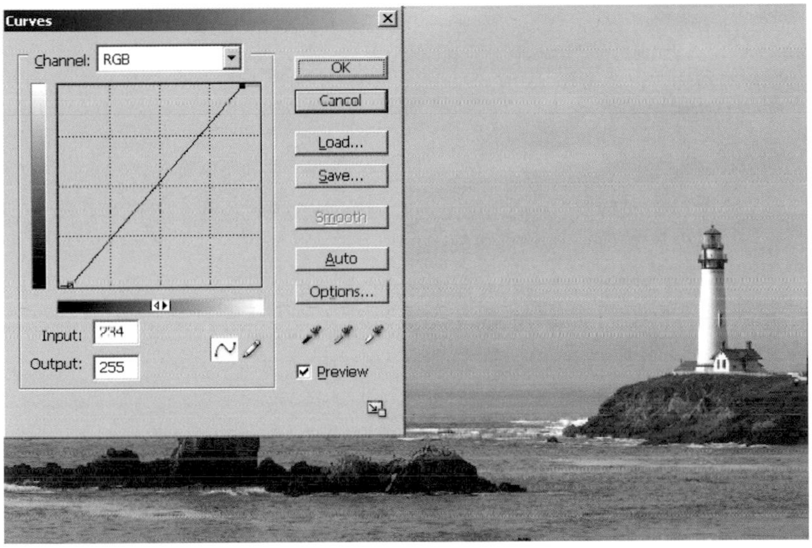

◂ *Figure 4-10:*
Linear transformation with Curves.

Of course, in some of these cases, it would be advisable to use Levels. But a linear curve can provide a good starting point for more advanced curve corrections.

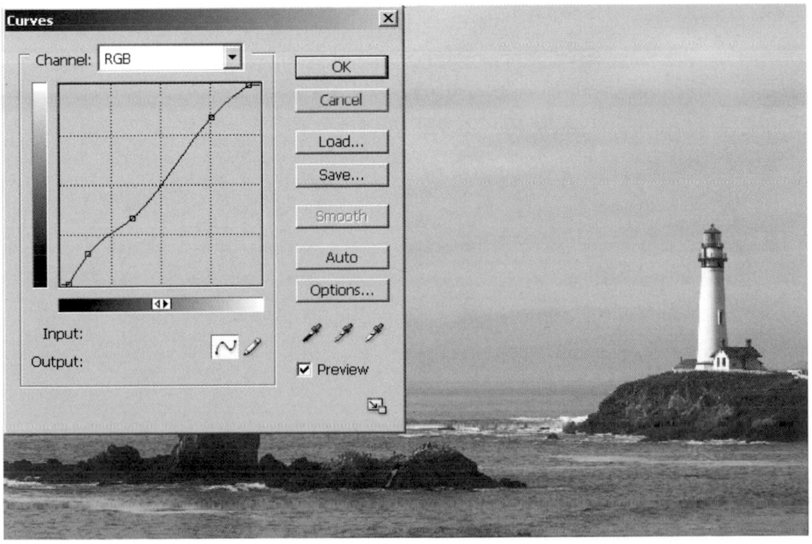

◂ *Figure 4-11:*
Some more advanced curves

Here (Figure 4-11), we start with the linear curve of Figure 4-10 and try to achieve the following:

→ *A flat curve part will lead to low contrast in those tonal areas and steep curve parts will result in high contrast and may result in some banding.*

▸ Slightly brighten the shadows (foreground rocks)
▸ Increase contrast in the midtones and highlights (S-Curve)

Be careful that no section of your curve becomes too flat or steep, as the latter may result in posterization.

Some useful standard Curves shapes

For minor global **brightening/darkening,** we use these curves:

→ *Photoshop supports two sizes for the Curves (and Levels) dialog. You may switch by clicking at the symbol (▨ or ▨) at the lower right side of the dialog box.*

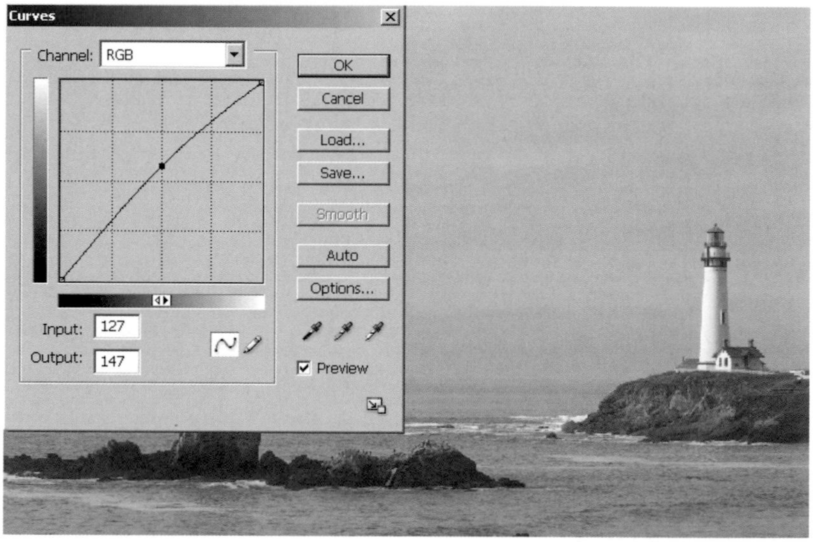

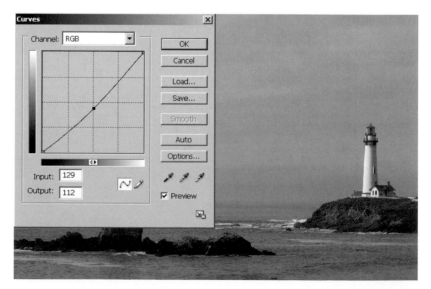

Figure 4-12: ▸
Brightening curve

Figure 4-13: ▸
Darkening curve

Why do we use Curves here and not Levels? With Curves, we are able to tweak behavior more easily than with Levels, where we are unable to change the gamma curve used by Levels.

We use **S-curves** to enhance contrast (Figure 4-14). This curve looks like a shallow S-curve, but it has a strong effect on an image. In our view, a major down side of curves is that minor changes often have dramatic (and even negative) results.

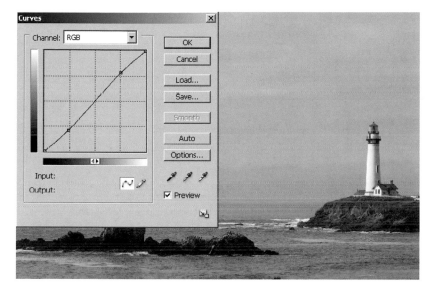

◀ Figure 4-14:
S-Curve to improve contrast

What also happens, in this case, is that midtone contrast is nicely improved without compressing shadows and highlights too much. Especially in this image, shadows are very delicate, and we want to avoid this type of compression. We use Adjustment Layers for Curves adjustments, and fix some problems by changing the Advanced Blending Options:

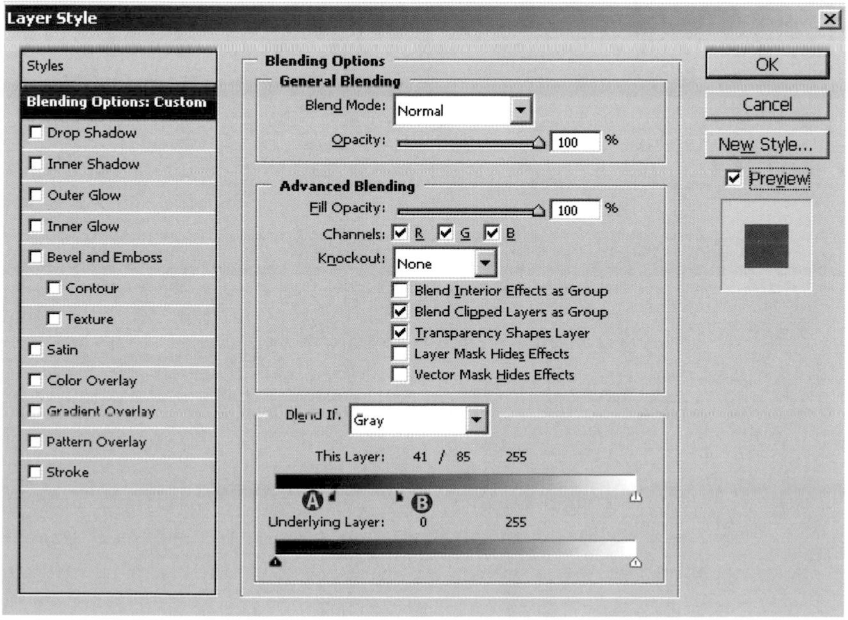

◀ Figure 4-15:
Advanced Blending settings to preserve the original shadows. Here, blending is controlled by sliders Ⓐ and Ⓑ. At first the sliders will look line this: By pressing the Alt key while dragging the left or right part, you may split the slider into two separate parts. In the tonal values in-between, the effect will gradually diminish.

Alternatively, we use a different curve that restricts the effect of the S-curve entirely to midtones:

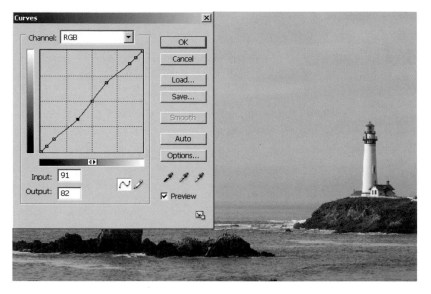

In this case, we prefer the latter solution. Overall, the S-curve can be very useful in many situations.

Local tonality tuning

We assume that, in most instances, you have done essential global tonality tuning before beginning your printing workflow. In fine-tuning your prints, it is vital to understand how to perform local tonality corrections that only apply to certain parts of the image. Here are some major ways to improve local tonality:

▶ Adaptive shadow and/or highlight correction[*]
▶ Corrections to selected areas using masks
▶ Corrections related to certain tonality ranges (shadows, midtones and highlights)
▶ Painting techniques (mainly dodge and burn)

* Shadows/Highlight *was introduced in
Photoshop CS1 (Photoshop 8).*

Adaptive shadow and/or highlight correction

We have described some information about shadows in the section on local tonality tuning. In fact, Levels and Curves understand shadows differently than we normally do. They consider a shadow as pixels with reduced brightness. Let's demonstrate what we mean with the following example:

This picture contains dark letters, but also real shadows that have detail within them. From their pixel brightness, the black letters, although in the sun, may be as dark or even darker than the real shadows. Both

Curves and Levels would treat both the same way. That is not really what we intend when we plan to open up shadows a bit.

In situations like this, there exist more useful tools that work *adaptively*; they take into account the context in which the pixels reside and not merely a single pixel value alone. Currently, the best known tool is Photoshop's Shadow/Highlight tool. Below is a demonstration target to show the principles of Shadow/Highlight:

There are five incrementally darker dots that are identical in each column. It is well known that we perceive the same brightness differently, depending upon its context or contrast:

▸ Bright spots look brighter in a dark context
▸ Dark spots look darker in a bright context

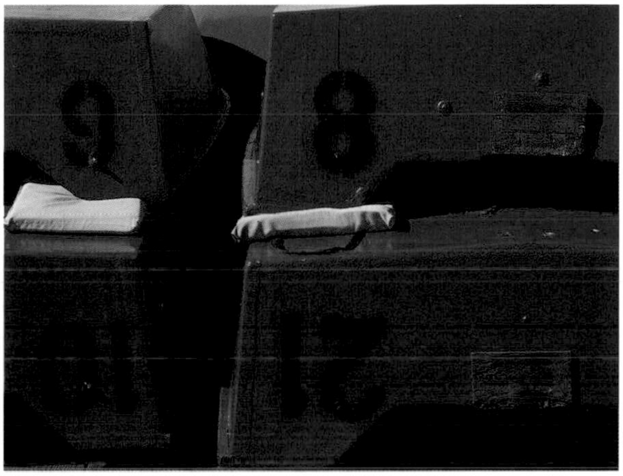

The above example should illustrate that treating all pixels equally, as with Curves and Levels, is not always helpful. Why don't we see more of these adaptive tools today? Because they:

▸ Are computing intensive
▸ May have color-shift side effects
▸ Sometimes create issues at their edges
  (e.g., show halos, so watch out for them)

Figure 4-17: Shadows and dark areas

Shadow recovery

When Shadow/Highlight is used to open up shadows, we see the following result:

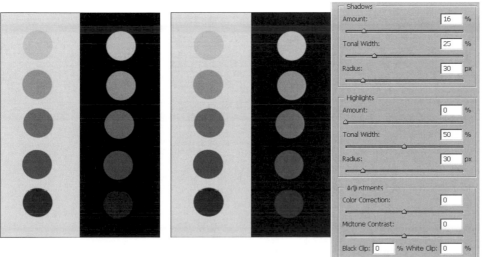

▲ *Figure 4-18a: Shadow/*
   Highlight test chart

▲ *Figure 4-18b: Shadow/Highlight used to open up the*
   shadows

Based on the result in Figure 4-18, we observe the following:

▸ All spots in the bright area remain unchanged
▸ The dark background brightens up
▸ The three darker spots on the darker background changed brightness

Highlight recovery

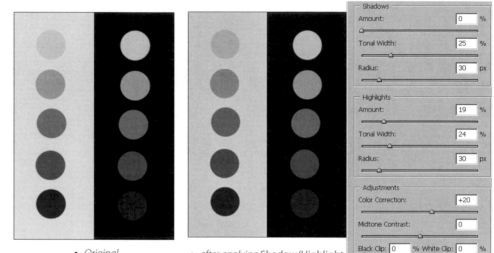

Figure 4-19: ▸
Shadow/Highlight *used to*
tone down highlights

▲ *Original*   ▲ *after applying* Shadow/Highlight

We observe the following in Figure 4-19:

▸ All spots in the dark area remain unchanged
▸ The bright background darkens
▸ The four brighter spots on the brighter background change their brightness

True, you could accomplish the same task with complex masking, but the main drawbacks would be:

▸ More complicated, involving much more work
▸ With real-world images and fine details, masking can become quite challenging

Corrections to selected areas using masks

This book does not cover all possible techniques in using complex masks. The fact is, we rarely use them anyway. But here is a technique that often works well.

We wish to make the shadows on dune shot (Figure 4-20) a bit brighter. It looks satisfactory on the screen, but when printed, we found it a bit too dark.

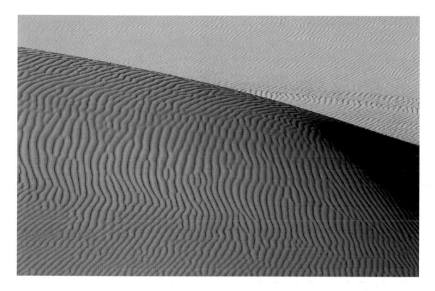

◀ *Figure 4-20:*
Start photo

So, we selected the shadow using the tool lasso ⤳ (Figure 4-21 shows just the relevant part of the image).

Then we switched over to the Quick Mask mode (use the key ⌨) and could see that mask edges are too difficult to make a clean selection (Figure 4-22).

We therefore feathered the selection (with values between 25–150 depending on the image and the selected area, see Figure. 4-23).

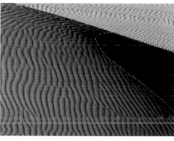

◀ *Figure 4-21:*
Select the shadow area with the lasso tool.

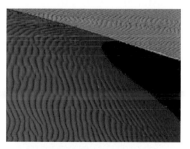

◀ *Figure 4-22:*
Same selection shown in Quick Mask mode

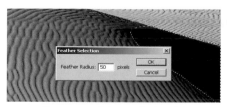

▲ *Figure 4-23:* *Selection feathered at 50*

The result is shown in Figure 4-24.

Now, we needed to tune the selection a bit at the upper dune shadow edge. Finally, we used a Curves Adjustment Layer with this selection as a layer mask to brighten up the shadow:

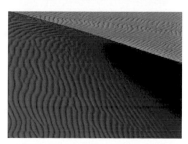

◀ *Figure 4-24:*
Selection after applying feathering

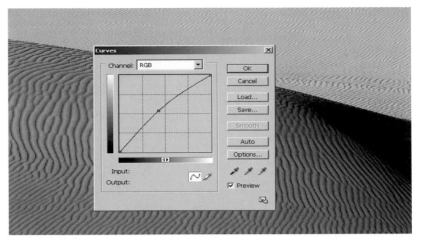

Figure 4-25: ▶
Using a Curves Adjustment
Layer to brighten the
shadow

This technique is useful when the area you work with does not have compli-cated edges as its boundaries.

Corrections related to certain tonality ranges (shadows, midtones, and highlights)

Often, we use a technique to restrict the effect of Curves and other tuning tools to only certain tonal areas:

▶ Shadows (e.g., opening up shadows)
▶ Midtones (e.g., adding contrast, brightens and darkens)
▶ Highlights (e.g., toning down aggressive highlights)

All our masks are based on a Luminosity mask similar to the black-and-white image of the original photo. We may invert this mask and also restrict it to certain tonal regions. Because this process can be quite tedious, we created our DOP Tonality Toolkit [15]. Here is an example:

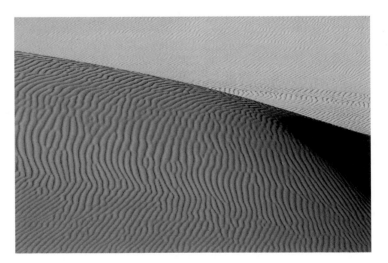

Figure 4-26: ▶
Original dune photo

As before, we want to open up the shadows. First we create a shadow tonality mask (using our DOP Tonality Toolkit):

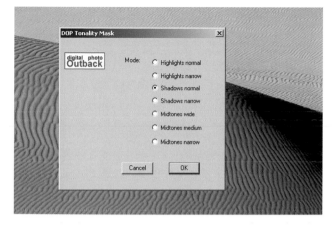

◀ *Figure 4-27:*
Use the Tonality Mask automation plug-in to create a shadow mask

We get the following selection:

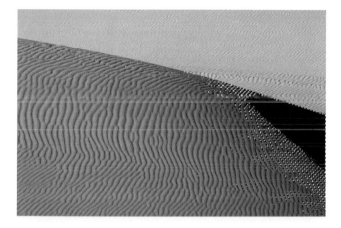

◀ *Figure 4-28:*
Shadow selection

Again, we use Curves with the selection applied to a Layer Mask:

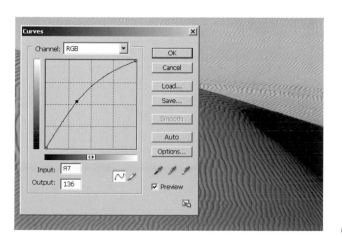

◀ *Figure 4-29:*
Curves applied to shadows only

Here is the Layer Mask that we created:

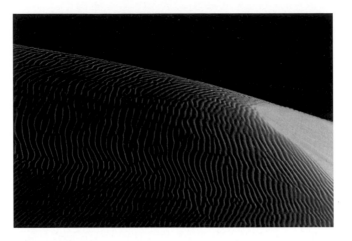

Figure 4-30: ▶
Tonality Mask (shadows normal)

Just for demonstration, we show the mask that would be created if we had chosen the "shadows narrow" option.

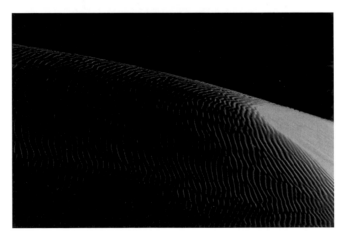

Figure 4-31: ▶
Tonality Mask (shadows narrow)

Different from the mask in the last section, we created these tonality masks that include all the shadow parts (even the dune ripples). Whether this effect is intended by you is based on how you want to present the print. This last method exaggerates the soft character of the shapes (reduced contrast), while the previous method shows more highlights in graphic patterns of the shapes. It is always helpful to have multiple ways to explore the potential of your photos for printing.

It is fairly easy to modify these masks using the following painting techniques.

Painting techniques (mainly Dodge and Burn)

In principle, you can paint all your masks (layer masks) with soft brushes (we usually use *Hardness* set to zero).

Painting using Layer Masks

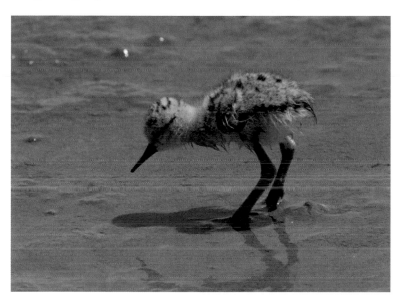

◀ *Figure 4-32:*
Original image

In this example, in Figure 4-32, the eye and part of the head of the Avocet chicken are in the shadow. We would like to brighten them up.

1. We create a Curves Adjustment Layer to brighten the whole image (see Figure 4.33). The resulting image of Figure 4-34 is clearly too bright, but don't worry.

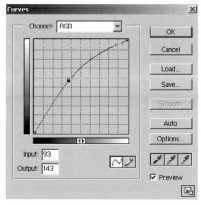

▲ *Figure 4-33: Curve to brighten up*
the image

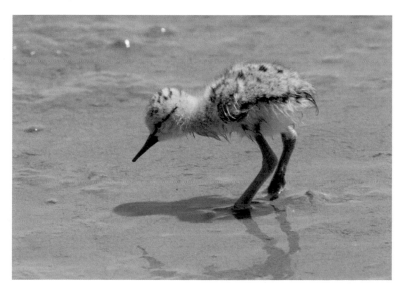

◀ *Figure 4-34:*
The image in Figure 4-32, brightened up by
Curves, is too bright.

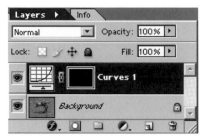

▲ *Figure 4-35: When the layer mask is completely black, the adjustment layer has no effect.*

2. Using the paint bucket 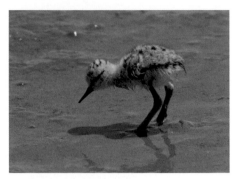, fill the layer mask with black. Ensure you have selected the layer mask when applying the black paint bucket). The black layer mask hides all the brightening effect of this layer:

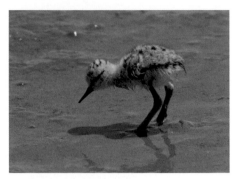

◄ *Figure 4-36:*
The effect of the Curves Layer is completely masked by the black layer mask.

3. Using a soft, big brush
   ▶ Color White
   ▶ Opacity 15%

   paint a few strokes over the face. By using 15 % opacity, you have a lot of control in brightening the face (try even higher opacity to experience the difference).

   A look at the Layer Mask by clicking on the layer-mask thumbnail) reveals the secret (see Figure 4-37):

This is a universal technique for selective image enhancement and can be used with many different types of layers:

▶ Layer with a sharpened version of an image
▶ Layer with a noise-removed version of an image
▶ Hue/Saturation Adjustment Layers
▶ Curves Adjustment Layer using S-curves

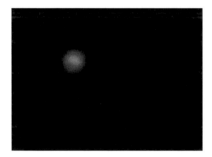

▲ *Figure 4-37: Layer mask after painting with the soft white brush.*

Figure 4-38: ▶
Optimized image. Here, the head is somewhat brightened up.

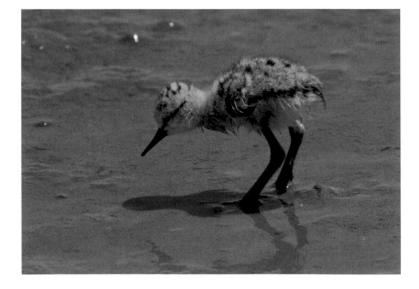

Dodge and burn using Layers

With the same sample image we show a different technique we learned from Mac Holbert. Again, the image would be good if those parts of our Avocet chicken could be lightened up a bit.

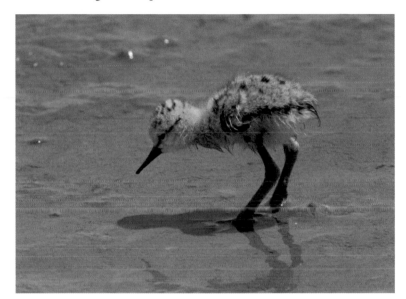

◄ *Figure 4-39:*
We want to brighten up the bird's body

1. Create a new layer in the layer palette

◄ *Figure 4-40:*
Create a new layer with Overlay
Blending mode

2. Set *Mode* to *Overlay* and select Fill with Overlay-neutral color (50% gray).

   Overlay is a very special blending mode with the following properties (for more details, consult Photoshop Help):

   ▸ 50 % gray   leaves the image unchanged (our starting point)
   ▸ values > 50 % gray   will darken the image (black being strongest)
   ▸ values < 50 % gray   will lighten the image (white being strongest)

   For painting in your grey level, you may use any of the painting tools e.g., a white or black brush (you should usually use a soft brush and a low opacity of about 10–15 %). We, however, will use the Dodge tool 🔍 for lightening and the Burn tool ✊ for darkening.

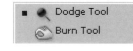

3. Select the Dodge Tool (🔍).

4. Set exposure to 5–15 %. Enable the Airbrush option and use a reasonably large, soft brush.

Figure 4-41: ▶
Select your dodge options

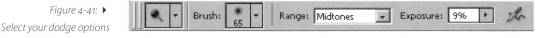

Now, when you paint on areas that are too dark for your taste, they will brighten the more you paint in that area. The lower the exposure, the more you need to paint, giving much greater control.

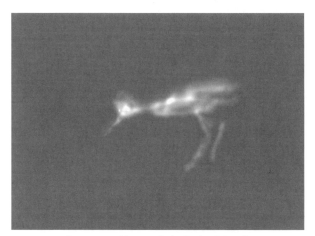

▲ *Figure 4-42: Shows only the Dodge & Burn layer*

5. Dodge the bird's head and body with a few careful brush strokes.

   If you make all other layers invisible, you can see what your "dodge & burn" layer looks like.

   Dark areas would show portions used to burn (no burning here) and the bright ones are those used for dodging. The following picture (blending of the original picture and the "Dodge & Burn" layer) illustrates our point.

Here is the original image (Figure 4-43a) and the optimized image (Figure 4-43b).

   As you have seen, most of the time there are several ways in Photoshop to achieve a certain optimization.

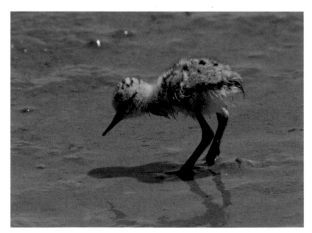

▲ *Figure 4-43a: Original image*

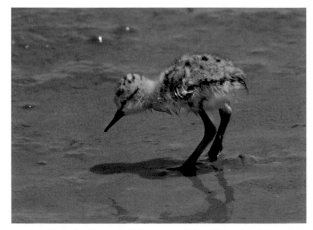

▲ *Figure 4-43b: Avocet now has improved brightened shadow while the rest of the image kept its tonal values*

4.3   Tuning colors

We assume you have the white balance of your image as you like it. Color tuning involves fine tuning of colors and not major color corrections.

A key issue is to achieve correct saturation. Ensure the contrast is correct before even thinking of tuning saturation. Often simply tweaking the contrast automatically alleviates any problems with saturation.

Selective saturation improvements

Sometimes we perceive an impression that a digital photo may need more saturation. Actions and filters to do this are quite popular. Let me open with some general comments:

Films like Velvia often produce high saturation of colors in photographs, i e , they appear "larger than life," and thus the image seems to lose other subtle, more natural colors. When you place two photos side-by-side, differing only in saturation, the one with greater saturation draws your attention more. Does that imply it is better? Not necessarily. Again, before you even consider enhancing saturation, adjust the contrast. Some S-curves might do the trick.

What about those times when you absolutely must enhance the saturation of an image? What's the best way to go about it, given the hundreds of possibilities?

An excellent tutorial on this subject can be found in an article by *Ben Willmore* in the Photoshop User magazine: "Saturate your World." It certainly has changed our view on saturation.

As a side remark: whenever you come across an article by Ben, read it. Also his excellent book on Photoshop CS2 [11] is now part of our library.

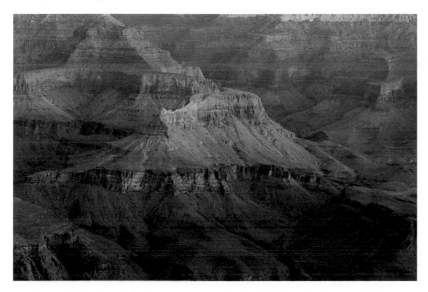

◄ *Figure 4-44:*
Grand Canyon: Mather Point

At first, his message sounds pretty obvious: "Use selective saturation in Photoshop." Why hadn't we considered this before? It seemed complicated, and it actually is when you try it on your own without Ben's guidance. But he gives a wonderful practical tutorial on how to master the art of selective saturation.

Global saturation enhancement seems an inappropriate method in most cases. In the following example, we use selective saturation enhancement only to selective areas of our photos:

We want to enhance saturation in the top part of this photo, yet keep the bottom as is. Create an adjustment layer using Hue/Saturation. Change the layer mask in this layer to something resembling Figure 4-45.

The black portion prevents saturation changes at the bottom but allows a soft transition to white in the upper areas.

Then, open the Hue/Saturation dialog, but do not change the "Master" settings. We altered the reds using the "Red" settings.

Figure 4-45: Black to white gradient used as a layer mask

Left Figure 4-46a: ▸
No changes done in "Master"

Right Figure 4-46b: ▸
For our image of Figure 4-44 we do our settings in "Reds".

We encourage you to learn for yourself what the different sliders mean, and thus do not include all the details from Ben's article.

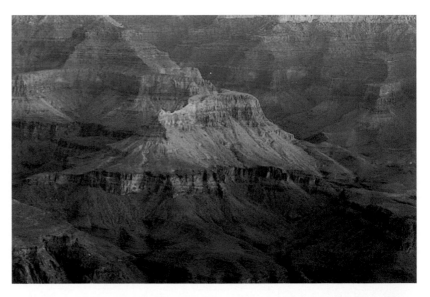

Figure 4-47: ▸
Image after selective Hue/Saturation corrections in "Reds".

Here is the result of this operation. We concluded that the change might be a bit too strong and considered changing the saturation settings. Instead, we modified the opacity of the adjustment layer.

Figure 4-50 shows our final version. The differences can be subtle, but this is precisely what selective saturation is all about: **think selectively!**

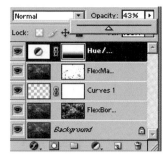

▲ *Figure 4-48: Different tuning layers (Adjustment Layers) of the final image*

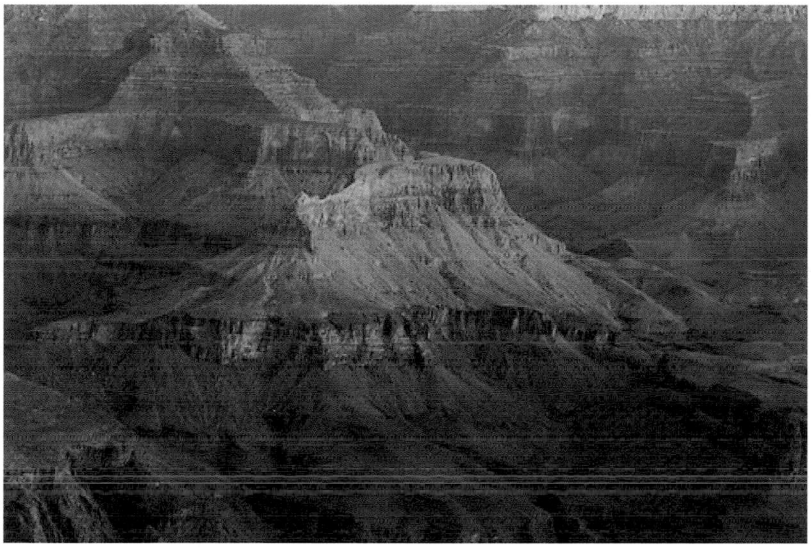

◀ *Figure 4-49: Final version of our image*

More saturation and contrast tricks

As all photographers learn, there is rarely anything better than the "right light." In our recent book, *Earthframes*, we made the following choices:

▸ Midday sunlight creating harsh shadows and burned-out highlights
▸ Evening sun with better light but longer shadows
▸ Overcast skies providing flat light

From these three alternatives, we favored "overcast," the lighting from which is like a good light box.

We probably get some flat images directly from the raw converter. Of course, we could tweak the raw converter (and sometimes we do that), but usually we prefer to do this work with layers in Photoshop. Then we are able to revisit all changes and improve on them at a later time. The first step is most often an adjustment layer using Levels:

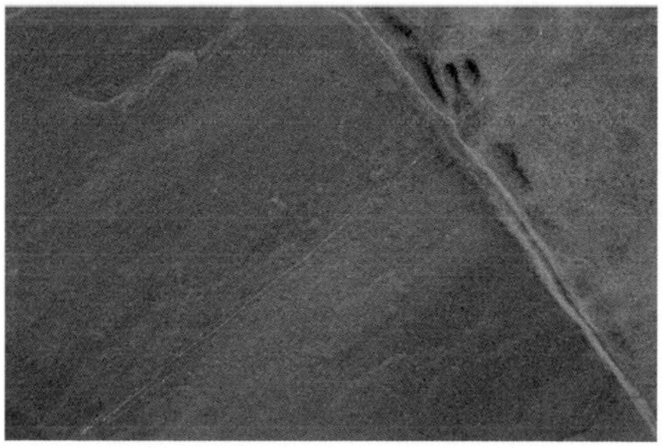

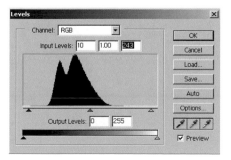

▲ *Figure 4-50: We start with a flat image*

◀ *Figure 4-51: Levels Adjustment Layer*

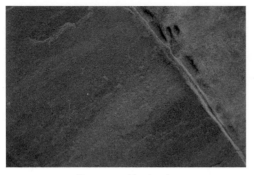

Figure 4-52: After Levels

As you see, we moved the white point only slightly, so the photo would not get too bright and retain only truly white details.

Now, increase the contrast using some S-curve in a Curves adjustment layer.

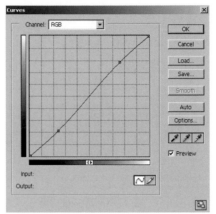

◀ *Figure 4-53:*
Slight S-curve for a bit more
contrast, resulting in image of
Figure 4-55

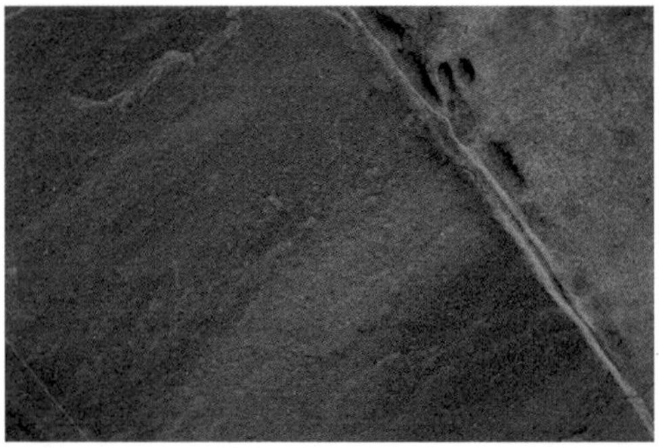

S-curves tend to create color shifts that can be removed by changing the blending mode of the layer to *Luminosity*. This change is subtle, so experiment with it.

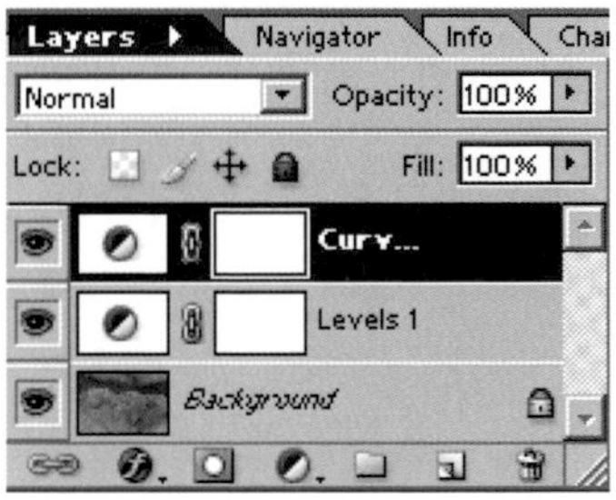

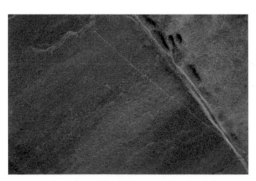

Figure 4-55: After Curves

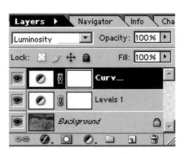

◀ *Figure 4-55:*
Our layer palette up to now

◀ *Figure 4-56:*
Changing blending mode to Luminosity

Some still may want to increase saturation and tweak contrast just a bit, so there are several ways to go, in particular a technique explained to us by Katrin Eismann, author of "Photoshop Restoration & Retouching" [1].

Figure 4-57: After change to 'Luminosity'

Using an adjustment layer with "Hard Light" blending mode

Create a new Curves adjustment layer and change the blending mode to *Hard Light (Figure 4-59)*.

This effect – as seen in Figure 4-59) is probably not what you want, but don't worry.

The right selection of layer opacity allows us to tone down the effect to a more pleasing level.

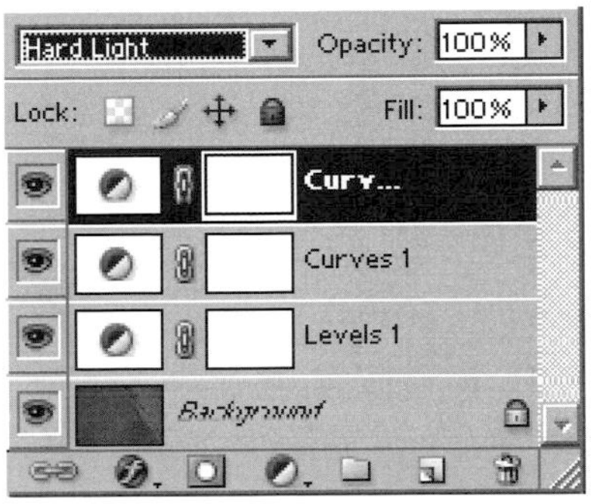

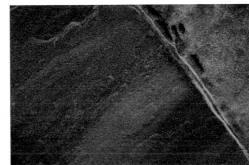

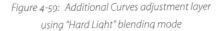

Figure 4-58: Image with 100 % "Hard Light"

Figure 4-59: Additional Curves adjustment layer using "Hard Light" blending mode

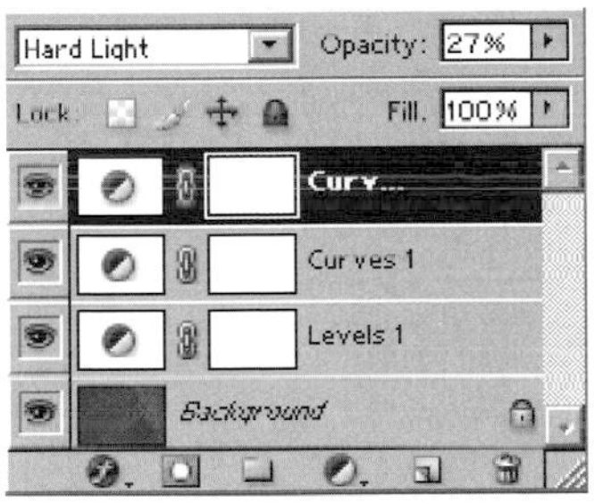

◀ Figure 4-60:
Changing the Opacity

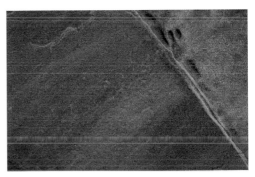

A problem can occur in using this technique: shadows might become too dense. Since we use a Curves adjustment layer, we could use curves to control the impact on the shadows, but there is a more elegant solution. Open the layer's blending options and move the left slider for the *Underlying Layer* to the right. Below 46, values are no longer affected.

Figure 4-61: Opacity of "Hard Light" layer reduced to 27 %

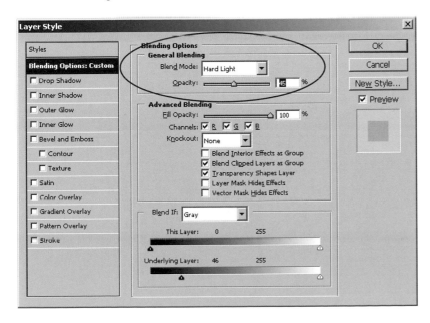

◀ Figure 4-62:
Setting the "Blending Options"

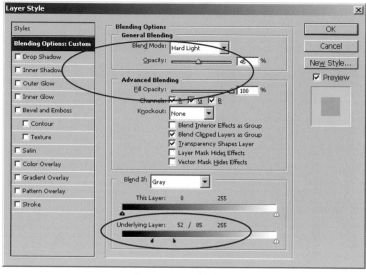

Figure 4-63: Split sliders

This is still not what we want, as the transition would become visible. If you look carefully, notice that the tiny triangle sliders are split. You can separate them by using the Alt key and moving the right portion of the triangle to the right (Figure 4-63). Voilà:

Now, all shadows below 52 are protected from our "Hard Light" layer, and there is a smooth transition zone up to 85. Finally, the layer effect is fully visible above 85.

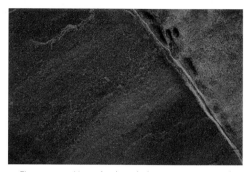

Figure 4-64: Here, shadows below 52 are protected from the 'Hard Light' correction

Variation with "Soft Light"

You can do the same thing using the *Soft Light* blending mode. This time, the effect is less dramatic.

Be careful or your photos will become too dramatic and punchy. Also, photos directly contrasted using strong saturation appear even flatter than they really are. This is one reason naturally saturated photos are perceived as flat. We are bombarded with too many overly saturated photos today, and sometimes call it the "heavy metal of photography."

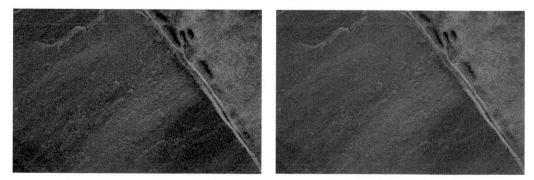

Figure 4-65a: Soft Light at 100% opacity   *Figure 4-65b: Soft Light at 27% opacity*

Removing blue shadow casts

We revisit our dune photo again.

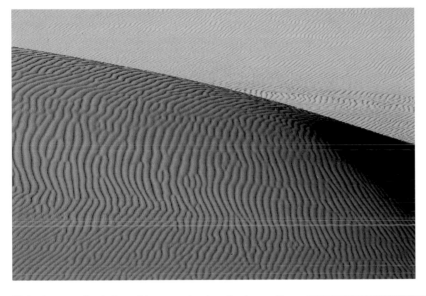

◄ Figure 4-66:
Initial Dune image

This time we look for a blue cast in the shadows. Be aware that this scene was actually illuminated by two light sources:

▸ Sun or sun-in-overcast
▸ Sky in the shades

The light actually has two different color temperatures. In this situation, the global white balance should be selected to correct for the main light source, in this case, the sun.

In shadows, we detect quite a bit of blue shadow cast, which is often not too easy to see on a monitor. We don't like an extreme blue cast in our prints and usually try to tone it down. The techniques here are shown at a 100% magnification crop (all screen shots).

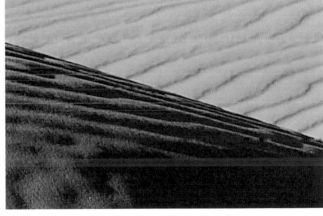

Figure 4-67: Crop of the original photo

We added a Hue/Saturation adjustment layer to pump up the blue, and to intensify the cast (see Figure 4-69).

Pushing up saturation temporarily is a very general technique when doing color corrections. This will show up the colors in your image and where they are. First do this in Hue/Saturation dialog selecting *Master* in the Edit pull-down menu. You may be surprised what colors your image will show. Having seen them, set saturation back to normal and go to the color tint you want to correct and there fine tune – using your sliders – the colors you want to correct. In our example this is Blue.

Figure 4-68: Adjustment layer to increase the saturation

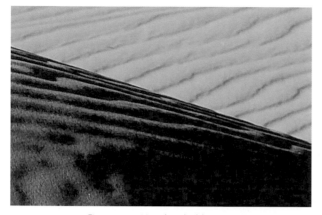

Figure 4-69: Visualize the blue cast

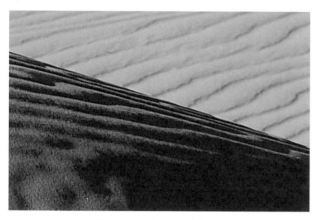

Figure 4-71: Blue, toned down

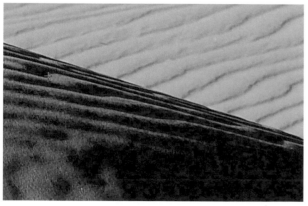

Figure 4-72: Reduced blue removal

As stated, the blue cast looks much too strong, but it gives an idea where blue cast resides. As shown in our workflow book [8], we use selective Hue/Saturation to tone down this cast. We keep the test Hue/Saturation layer on top, just to show the effect:

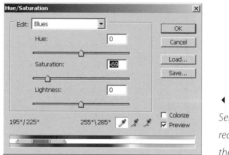

◀ *Figure 4-70: Selective reduction of the blue cast*

A nice side effect is that shadows get a bit brighter when we tone down the blue. It is possible that this strong removal might be too much, and we may want to limit the blue reduction to shadows. This is why we used our Tonality Tuning Toolkit [15] and created a mask to limit the Hue/Saturation layer only on the shadow portion of the image:

Note: We often use the same shadow mask to limit the effect of a noise-removal layer to the shadow part of the image. These shadows sometimes contain a lot of noise.

Remember, our Hue/Saturation test layer still strongly amplifies the blue. The next page shows the final version, after disabling the Hue/Saturation test layer (Figure 4-69):

Keep in mind that sometimes the difference is not as impressive on screen as it can be in a print, so you also must test these effects by actually printing some test prints and studying them under optimum lighting.

Of course, you must be careful if other blue areas reside in your image (e.g., sky). In that case, you may use masking techniques to protect those areas.

If you want to create a luminosity mask using the standard selection mechanism (instead of using our Tonality Tuning Toolkit), choose Select ▸ Color Range and *Sample Colors* in the *Select* drop-down menu. Control the width of your Luminosity using the *Fuzziness* slider. You can then invert the mask it necessary (⇧-Ctrl-I, Mac: ⇧-⌘-I).

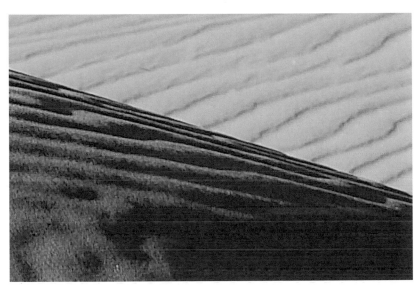

◀ Figure 4-73a:
Initial (above) and final
version of the image

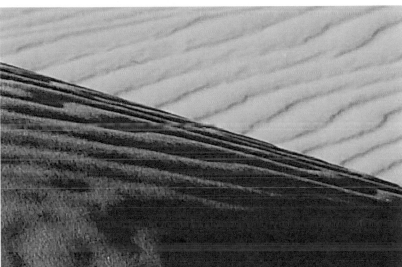

◀ Figure 4-73b:
Initial (above) and final
version of the image

4.4 "Ring Around" and Variations

This chapter covers material strongly influenced by our friend Brad
Hinkel.

Finally, only an actual print can show how a print will look in its final
form. Soft-proofing is just one way to get as close in quality to the final
print as possible. We want to cover here two important techniques in fine-
tuning your prints:

▸ Ring Around
▸ Variations (on screen and in print)

Both techniques are based on seeing the same image (or partial image) in variations of the original to verify you get the interpretation of the image you prefer.

This text is from Brad Hinkel (see www.bradhinkel.com).

Ring Around

Printing a "ring around" is a traditional technique for evaluating images in the wet color darkroom. We all did it for a basic color printing class. I found the process useful, but far too tedious to repeat for any image other than that particular assignment.

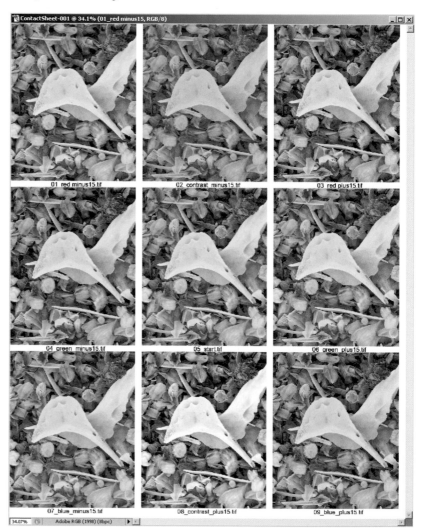

Figure 4-74: ▶
"Ring Around" scheme

In the digital darkroom, this procedure is still effective, but much easier. The "ring around" is designed to help evaluate if an image has the appropriate color balance and/or density. It can potentially be used for a wide range of options, i.e., anything that can be placed on an adjustment layer. We will be investigating more options in the future. The basic "ring around" shows some variations of an image for +R, +G, +B, -R, -G, -B, darker and lighter.

Use a "ring around" when you have an image:

▸ that you feel looks great – but just to test the final evaluation
▸ that you just can't seem to color-balance well

It is important to remember that our eyes/brains will sometimes compensate for color balance issues in an image, to make it appear better than it really is. So, take time away from an image, say, a couple of minutes, and return to it to evaluate its color. A "ring around" forces a better evaluation of color.

We automated the whole process. The action provided helps to create a "ring around" quite easily.*

1. We create a folder (PC: "C:\tmp\ring around").
2. Empty the folder.
3. Run the action.
4. Browse to the folder in Bridge or the Photoshop file browser.
5. Run the Contact Sheet II tool from Bridge or Photoshop (Figure 4-75 and 4-76).

* Sorry, this action is for Windows only, as we need to write to disk, but the action is a blueprint for your own actions on a Mac.

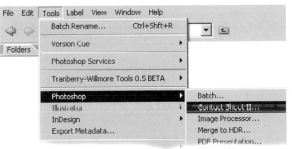

Figure 4-75: Calling Contact Sheet II from Bridge

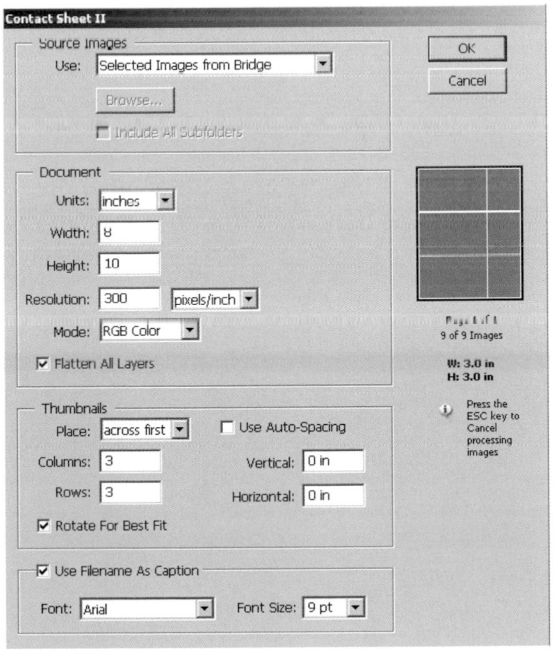

◀ *Figure 4-76: Contact Sheet II dialog*

6. Select a 3 × 3 matrix.
7. Enable a filename as a caption.
8. Confirm OK.
9. Photoshop will create a one-page proof sheet.
10. Print the contact sheet using the appropriate profile (suiting printer, inks, paper, and printer driver settings).

You can find and download our free Photoshop action for "Ring Around" at [17].

Using Variations

Fine-tuning an image takes at least as much effort as getting the image in the first place. Here is a technique to help you visually optimize pictures. These routines look simple, yet they really help for that which they are designed: fine tuning.

We have implemented this technique in a "DOP Variations plug-in," and you can do the same steps by hand.

Comparison is a powerful tool in optimizing color, brightness, contrast, saturation, and more. There is a nice tool in Photoshop called *Variations* (Image ▸ Adjustments ▸ Variations) that guides you through a sequence of image variations (Figure 4-77).

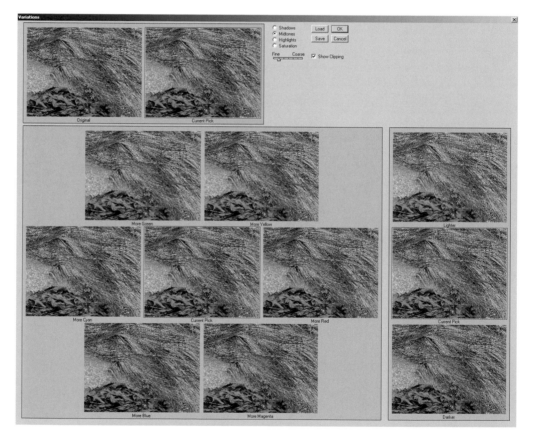

Figure 4–77: ▶
Photoshop Variations

It is a nice tool, but has some major shortcomings when seriously fine tuning:

▸ Images are much too small

▸ Once confirmed, a change is "cast in stone" and cannot be edited; it would be nice to make it an adjustment layer.

▸ Not easy to customize

When our friend Brad Hinkel introduced us to "Ring Around," it stimulated us to design a better way to use variations. Our goals were:

▸ Use the full Photoshop image to compare
▸ Have different comparison patterns
▸ Correct in iterations
▸ Leave all corrections in adjustment layers (let nothing be "cast in stone"!)
▸ Preview before and after at any time
▸ Easy to customize
▸ Not waste too much disk space

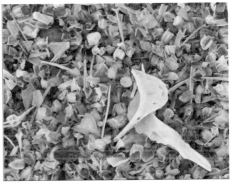

Figure 4-78: Starting image

DOP Variations

Though this is our own tool, feel free to create your own variations workflow using Photoshop actions. You will find our tool here: [16].

As with many good ideas, it is really very simple. The plug in creates adjustment layers with layer masks that are used to compare before/after scenarios. Here are the masks you can select:

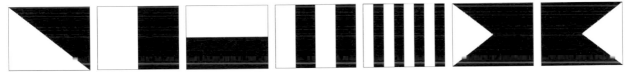

Figure 4-79: Masks, you may use with our Variation Plug-in

The two masks to the right will be used for the "left/right quarter" option, and provide an alternative method of comparing. We use this same image also in our full variations workflow:

Let us assume that you use mask #1 ("Diagonal Split"). Then, the action "*DOP Variations Layers*" will create a layer group (or layer set) with layer masks that use mask #1. It would look like Figure 4-81 and result in an image displayed like in Figure 4-82.

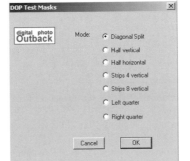

Figure 4-80: Different comparison masks (only available in the Windows version of the plug-in)

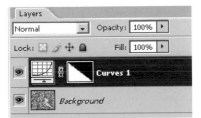

◂ Figure 4-81: Layer palette showing the Curves adjustment layer with its layer mask

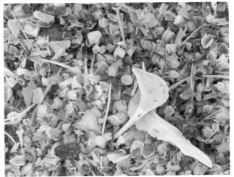

Figure 4-82: Image with split layer mask #1

The goal of the mask is to provide an aid to see the difference between "before" and "after." The adjustment layer is easily tuned using opacity to reduce the brightening effect. Its full benefit is seen in our next example. Here, we provide information on how these variations work, at least in principle.

The full optimization workflow:

Again, we start with an original file. This time we use the supplied action called "*DOP Variations Layers*" and use option 1. This creates the layer structure of Figure 4-83.

The plug-in, together with the actions, creates a layer group (before CS2, called *layer set*) with all layers disabled. We get 12 Adjustment Layers:

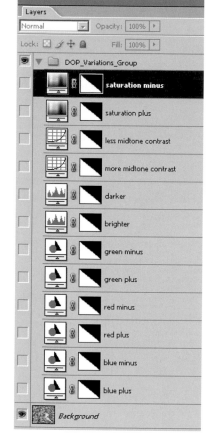

Figure 4-83: Layers

▸ Blue plus/minus color balance (+30/-30 at 50 % opacity)

▸ Red plus/minus color balance (+30/-30 at 50 % opacity)

▸ Green plus/minus color balance (+30/-30 at 50 % opacity)

▸ Darker/brighter levels (0.8/1.2 midpoint at 72 % opacity)

▸ More/less midtone contrast S-Curves (at 80 % opacity)

▸ More/less saturation (+20/-20 at 75 % opacity)

▸ Warmer/cooler (Photo Filters at 50 % opacity)

The task is now to inspect each pair of corrections and decide whether a picture benefits from one of the corrections.

Sample #1 Darker

We enable the "darker" layer and see the image of Figure 4-84. We can now tune the opacity of this layer to darken it as much as we like (here, less is probably more). When we are happy with the result, we disable the Layer Mask:

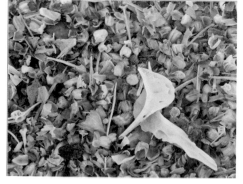

Figure 4-84: Image when layer "darker" is enabled.

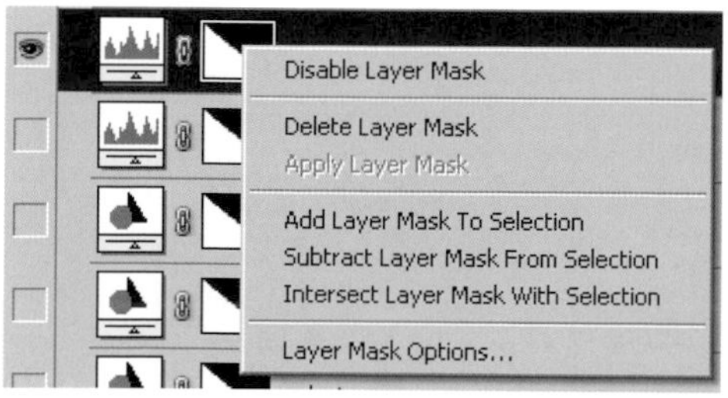

◀ Figure 4-85:
"Disable Layer Mask" to
remove the partial disabling
of the layer effect.

You will get the layer structure of Figure 4-86:

Now "darken" with opacity 25% is applied to the full image. Also we can check the global effect at any time by enabling/disabling the complete layer group.

As we perform these tests for each of the layers, in many cases we see right away that this sort of correction may not make sense.

Don't these many adjustment layers blow up a file size? We tested it on a full Canon 1Ds Mk. II file (16.7 MP):

Name	Size ▲	Type	Date Modified
1ds2_0000_2861_no_layers.tif	35,314 KB	TIF File	11/2/2005 7:06 PM
1ds2_0000_2861_one_adjustment_layer.tif	81,230 KB	TIF File	11/2/2005 7:13 PM
1ds2_0000_2861_with_layers2.tif	83,384 KB	TIF File	11/2/2005 7:11 PM
1ds2_0000_2861_with_layers.tif	85,708 KB	TIF File	11/2/2005 7:08 PM
1ds2_0000_2861_one_layers.tif	127,414 KB	TIF File	11/2/2005 7:12 PM

▸ Image without any layers: 36 MB
▸ Image with a single adjustment layer: 81 MB
▸ Image with the full layer group: 85 MB

This means the overhead is significant compared to not using layers at all. But because layers are the way to go for fine-tuning anyway, our base size is at 81 MB. In this case, we have about 4–5 MB overhead and this means no more than 5% more than the minimal size for just one adjustment layer.

All this fine-tuning will take some time and is only worth it for prints you really care for – but that's all this book is about.

If you finally like your image, and you have scale and sharpened your image as described in the following sections 4.5 and 4.6, you may start the actual printing, described in the next chapter.

4.5   Further preparations for printing

Before you resize and sharpen your image, (which you should do on a copy of your image), you might consider flattening your various layers down to one layer. We recommend you save your layered image first (as a new master image) make a copy of it and only flatten your layers in that new copy. This is the copy you should do your resizing and sharpening on.

Give your various copies consistent file names linking the different versions of your photo together by their file names. According to our experience, you will often want to go back to a previous version (e.g., the version with the correction layers still intact) and do some more fine-tuning there or use it as the base for a print on another output device or for another print size.

The final step in print preparation should be restricting the tonal values of your image to those the printer can reproduce. How this is done is described in Chapter 3.8, page 79/80. You may perform this operation either before or after scaling (sizing) your image copy.

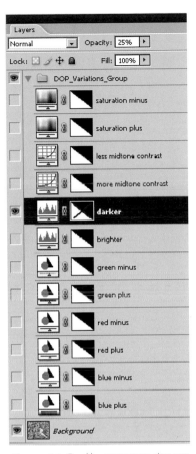

Figure 4-86: Final layer structure after our optimization using the "Variation plug-in". If you keep all disabled layers, you may activate them later for further tuning.

➔ *Your image may lose some visual on contrast on screen when you reduce your tonal values. But don't worry, it won't reduce the quality of your print but will result in more details in shadow and highlight areas!*

4.6   Resizing

As in Sharpening, *resizing* is a complex topic. For printing, we mainly deal with increasing the size of an image only after the print sizes becomes larger. There are two main reasons to increase the size:

▸ Bring the ppi (pixel per inch) up to a value that is optimal for your printer. Most printers work fine with the original ppi between 240 to 360 ppi. Some even use 180 ppi and leave the further "up-sizing" to the printer driver.

▸ Make significantly larger prints than the original image size and ppi would normally allow. We rarely try this, as it always means extrapolation of many new pixels. Admittedly, good up-sizing algorithms can create wonderful illusions.

When you perform major up-sizing, you normally need to add final sharpening.

In Chapter 6, "Printing with Printing Packages and RIPs," we feature Qimage, because it does all these things:

▸ Use first-class up-sizing algorithms

▸ Up-sizes to a printer's native resolution (Epson 360 ppi or 720 ppi, and HP 600 ppi and Canon 360 ppi)

▸ Applies some mild amount of final sharpening that often results in some nice local contrast enhancement.

If you really must up-size your image first, which you should do if you want to print a larger image using Photoshop and the standard printer driver, we recommend the following up-sizing tools:

When using "Bicubic Sharper" for downsizing an image, you may use less sharpening as the image already underwent some sharpening by the scaling process.

▸ Photoshop *Bicubic Smoother*: does a nice job for moderate up-sizing*

▸ DOP Up-sizing [27]: Our free automation plug-in that implements a strategy by our friend Jack Flesher.

▸ Genuine Fractals [37]: the classic up-sizing tool, but slightly expensive.

For down-sizing, Photoshop *Bicubic Sharper* will do the job in most cases.*

If you have to up-size more than 50–80% you may consider using one of those numerous up-sizing Photoshop plug-ins like Genuine Fractals [37] (as mentioned), plx SmartScale [37] or Sizefixer [32]. But most of these plug-ins are costly and are only worth their money if you do a lot of up-sizing and scale up considerably.

When you are shooting RAW and intend to print large, you may prefer to do your up-sizing in the RAW converter. In most cases, the results are slightly better than scaling in Photoshop.

Note: If you have to resize an image, never do it to your master image but only to a new copy of the image file!

4.7 Sharpening

All images produced by a digital camera need some sharpening, as some softness is introduced internally by the anti-aliasing filter of the digital camera (in front of the sensor). Some additional softness is introduced by the demosaicing filter. With digital scans, some softness is produced in the digitizing process.

Sharpening usually should be performed as the last optimization step. After removing noise, sharpening may make noise more visible. There actually are two types of sharpening you should apply to an image:

A) **Some general sharpening** to improve an image, independent of the output method

B) **Output-specific sharpening.** If the output method produces additional softness, e.g., due to dithering as used for offset or inkjet printing, you would apply more sharpening to compensate for this. If your output method does no dithering, e.g., say for presentation on monitors, or when using dithering-free printing such as LightJet printing (direct photo printing) or output on a dye-sublimation printer, no additional or only slight sharpening after step A is required.

The second kind of sharpening should be done after final scaling for output, as sharpness is influenced by increasing or decreasing the size of an image. Ideally, scaling and sharpening may be left to the printing process (e.g., RIP), if this process offers such a feature.

With some printing packages or RIPs you may leave sizing and sharpening to those packages (e.g., Qimage, ImagePrint, and Adobe Lightroom).

Please consult our e-books DOP2000 ([8]) and DOP3002 ([9]) for more on sharpening.

> **Uwe's personal note on sharpening:**
>
> I try to sharpen an image at the camera's resolution so that I can see as few artifacts as possible (at 100% magnification), but still keep the image in focus. Later on, I try to avoid too much up-sizing (see next section) and do hardly any extra print sharpening. This ensures a natural sharpness for the print. Too much sharpening always makes prints look so *digital* or *less smooth*. Even though I use my own sharpening tool, EasyS Plus Sharpening Toolkit,* there are many other valid sharpening strategies that will suit your needs.

* For EasyS Plus Toolkit see [18].

We do our sharpening using a separate pixel layer. For this we reduce all visible layers down to a new layer ([⇧]-[Ctrl]-[Alt]-[E], Mac: [⇧]-[⌥]-[⌘]-[E]).*

With the techniques demonstrated in this chapter, your image should be fine-tuned and ready for printing. Now, you are actually ready to print, and we will show you how in the next chapter.

* With Photoshop 7 and Photoshop CS1 you have to use two steps: first create a new empty layer ([⇧]-[Ctrl]-[N]) and then do the flattening ([⇧]-[Ctrl]-[Alt]-[E]).

Fine Art Printers in Practical Use

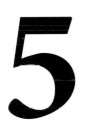

When everything works correctly, printing with today's fine art printers can be a pleasure. Unfortunately, many things can go wrong and spoil the fun, which implies that you need to know when to use or not use certain features of your printer and the various set-ups for proper color management. Knowing the basics gives you the freedom to experiment.

5.1   Printer installation

The physical installation of a printer is similar, whether connecting to a Mac or PC. Unfortunately, the software is usually quite different. Typically, we install a new printer in about 15–30 minutes.* With some large-format printers, the ink charging time may take longer. In most cases, printer installation is a very smooth process (HP, Canon, and Epson).

* With some large-format printers, it may take a bit longer, as the loading of the ink may take some time.

Connection types

USB/USB 2.0: Currently, USB is the most common type of connection offered by all new printers, although there is usually no cable supplied in the box. A connecting cable can extend from about six to 20 feet. Avoid cables that are too long. Additionally, you can connect most USB printers via a USB hub that has its own power supply. Often, passive USB hubs do not allow adequate power to reach the various devices connected to it. USB hubs may, in some cases, cause problems with certain printers e.g., HP Designjet printers, as we discuss later. USB 2.0 ensures a better throughput, and is also the current standard for the newest printers. Sadly, the speed of most printers is not high enough to even challenge the USB 1.0 connection.

➔ With some HP printers we encountered problems when connecting them to the PC via a USB hub.

Firewire (IEEE-1394): Firewire is less common and not significantly faster than USB 2.0. Firewire allows slightly longer cables, however.

Ethernet (LAN): Ethernet allows the longest cables, easily 50 feet or longer. Printers like the HP Photosmart 8750 come with USB and Ethernet, or you may add an Ethernet network card, as is true with some Epson large-format printers. This throughput is adequate most of the time, and using Ethernet allows you to easily share printers among multiple computers. On the other hand, networking can be challenging. If you don't like dealing with a network, we suggest using one of the other kinds of connections.

➔ Do not connect a printer to your computer until you are prompted to do so by the printer's manual.

Parallel: This was the classical type of PC computer-to-printer connection, but has been largely replaced by USB. We would not recommend using parallel with today's printers because of their short/thick cables offering less flexibility.

Unpacking

During physical set-up, follow the manufacturer's set-up instructions word-for-word. Place the printer at a location where you can handle all paper input/output easily, provide adequate space for cooling (most printers don't generate excessive heat), and allow for proper ventilation of various ink, paper and other printer chemicals that discharge during printing.

Installing the print heads

Some printers (HP and Canon) have removable heads, while others (Epson) have fixed ones. Both are related to the inkjet technology used; there are pros and cons for both technologies. Overall, this aspect should not affect your choice of a printer, other than that you must take into account the cost of new heads in your cost analysis. If you need to install heads (HP and Canon), follow the manufacturer's instructions carefully.

Installing the ink cartridges

Follow the manufacturers instruction carefully. Never touch the electronic contacts. If you do, clean them with a lint-free cloth and isopropyl alcohol, as the perspiration on your fingers can cause the contacts to corrode.

If you install cartridges with pigment inks, carefully shake them before installing to stir up the pigments.

Calibration, printer tests and head alignment

Some recent printers ask you to insert plain paper to perform an automatic head alignment or color calibration (usually, it is not really a color calibration, but a density calibration for the individual inks). Both steps may be repeated later, but it is best to do the printer set-up as early as possible. Normally, the final test sheet indicates that the printer passed all its tests.

Installing the drivers and other software

> **Repeat Note:** Do not connect the printer to your computer before the manufacturer's manual or the installation software prompts you to do so (usually, after a printer driver is installed).

We repeat this to save you potential problems.

All the printers we cover in this book ship with software installation programs to safely guide you through the entire driver-installation process, step-by-step. Follow the instructions carefully and take your time. Some printers come with software other than the driver itself. We rarely install this extra software, as we are familiar with our printing software (Photoshop CS/ CS2, Qimage or ImagePrint), and none of the software packages we recommend needs more than their drivers.

Once you have installed the drivers, it is time for a test print. This is merely a print confirming that the connection and the drivers work correctly. It is not to test the print quality and colors you want. We will check that later.

Installing printer profiles

Many modern printers come with generic profiles for the printer. Sometimes these may require an additional installation step. In most cases, these profiles are installed with the printer drivers. Without them, you will have a difficult time getting good prints.

➜ It may be well worth it to look for updated, improved or additional ICCs profiles at the Internet site of the printer's manufacturer.

5.2   Printer adjustments

Though most printers are ready to go after the installation process, some require fine-tuning their behavior.

Head Alignment

Head alignment is crucial for optimum print results without banding. Fortunately, many new printers now use sensors inside the printer to perform this alignment automatically. Check the user manual to perform head alignment, if necessary.

Nozzle Check

➜ *You should use your inkjet printer regularly – once a week should be a good time frame. This will prevent the nozzles of the print heads from clogging. It may be sufficient just to switch it on and off after a few minutes.*

Especially when not using your printer every day, some nozzles may become clogged. The Nozzle Check prints a test pattern to show you whether any nozzles are clogged or not. If possible, you should use your printer at least once a week.

Clean nozzles are an important issue for high quality prints, For this reason we run a nozzle check every time before we start printing when the printer was not used for some time. Professional services do this every morning!

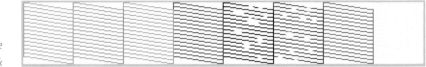

Figure 5-1: ▶
Nozzle check pattern showing some clogged nozzles with the black and blue ink

Head Cleaning

If some nozzles are clogged, you must perform one or more head-cleaning cycles. Unfortunately, this procedure uses up some ink that adds to overall ink cost.

Color calibration

* Actually, this is a density calibration and not real color calibration but will improve color accuracy.

Some printers perform a color calibration on the printer, e.g., HP Designjet 30/90/130. This has the advantage that a printer can more easily be used with generic profiles, as the printer is set to a defined state. Color calibration is best performed after changing heads or inks.*

With its new, large-format printers, Epson (4800, 7800, 9800) has tried to avoid this step by using the following measures:

▶ Very low production variations between printers of the same make
▶ Fixed heads
▶ Factory printer linearization

5.3   General driver tasks and settings

Printer drivers seem to be simple tools, yet there are many aspects that influence image quality, not to mention comfort of the user. Here, image quality should clearly be a high priority.

Settings that influence print quality

> **Note:** All these parameters may influence your choice of profiles. Remember that any given printer profile is only valid for a specific paper, ink set and driver setting combination.

Paper type

Paper type is one of the most important settings in your driver. Be aware that most drivers only allow a choice between papers of a specific printer manufacturer. Third-party papers may be a close match or completely wrong. Expect the least problems by staying with the family of papers a manufacturer provides or suggests.

> ➜ *When using third-party papers, you should look for instructions for the proper printer settings when using their paper. You will probably find this information at the Internet site of the paper manufacturer (see Appendix B for some of the URLs).*

With paper type selected, you implicitly select many other parameters of the printer driver, and often there is no other way to select them directly. How these settings work is known only by the manufacturer. Often, there is a lack of a reasonable description of the settings in the printer manual.

▸ Paper thickness (distance from heads to paper)
▸ How much ink to lay down
▸ Drying time
▸ Paper transport speed
▸ Possible print quality selections (dpi)

Print quality settings

DPI (dots per inch): Each paper is assigned a certain dpi setting.* Often, higher values give better results, print slower, and often use more ink. Also, in many cases, you may distinguish the difference only upon close inspection with a magnifying glass. With newer printers and drivers, quality settings do not name dpi values but use names like *Standard*, *Photo* or *Best Photo*. We are usually quite pleased with the settings referred to as *Best*.

> * *With newer printers and printer drivers, the print resolution is not given in dpi but terms like "Draft", "Photo", "Best Photo" or "Maximum dpi" are used.*

Color and color management settings

These settings make or break good prints. We provided a full chapter on Color Management to ensure you get the best possible prints.

There are three different strategies in working with printers to create the colors you want.

1. **Let the client application, e.g., Photoshop, handle color management** (File ▸ Print with preview).

    This means the printer should not do color changes at all.

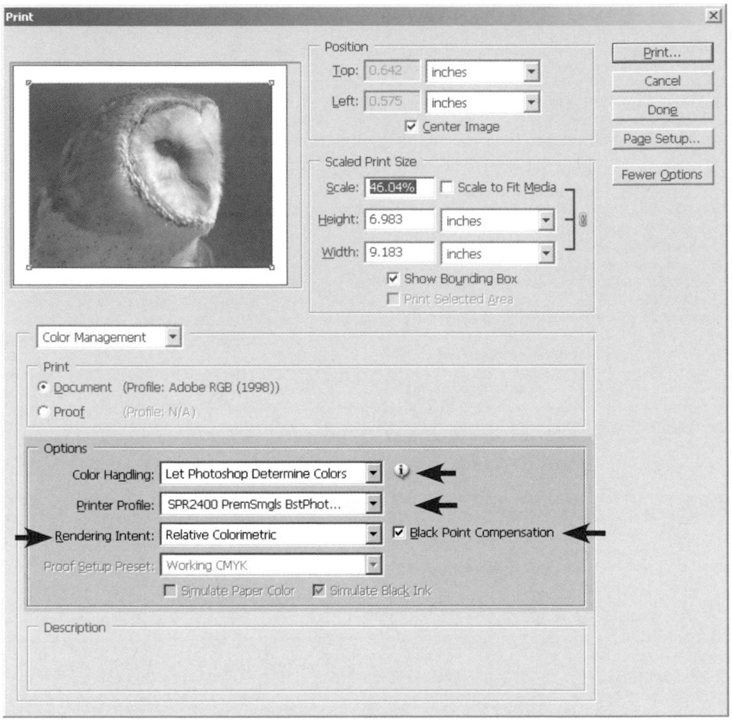

Figure 5-2a: Select your CM strategy in Photoshop CS2

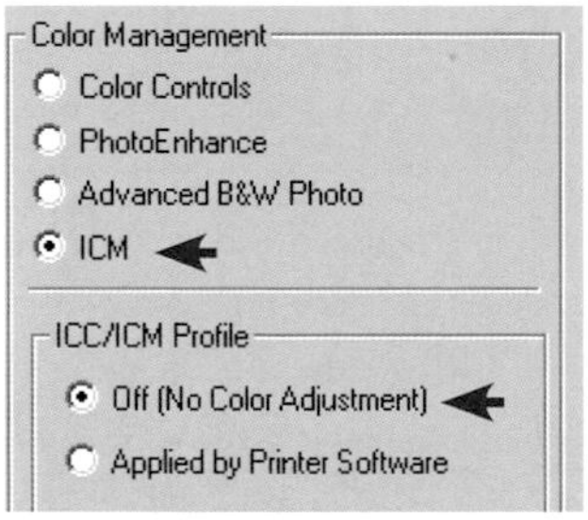

Figure 5-2b: Settings to turn color handling off in the printer driver

Important settings are marked in red in Figure 5-1a. When color management is done in an application, you must disable it in the driver (Figure 5-1b). In other words, **do not** enable it in the application and in the driver!

This is our preferred option used most of the time. It is much easier to understand what a client application does than what the printer is doing in the background.

2. **Let the printer handle color management.**

    In this case, the client application does not handle profile conversions, and leaves it to the printer driver (see Figure 5-3). In almost all cases, this is not a good idea, as you rarely understand what the driver is doing. Only on some printers, especially when printing in black-and-white, do we use this option, which is covered later in Chapter 7 "Black-and-White Prints".

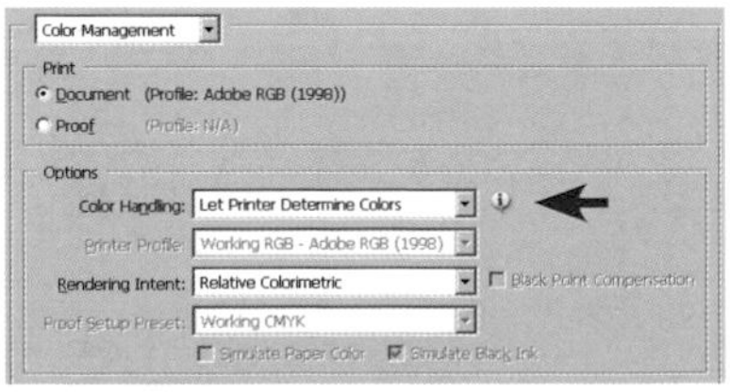

Figure 5-3: With these settings, Photoshop lets the printer driver handle color management.

3. **Use manual or automatic color settings for a printer.**

    We never use such settings, as they eliminate proper color management and make printing of correct colors more of an undesirable gamble. If you do not use color management, then you should, at minimum, leave your original image in the sRGB color space, as in most cases the driver will assume the picture is in this space.

As mentioned earlier, to get the results you want, work on your profiles, and improve them.

Good profiles are your ticket to accurate prints!

Printing Speed

Some printers are faster when printing bidirectionally.* In some cases, this somewhat decreases image quality. We recommend using this setting only if you can see no difference in quality or when you need sample proofs quickly.

With some printer drivers, this feature is named "High Speed":

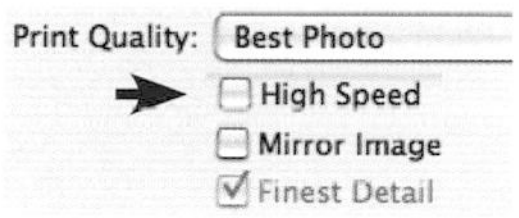

Advanced Settings (ink volume, color density, drying time, etc.)

Most of the time, you won't need to change any of these settings.

Yet, we have had situations where, for example, the prints on Epson Enhanced Matte paper came out too wet, which caused warping. To solve the problem, we reduced color density to -5 or -10. If you do this regularly with a paper, you might be wise to create a special profile with these settings.

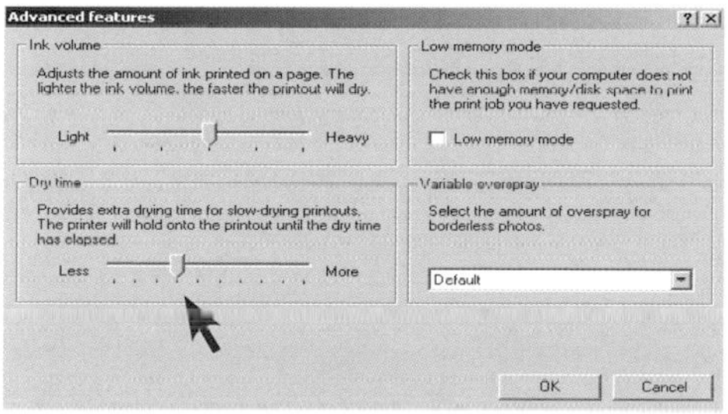

Figure 5-4a: HP Photosmart 8750 advanced settings

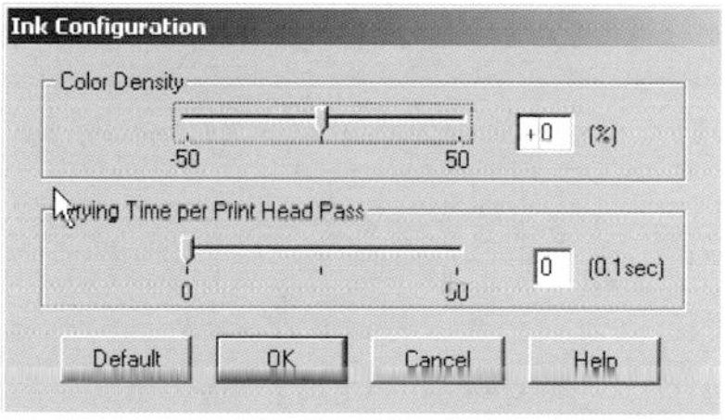

Figure 5-4b: Epson R2400 advanced settings

More settings

The settings listed here are not related to image quality, but more to controlling the layout, paper feed and more.

Paper Size ▸ Quite obviously, an important setting. The drivers also allow creation of your own custom paper sizes.

Paper Sources ▸ Most printers have different paths to feed paper:

▸ Different trays

▸ Single-sheet feed

▸ Roll feeder, (which also involves automatic or manual cutting; check whether a built-in cutter can handle your paper's weight)

Paper orientation ▸ Select landscape or portrait mode.

Borderless printing ▶ We have little experience using this mode, as fine art prints nearly always have a border, (at least an inch), to allow proper space for matting.

Number of copies ▶ Normally, you can select the number of copies in the client application's printing dialog.

Scaling ▶ We recommend performing any scaling in the client application, e.g., Photoshop.

Print preview option ▶ We rarely use this option. Sometimes it makes sense to check whether your prints have the expected orientation and size.

> **Warning:** We have heard users say that their prints look "wrong." Eventually, we learned these users had never actually printed their images, but were merely viewing the Epson print preview screen. Do NOT judge the ultimate colors of prints using the Epson print-preview window. They display without color management and can be completely inaccurate, often tending towards magenta.

Ink-level monitor

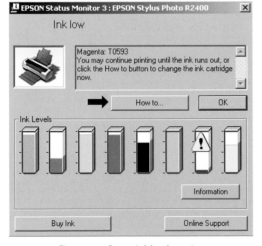

Figure 5-5: R2400 ink level monitor

Checking ink levels is important, but can also be confusing. When some ink indicates as low, have replacement cartridges available. Manufacturers want you to change ink as early as possible (for obvious reasons). The following has been our experience with two different printers:

Epson Stylus R2400   We wait until the printer stops printing before changing an ink cartridge. So far, we find that we have not lost a single print in doing this.

HP Photosmart 8450   We do not switch the cartridge immediately when we get a warning. It may be a good idea, however, not to wait until the cartridge is completely empty as these particular cartridges contain 3 different colors of ink, and you may be low on only one. Waiting too long may cause pages to print with degraded quality.

Printer driver settings in Mac OS X

There are many variations of a Windows-version printer driver interface; the look of the interface depends on the printer manufacturer. Even the driver dialog boxes of the same manufacturer show many variations when handling different printers from the same manufacturer. While we will use Windows-based examples later in this chapter, we would also like to show the driver setting scheme for Mac OS X. Apple has designed a very clean and consistent framework for various driver dialogs.

The basic Mac OS X driver dialog hierarchy looks like this:

Printer Choose the printer you wish to print on.

Presets If you have saved some printer settings previously, you will find those names in the drop-down menu. Load a set by selecting its menu item. Otherwise, use *Standard,* and make individual settings in the various dialog boxes selected from the following drop-down-menu:

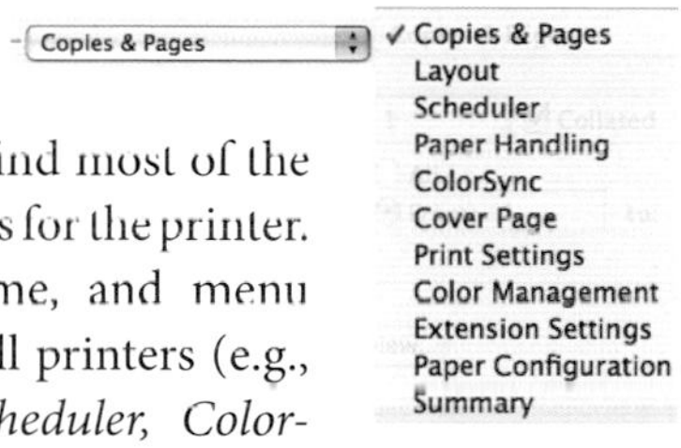

This is a menu where you find most of the various settings' dialog boxes for the printer. There is a standard scheme, and menu items are there for nearly all printers (e.g., *Copies & pages, Layout, Scheduler, Color-Sync,* and *Summary*). Some menu items are printer and manufacturer specific: e.g., *Print settings, Extension Settings* and *Paper Configuration.*

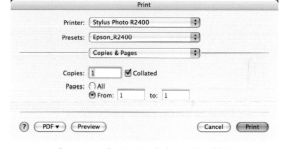

Figure 5-6: Basic print dialog in Mac OS X.

◀ *Figure 5-7:*

Typical hierarchy for printer driver settings and print dialogs in Mac OS X

Here is a short explanation of the various menus and settings:

Layout Lets you specify the number of images you wish to place on one sheet. For fine art printing this is not useful, as placement is arbitrary. If you want to do an index print or place several images on one sheet, you can use Photoshop or other applications to do this. This dialog box changes slightly when a different printer is used.

Schedule You may specify when the print job should begin. With fine art printing, you usually want it to start right away, which may be the default in the print queue.

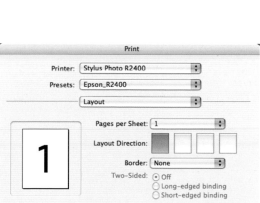

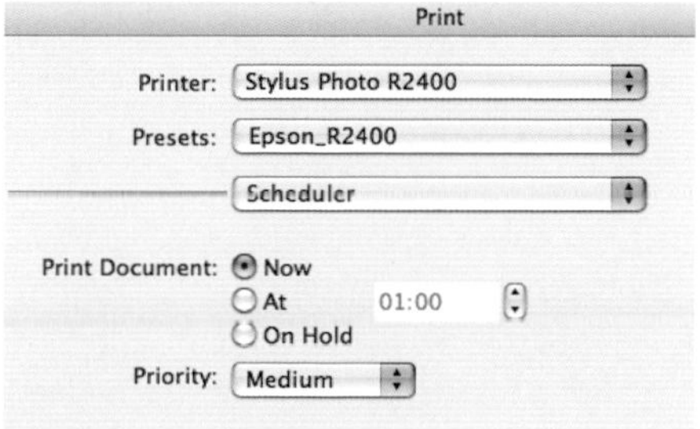

Figure 5-7: Mac OS X Printer Layout tab

◀ *Figure 5-8: Mac OS X printer Schedule tab*

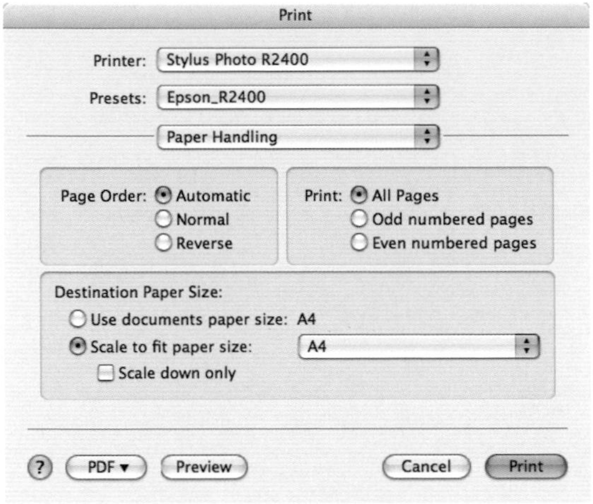

Figure 5-9: Mac OS X Printer Paper Handling

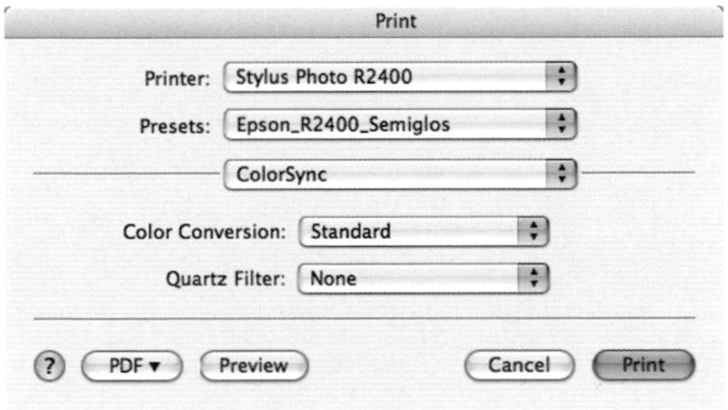

Figure 5-10: Mac OS X ColorSync tab

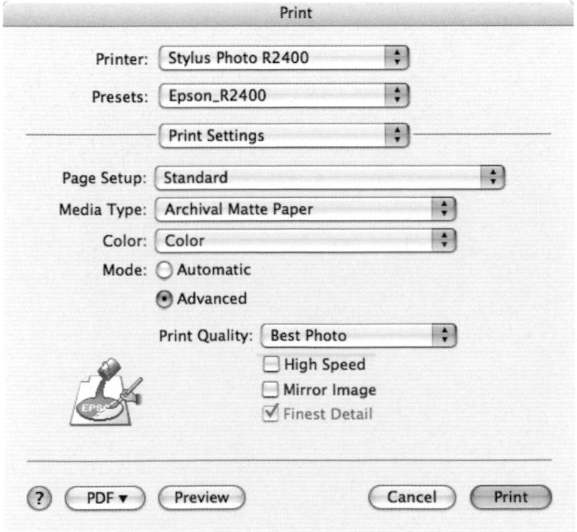

Figure 5-11: With 'Printer Settings' you do most of the settings for your print.

Paper Handling You may scale your print here, which is fine when slight scaling is required. For fine art printing, scaling should be done either when preparing the image for print (see Chapter 4) in Photoshop, or should be left to the RIP when using one. If you print a portfolio with a multi-page document, and want to print duplex without having a printer equipped with duplex capability, you may use the strategy of first printing all *Odd numbered pages*, re-inserting the paper stack and then printing *Even numbered pages,* while activating *Reverse.*

ColorSync Here, you select how the Mac OS X color-management system is involved. You may do some image preprocessing using Quartz filters, which we do not recommend, however, when printing directly from Photoshop.

ColorSync settings are useful when printing from an application that is not color managed. In this case, ColorSync may take over and provide color management, e.g., mapping image color from the image color space to the printer color space. However, you can't select the printer profile from this printer driver dialog, but must do that set-up using the ColorSync Utility (found in Applications ▸ Utilities ▸ ColorSync Utility). See Mac OS X help for more information.

Cover Page allows you to print a cover page. In fine art printing, this may be undesirable, considering the cost of fine art paper and expensive ink.

Printer Settings

These are the most important settings in fine art printing. This dialog box is printer and manufacturer specific, resembling Windows printer driver dialogs. Figure 5-11 shows an example of the dialog for the Epson R2400 printer:

▸ **Page Setup** With the R2400, you are given a choice between *Standard* (Sheet Feeder) and *Paper Roll.*

▸ **Media Type** Select your media (paper) here. The R2400 printer driver only offers those media working together with the type 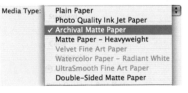 of black ink cartridge in place, either *Photo Black* or *Matte Black* (the latter was inserted as the screen shot was taken). All unsuitable media are grayed out and therefore not accessible. The driver interface only offers Epson media.

If you use a third-party paper, you must estimate which Epson paper is the closest equivalent.

▸ **Color** For the R2400, you may either print in *Color*, *Advanced B&W Photo*, which we select for black-and-white printing (see Chapter 7) or *Black* only, which is useless for our purposes.

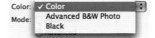

▸ **Mode** For fine art printing, select *Advanced*, so that the dialog will show the advanced settings for the printer as shown in Figure 5-11.

▸ **Print Quality** The drop-down list will offer different printing qualities, depending on the media type selected (e.g., for plain paper, only *Economy* and *Fine* are enabled). For fine art prints using the Epson R2400, we recommend *Best Photo*. Below that, we disable *High Speed* and activate *Finest Detail*.

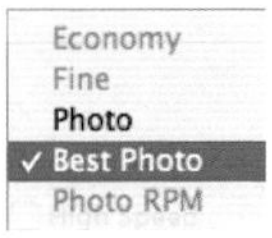

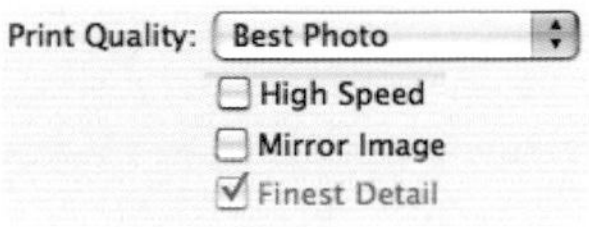

Color Management You may define how color management is done and by which application. If printing directly from Photoshop, turn color management off as shown in Figure 5-12. If you print from a non-color-managed application, you should activate *ColorSync* and do your printer specific set-up in ColorSync (Applications/Utilities/ColorSync Utility).

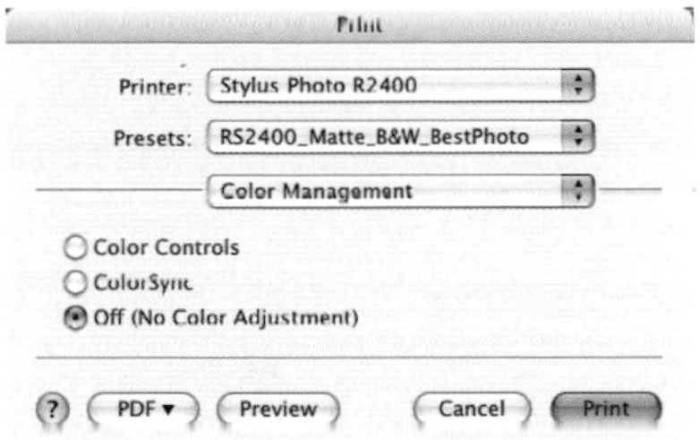

Figure 5-12: Color management tab

Extension Settings This is printer specific and only available for some printers. For the Epson R2400, for example, you may specify using *Thick paper*. We only activate Thick paper if the paper has more than 200 g/m².

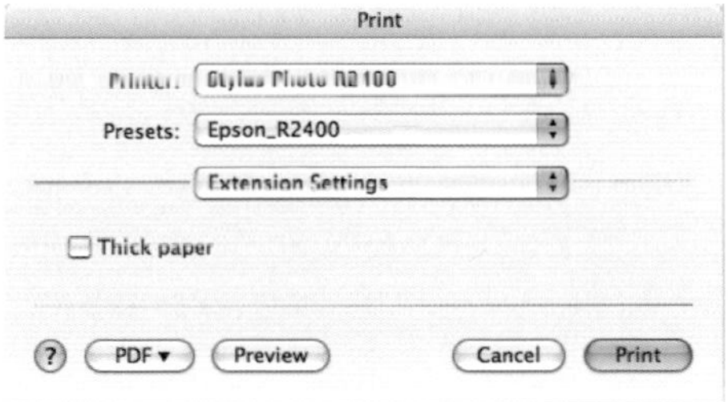

◀ *Figure 5-13: Extensions Settings with the Epson R2400 driver*

Paper configuration This item is only available with some printers (such as the Epson R2400). You may reduce Color Density (actually ink density), which may prevent paper warping when printing on thinner paper.

Summary

This can be very convenient, as all settings are summarized here and the individual details may be shown or hidden by clicking on the small ▸ icon (see Figure 5-15, next page).

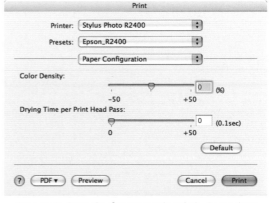

Figure 5-14: Paper Configuration tab with the R2400 driver

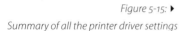

Figure 5-15: ▶
Summary of all the printer driver settings

Save settings

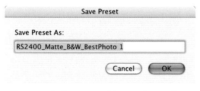

Figure 5-16: Save your driver settings using a descriptive name.

After testing various settings and having discovered the proper settings for a printer and a specific type of print job, you should save those settings so you may recall them at a later time. To save your settings, go to the menu item *Save As* under the drop-down menu for Presets.

Give a descriptive setting name that states the type of paper and other important parameters. This name will then show up in the drop-down menu for Presets.

Printer-maintenance utilities

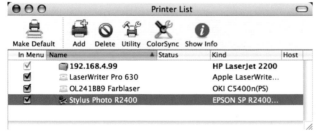

Figure 5-17: You may find the Mac OS X "Printer Setup Utility" inside your Dock. It shows a list of all printers installed.

You will find printer maintenance utilities for inkjet printers in the dock: *Printer Setup Utility.* 🖶

Here you should select your printer (we did it for our Epson Stylus Photo R2400), and click on *Utility* (🖶). This utility, used with the Epson inkjet printers, will bring up the Epson maintenance utilities as shown in Figure 5-18:

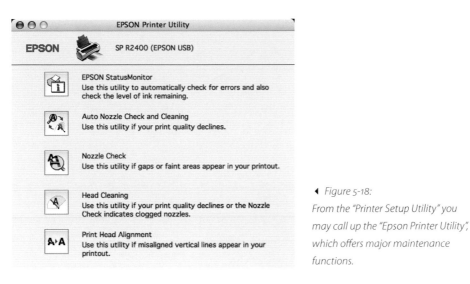

◀ *Figure 5-18:*
From the "Printer Setup Utility" you
may call up the "Epson Printer Utility",
which offers major maintenance
functions.

Here, you find those maintenance functions already described in section
5-2.

Starting from the "Printer List" (actually, it is the "Printer Setup
Utility"; see Figure 5–17), you may also call up the Mac ColorSync Utility.
(Click ✂). When Color Sync Utility appears, select tab ⬚ *Devices* (Figure
5-19). There, you may assign profiles to a device (here, a specific printer).
This is useful if you print from a non-color-managed application, and
ColorSync must do the color mapping.

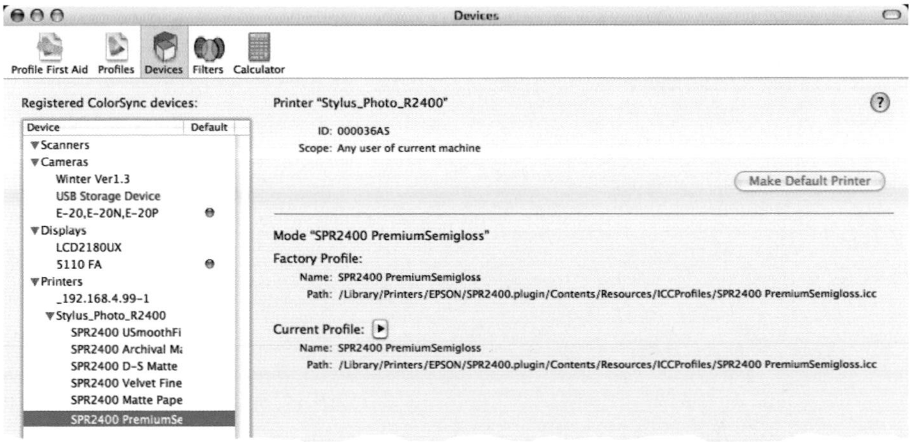

◀ *Figure 5-19: You*
should assign the appropriate
profiles to your devices using
the "ColorSync Utility." This helps
when printing from a non-
colored-managed application.

5.4   Printing from client software

Quality printing requires applications that are color managed: Photoshop, ImagePrint, Adobe Lightroom, Apple Aperture, Qimage, and many others. We describe printing only from these applications that are mature products and come with good documentation. If you do not own any of these programs, we recommend keeping all your documents in an sRGB working space. With some trial and error and a little luck, you are likely to get some decent prints.

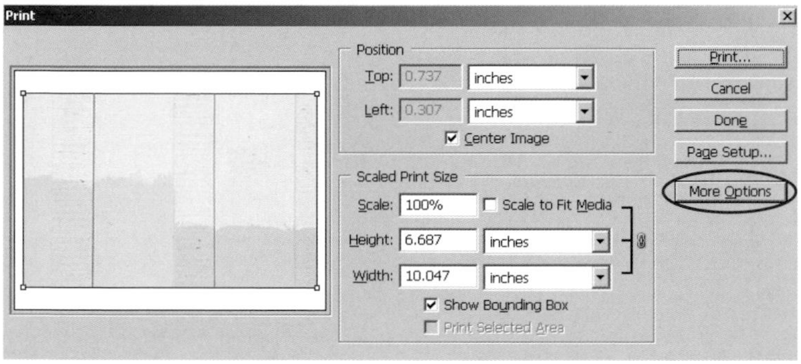

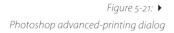

Figure 5-20: Photoshop basic print dialog

We only cover printing from Photoshop CS2 here, but the principles are the same with all applications that are color-managed.

For printing we use the Photoshop function Print with preview. Initially, Photoshop shows the following dialog (Figure 5-20):

This dialog does not offer color management settings. Therefore, you should activate the advanced dialog by clicking the button More Options.

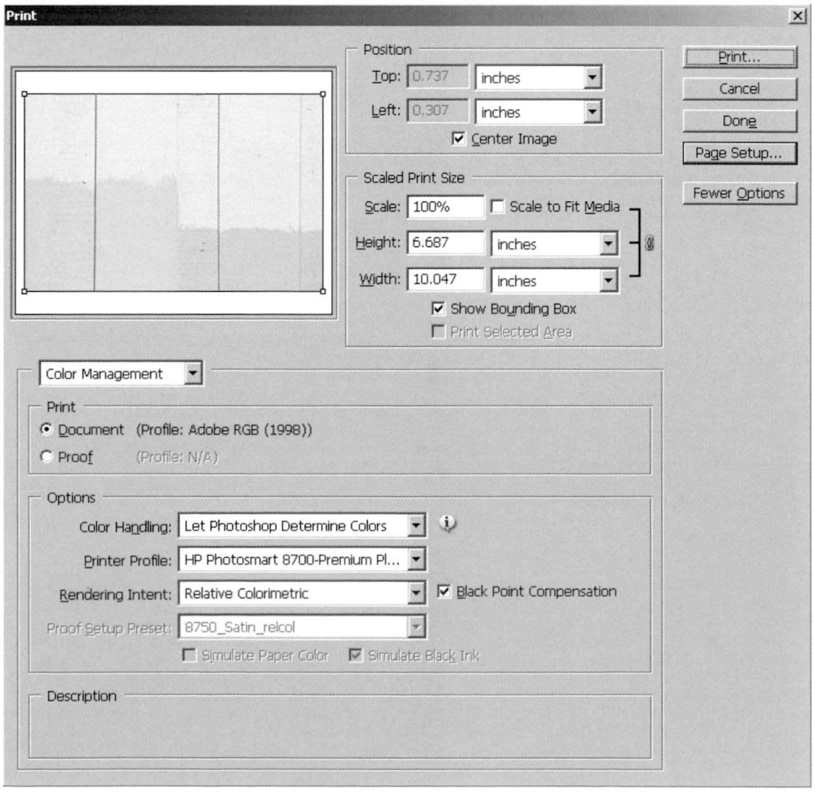

Figure 5-21: ▶
Photoshop advanced-printing dialog

These are the recommended settings:

▸ Before changing any other settings, be certain you have the correct page set-up (see Figure 5-22).

Here, you will be able to define the paper size, the feeding option (paper source) and the page orientation. Before changing any of these parameters, select and set up your printer (click on the Printer button):

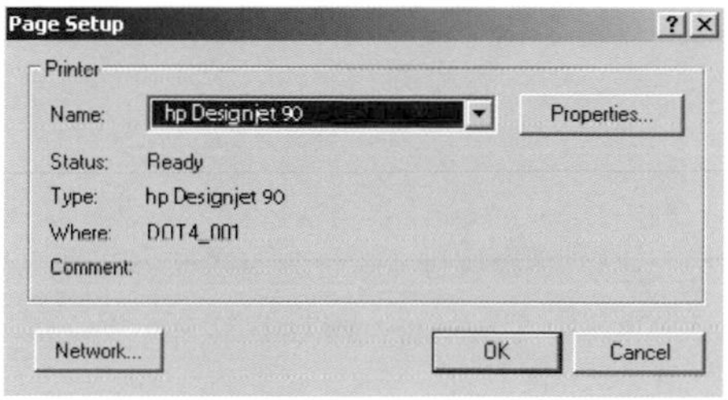

◀ *Figure 5-23:*
In Page Setup, click Properties
to display more printer driver
settings.

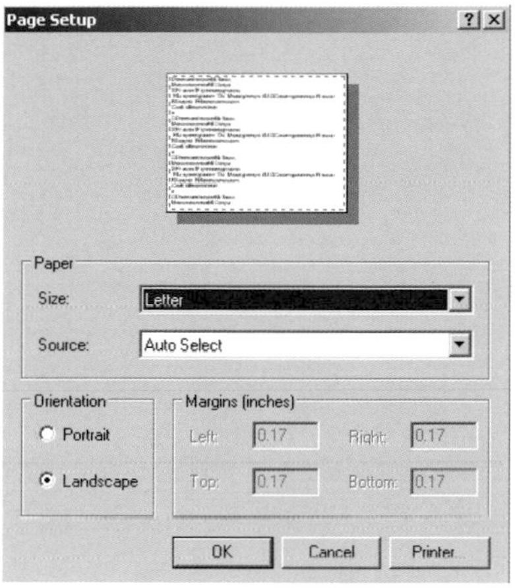

Figure 5-22: Page Setup

Once you have selected your printer, you must set up the correct printer driver options (click on Properties). These are the options we discussed earlier in the section on printer driver settings.

You can change the size of the image. Normally, we do this in Photoshop before entering the printing dialog, because all this option does is to change the ppi of the document to match the new print size. This is fine for minor resizing, but in other situations you are better advised to use the more advanced scaling techniques in Photoshop, or perhaps a dedicated Photoshop plug-in.

The drop-down box below the image preview is set to **Color Management.**

① We select the **Document Option,** which shows our document's working space; here it is Adobe RGB (1998).

② Color handling allows selecting from four options:
Normally, we would use *Let Photoshop Determine Colors*. This way, Photoshop controls the mapping of colors to the printer. There are situations where we may use different settings:

– Black-and-white printing. If we have no special black-and-white profile (as described in Chapter 7.2), we let the driver to the tonal mapping.
If, however, we have a black-and-white profile, we again use this profile and use *Let Photoshop Determine Colors*.*

– Printing of color targets to create printer profiles. Here we need to set Color Handling to *No Color Management*.

③ In Printer Profile you select the correct or most appropriate profile for your combination of printer, paper, and ink. As stated previously, good profiles produce good prints. Currently, many printers come with adequate generic profiles to get you started.

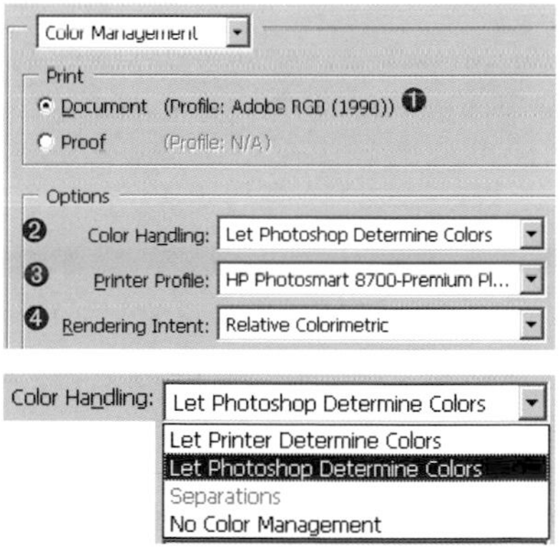

Figure 5-24: Color Handling Options in
Photoshop dialog Print with Preview

* *In Chapter 7.5 we describe how you may*
produce a black-and-white ICC profile

④ For **Rendering Intent** there are two choices when printing photos:

Perceptual: This is appropriate when your image has a lot of colors "out of gamut" (see Chapter 3.2, page 62).

Relative Colorimetric: Use this intent when colors in your image fit into the gamut of the printer color space. Check for this in Photoshop by activating gamut warning (⇧-Ctrl-Y, Mac: ⇧-⌘-Y).

No best rendering intent is suitable for all images. You need to experiment to learn which one fits your personal style. We prefer to print with the relative colorimetric rendering intent most of the time.

⑤ Check the box **Black Point Compensation**. This feature by Adobe compensates for a different level of black between the working color space and the printer color space.

➜ *Activating "Black Point Compensation" may not yield the best result with all RGB profiles. There seems to be a few profiles (actually profiling packages), where leaving this option deactivated will result in better prints.*

5.5   Test prints

Now is a good time to perform a test print. Sometimes it is best to use special test images that show a variety of printer properties and limitations.

Bill Atkinson assembled the following test image, allowing us to share it with our readers (see Figure 5-25). This 24 MB ZIP file is a LAB image.* Resize the test image, if necessary, to fit your paper size.

➜ *We had reports that with some printing applications there are problems using a LAB mode image. So, if you encounter a problem, convert the test image to RGB.*

Important checks:

▸ Possible casts in the gray ramps
▸ Handling of strongly saturated colors
▸ Skin tones
▸ Shadow details

5.6   Print quality related issues

Here is an additional short list of issues to be aware of:

Drying time   Refrain from judging a print critically without giving it sufficient time to dry. A safe bet is 24 hours, but for most prints, three to four hours is enough. Likewise, never use prints in profiling without allowing enough drying time.

Prints from some printers (e.g., HP) are especially delicate immediately after printing. Make certain you don't touch the surface of a print, and let it dry in a dust-free space.

Inspecting your prints   Inspect your prints using standardized daylight, D50 (Daylight at 5,000 Kelvin), as all color management is based on this. For information on how to obtain such light, and for more details on image inspection and judgement, see Chapter 8 "Image Judgement."

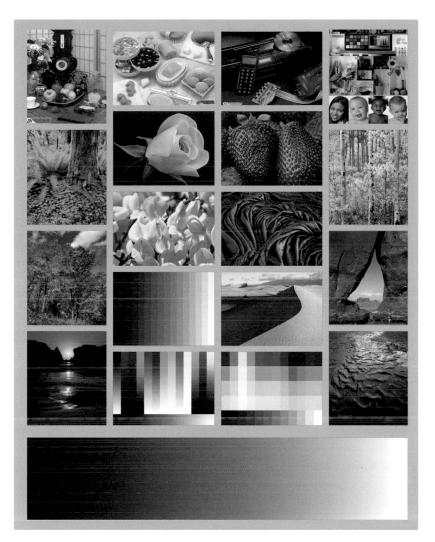

◀ *Figure 5-25:*
Test image (24 MB ZIP file in LAB mode,
composed by Bill Atkinson. It may be
downloaded from:
www.jirvana.com/resources/printing/
bills_lab_test_image.zip

Roller marks / pizza wheels   Sometimes you may encounter roller marks on a printed paper surface. There are many possible reasons. Check that the paper settings match the paper. Sometimes it is a good idea to consult printer-specific news groups to pick up ideas from experienced fellow users, maybe even things such as removing some printer wheels.

Banding   If you see banding, run a nozzle check and perform print-head cleaning, if necessary. The next step is to check head alignment and realign the heads, if needed. If this doesn't help, check your paper settings and turn off high speed. When not using standard paper, setting your printer to custom thickness may avoid banding.

Dust spots   Using some cotton papers, you occasionally see small spots after a print dries. This can be caused by cotton dust and/or scuffing. The paper has dust or other loose cotton particles on its surface. The printer places ink on these areas. After printing, the particles fall off and you get white spots. Always gently brush cotton-based paper before feeding it into the printer.

Water spots   Be careful not to get water on a picture. It is best to let it dry naturally. Trying to wipe the water off can smudge the print and/or leave a mark.

5.7   Most popular fine art inkjet printers

Though Canon also builds some very fine printers, we omitted their printers as, at the time of writing, no fine art printer using pigment inks was available. Canon announced the iPF 5000 and PIXMA Pro9500 Photo, two very fine printers from a glance at the data of their specifications. However, we have not had a chance to test them. So, we have to wait for the next issue of this book to include them.

There is also a fine art printer by HP which will use pigment inks – it's the HP Photosmart B9180. This printer was also not yet available when this book went to press.

We will discuss some of the most popular, currently available fine art inkjet printers. The market leaders are, as of this writing: Epson, HP, and Canon. These companies each have their own inkjet technologies, and produce printers with different features.

Epson printers

Epson was the first company to create a complete line of professional and semi-professional printers, using only pigmented inks to allow for better longevity. Here is a brief history on the Epson printers we have used:

Epson Stylus 2000P (13″ wide): First pigment-ink printer on the market.

Epson Stylus Pro 7500 (24″) /9500 (44″):   Professional printers using the same ink set as 2000P.

Epson Stylus 2100/2200 (13"): Introduced a new ink set called *UltraChrome*™ with eight inks (the 2200 uses only seven cartridges installed, and the user can switch between Photo Black and Matte Black for printing on glossy or matte media).

Epson Stylus Pro 4000 (18″)/ **7600** (24″) / **9600** (44″): Professional printers using the same *UltraChrome* ink set as the 2200, although the 4000 can use all eight inks installed simultaneously.

In this chapter, we will cover the newest models, introduced mainly in 2005. Epson has two major lines of ink sets:

▸ UltraChrome™ Hi-Gloss Ink (consumer printers, e.g., R800, R1800)

* See page 174 for a short data sheet for these printers .

▸ UltraChrome™ K3 inks (professional and semi-professional market, e.g., R2400, R4800, R7800, R9800)*

Printing with the Epson Stylus Photo R800/R1800

The inks

Both the R800 (letter-sized prints) and the R1800 (13" wide, A3) feature the same ink sets: eight Epson UltraChrome™ Hi-Gloss inks:

Gloss Optimizer, Photo Black, Matte Black
Cyan, Magenta, Yellow, Blue, Red

The R1800/R800 actually use only six true colors. The Photo Black and Matte Black are used for glossy and matte papers, respectively. So, for a single print, only one is used.

Gloss Optimizer is not a true ink. It controls colors by improving the glossy appearance of your print. It produces less bronzing and gloss differential. Unless printing on very glossy media, you may not need the Gloss Optimizer at all. In any case, test-print your papers both with and without Gloss Optimizer.

Note: Because R1800 and R800 only use a single black ink, these printers are not an ideal choice for photographers who want excellent black and white prints. These printers may, however, for some images produce nice, black-and-white prints, in spite of this apparent flaw.*

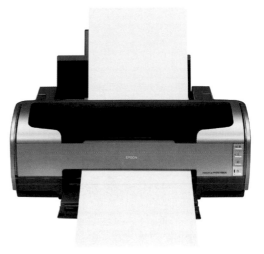

Figure 5-26: Epson Stylus Photo R1800
(Courtesy of Epson America Inc.)

* The Epson R2400, HP 8750, Canon PIXMA Pro9500 are a better choice for high-quality black-and-white prints.

Driver settings recommendations

What is covered here is not intended to replace your printer's manual. As usual, we assume you do all your color management inside the printing application (e.g., Photoshop).

Paper selection ▸ Most users choose single-sheet feeding with this printer (from the paper tray). When using roll stock, select it at this time.

Paper Type ▸ Here, try to make a very close match. If you use a third party paper, you will have to guess which HP paper would be right.

Print Quality ▸ The available quality settings will depend on the paper used. The highest-quality setting is *Photo RPM*, and this selection often produces

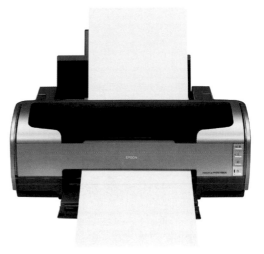

Fig. 5-27: Epson R1800: Main print driver dialog

the best results at a price of speed and ink. Often, a lower-quality setting may produce results close to maximum quality, but requiring less ink and resulting in faster printing time. We usually use "Best Photo".

Paper Size ▸ Most often you will find your paper size listed. But, in some cases you may also need to create a custom size. Select "User Defined," and follow the instructions.

Orientation ▸ Choose whatever is needed: Landscape or Portrait mode.

Print options

Gloss: Use only for highly glossy media
High Speed: Uncheck this option for best quality
Edge Smoothing: Off for fine art photos
Print Preview: We normally turn it off.
Be aware that preview colors may look incorrect, because they are not color managed.

Saved Settings

In most printing, you use only a small number of different papers, with few variations in their settings. Having found the proper settings for a certain type of print job and paper, you can save current settings and recall them much more quickly later on. This practice also helps avoid costly mistakes (ink, paper and time).

Color management in the printer driver

With the R1800 and R800 we always turn printer CM off, and do the profile selection and color control inside Photoshop. The dialog of the printer driver settings shows exactly how.

Ink monitor

With Epson printers we print until we see an ink-low warning. When you get this message, make sure you have a replacement ink cartridge available because the printer will soon be out of ink, and some printers will stop printing.

Maintenance tools

Most printer sets include some maintenance tools. With most Epson printers, the maintenance application may be called up from the printer driver interface. It offers some useful functions (see Figure 5-29, page 161):

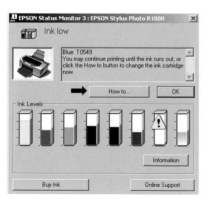

Figure 5-28: Ink-low-warning

Status Monitor: Shows the ink level dialog (see Figure 5-28).

Nozzle Check and Cleaning: Select this when you have not used the printer for some days. Check for banding or missing colors. Be aware that this procedure consumes ink.

Nozzle Check (manual) / Head Cleaning (manual): Use these only when you feel there is a major problem. Again, this will consume quite a bit of ink.

Print Head Alignment: Perform when you see banding.

Printer and Option Information: We rarely use these options. Check your manual when you think you may need them.

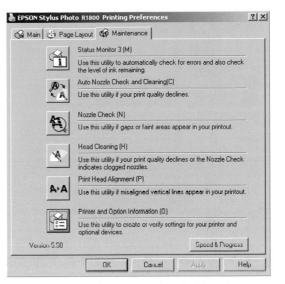

Figure 5-29: Maintenance tools called from the printer driver interface by selecting tab Maintenance.

◀ *Figure 5-30:*
Printer Information.
Here, you may activate
"Thick paper."

Manufacturer provided profiles for R800/R1800

Epson provides quite good generic profiles for their own papers. You can further improve color fidelity by using custom-made ones. Most profiles come specifically targeted to certain print quality settings. Check that your choice of profile (in the client application, e.g., Photoshop) matches your print quality settings (*Photo, Best Photo, Photo RPM*).

> **Note:** With the R800, some profiles showed some "smudging." Check for more details in our R800 review [25], which is written in a diary style, and which we update periodically.

SPR1800 D- S Matte Paper.icm
SPR1800 Enhanced Matte.icm
SPR1800 Matte Paper- HW.icm
SPR1800 Photo Qlty IJP.icm
SPR1800 Premium Glossy.icm
SPR1800 Premium Luster.icm
SPR1800 Premium Semigloss.icm
SPR1800 Velvet Fine Art.icm
SPR1800 WC Paper - RW.icm
SPR1800_DblSDMtte_BestPhoto.icc
SPR1800_EnhMtte_BestPhoto.icc
SPR1800_EnhMtte_Photo.icc
SPR1800_MtteHvyWt_BestPhoto.icc
SPR1800_MtteHvyWt_Photo.icc
SPR1800_MtteScrapbk_BestPhoto.icc
SPR1800_MtteScrapbk_Photo.icc
SPR1800_PrmGlsy_Photo.icc
SPR1800_PrmGlsy_PhotoRPM.icc
SPR1800_PrmLstr_Photo.icc
SPR1800_PrmLstr_PhotoRPM.icc
SPR1800_PrmSemgls_Photo.icc
SPR1800_PrmSemgls_PhotoRPM.icc
SPR1800_UltrSmth_Wtrclr_BestPhoto.icc
SPR1800_UltrSmth_Wtrclr_Photo.icc
SPR1800_VelvtFneArt_BestPhoto.icc
SPR1800_VelvtFneArt_Photo.icc
SPR1800_WtrclrRdWht_BestPhoto.icc
SPR1800_WtrclrRdWht_Photo.icm

Figure 5-31: ▶
Profiles provided by Epson
for the R800/R1800

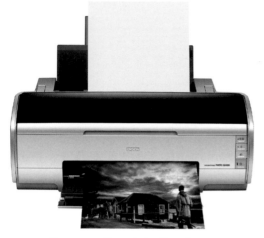

Figure 5–32: Epson Stylus Photo R2400
(Courtesy of Epson America Inc.)

Epson Stylus Photo R2400 / Pro 4800 / 7800 / 9800

The Inks

All four printers feature the same ink set (Epson UltraChrome™ K3, 9 inks). This set is different from the R800/R1800:

> Photo Black, Matte Black, Light Black, Light Light Black
> Cyan, Light Cyan, Magenta, Light Magenta, Yellow

These printers actually simultaneously use only eight inks out of the nine. Photo Black and Matte Black are used for glossy and matte papers, respectively. Unfortunately, it is required to switch the Matte Black ink for Photo Black ink when switching from matte to glossy media and vice versa. This procedure costs time and ink, and on the Pro printer line, it is a substantial amount of ink – about $75 is used up for every change of black inks.

These printers do not use a Gloss Optimizer, because the new ink formulas do not require it.

All four printers have three different blacks, Photo or Matte Black, Light Black and Light Light Black, allowing them to produce very good black-and-white prints with a highly neutral look and smooth gradients. We cover this in more detail in our Chapter 7 on black-and-white printing.

Driver settings recommendations

Figure 5-33: Driver settings recommended for fine art printing using the Epson R2400.

As stated earlier, what is covered here is not a replacement for the printer manual. And as before, we assume you do all color management in your printing application, e.g., Photoshop. We show only the settings of the R2400, as the same principles apply to the other more professional printers (Pro 4800 through the Pro 9800).

Paper selection Most users will print single sheets with this printer directly from the paper tray, but the R2400 also comes with a roll-feeder option out of the box.

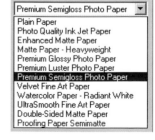

Paper Type The list offered here is dependent on which black ink is used in the printer (Photo Black or Matte Black). Here you should try to find a close match. Using a third-party paper, you'll have to estimate which Epson paper is closest to the characteristics of your specific paper. You may have to do some experimenting, using different paper type settings. With some luck, you may find advice on paper type settings at the Internet site of the paper manufacturer of your paper.*

* *See Appendix B, page 243, for the URLs of some of the well-known paper manufacturers.*

Print Quality The available quality settings depend on the paper type selected. The highest-quality setting usually produces the best results at the expense of speed and ink usage. A lower-quality setting may produce a result close to maximum quality, e. g., *Best Photo* instead of *Photo RPM*.

Paper Size Most of the time you will find an appropriate paper size listed here. In rare cases, you may need to create a custom size. Simply select and follow the instructions.

Orientation Choose either Landscape or Portrait mode:

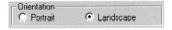

Print Options

▸ High Speed: Off, for best quality

▸ Edge Smoothing: Off, for fine art photos

▸ Print Preview: We usually turn it off. Be aware that colors may appear untrue. This preview is not color managed.

Save your settings

You will probably use only a few different papers with few variations. Therefore, having found the right settings for a certain type of print job and paper, save the settings and recall them later. It is much faster, and there is no danger you will forget to set all parameters correctly for this particular type of job.

Color Management

For the R2400, we turn printer *Color Management* off (unless printing black-and-white images) and do profile selection and color control inside Photoshop. The dialog of the printer driver setting shows exactly how.

For black-and-white printing we would use the *Advanced B&W Photo* mode, which we describe in our "Black-and-White Prints" chapter. If we have a black-and-white ICC profile, we use this profile and will select *Let Photoshop Determine Colors* in the Photoshop dialog Print with Preview and nevertheless deactivate color management in the printer driver and activate *Advanced B&W Photo* mode in the driver settings.

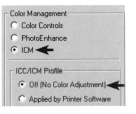

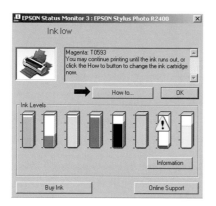

Ink monitor and maintenance tools

When using Epson printers, continue printing until the printer prompts you to replace an ink cartridge. When you get the Ink Low message, ensure you have a replacement ink cartridge available, as the printer will soon be out of ink and stop printing.

The dialogs for the ink level monitor and the maintenance tools are almost identical to those of the Epson R1800. See page 146 for the description of those dialogs.

Status Monitor: Shows the ink-level dialog

Nozzle Check and Cleaning: Select this when you have not used the printer for some days. Check for banding or missing colors. Be aware that this procedure consumes ink.

Nozzle Check (manual) / Head Cleaning (manual): Use these only when you feel there is a major problem. Again, this will consume quite a bit of ink.

Print Head Alignment: Check this if you see banding.

Printer and Option Information: This is the dialog used to indicate which black is currently loaded. Be sure it shows the black that actually is loaded into the printer, because the driver depends on this information to work properly.

SPR2400 Archival Matte.icm
SPR2400 D-S Matte Paper.icm
SPR2400 D-S Matte Paper_PK.icm
SPR2400 Enhanced Matte.icm
SPR2400 Enhanced Matte_PK.icm
SPR2400 Matte Paper - HW.icm
SPR2400 Matte Paper - HW_PK.icm
SPR2400 Photo Qlty IJP.icm
SPR2400 Photo Qlty IJP_PK.icm
SPR2400 PremGlsy BstPhoto.icc
SPR2400 PremGlsy Photo.icc
SPR2400 PremGlsy PhotoRPM.icc
SPR2400 PremiumGlossy.icm
SPR2400 PremiumLuster.icm
SPR2400 PremiumSemigloss.icm
SPR2400 PremLuster BstPhoto.icc
SPR2400 PremLuster Photo.icc
SPR2400 PremLuster PhotoRPM.icc
SPR2400 PremSmgls BstPhoto.icc
SPR2400 PremSmgls Photo.icc
SPR2400 PremSmgls PhotoRPM.icc
SPR2400 ProofingSemimatte.icm
SPR2400 UsmoothFineArt.icm
SPR2400 UsmoothFineArt_PK.icm
SPR2400 Velvet Fine Art.icm
SPR2400 Velvet Fine Art_PK.icm
SPR2400 WC Paper - RW.icm
SPR2400 WC Paper - RW_PK.icm

Figure 5-34: Profiles provided by Epson for the R2400

Profiles provided by Epson for the R2400

Epson provides good generic profiles, but only for their own papers. You may further improve color fidelity by using custom-made ones. Most profiles come specifically targeted to certain print quality settings. Check that your choice of profile (in the client application, e.g., Photoshop) matches the print quality settings done in the print driver dialog (*Photo, Best Photo, Photo RPM*).

Some help for paper feeding

With the R2400, we have encountered some problems when feeding sheet paper. If this happens, it may be helpful to apply slight pressure with a finger at the top of the sheet.

HP printers

While Epson printers use mainly pigmented inks to improve longevity, HP printers – until very lately – all featured use of dye-based inks to improve longevity with optimum paper-ink combinations. The prints using the printers we cover using HP Premium Photo Plus papers are rated at about 80 years by Wilhelm Imaging Research (WIR, [44]) – provided you use swellable HP inkjet papers.*

Newer models we feature were introduced mainly in 2005. These are the main models for fine art prints

▸ HP Photosmart 8450 and 8750
▸ Designjet 30 / 90 / 130

We here only cover those HP printer we consider suitable for fine art prints.

* Finally, in 2006, HP introduced some new printers also using pigment-based inks. The first of those is the HP 'Photosmart Pro B9280 Photo'.

HP Photosmart 8450 / 8750

Both the 8450 (letter-size prints) and the 8750 (13" wide, A3+), feature the same ink set. HP introduced the first true black-and-white printers featuring three blacks, and the 8750 was the first A3 using these inks. Shortly thereafter, Epson followed with its new UltraChrome™ K3 printers

The Inks

HP calls its archival dye inks *Vivera inks*. The 8750 can take three cartridges with up to three inks in each cartridge.

▸ HP 97 Tri-color (three colors) always needed

▸ HP 99 Photo (three colors), needed for fine art prints with the 8450, but the 8750 may work better with the 102 cartridge (see below)

▸ HP 96 Black (one black). This is okay for color prints, but should be replaced by a Gray Photo cartridge (HP 100/102) when you print black-and-white.

▸ HP 100/102 Gray Photo (3 gray/black at 15/23 ml) for excellent black-and-white images

▸ HP 102 Blue Photo (to enhance blue color gamut). Only used in the 8750.

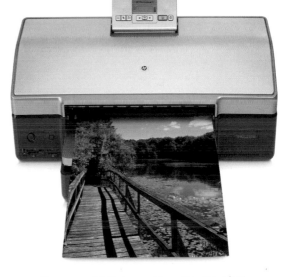

Figure 5-35: HP Photosmart 8750 (Courtesy of HP)

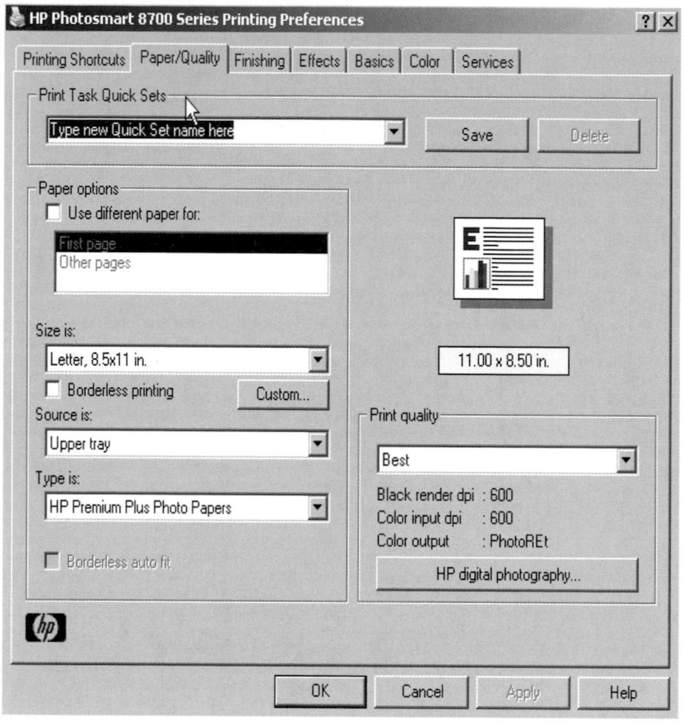

Figure 5-36: 8750 printer dialog with paper and print quality settings

Driver settings recommendations

What we cover here is not intended as a replacement for the printer manual. We assume you do all color management inside the printing application, e.g., Photoshop.

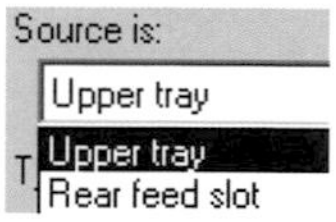

Paper selection (feed) Most users use single sheets with this printer (from the paper tray).

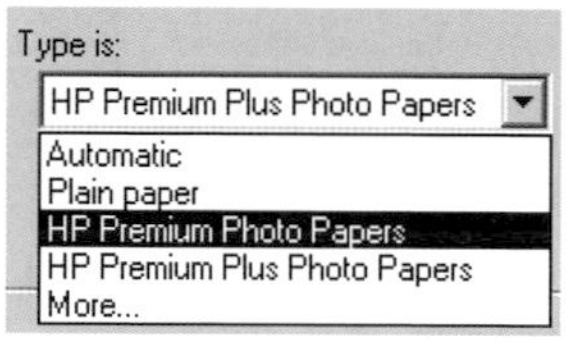

Paper Type Try for a very close match. Prints with non-matching paper type settings can be highly inaccurate. We do not recommend you use *Automatic*, as the printer, in some cases, does not recognize the paper in the sheet feeder. If your are using HP paper and it is not listed in the short list, select *More*.

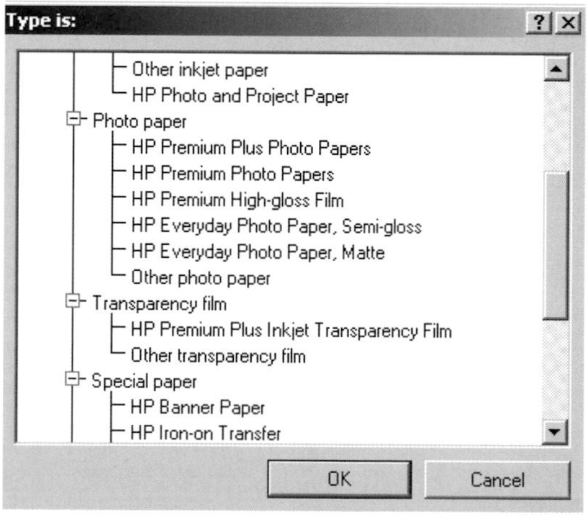

Figure 5-37: ▶
Paper selection

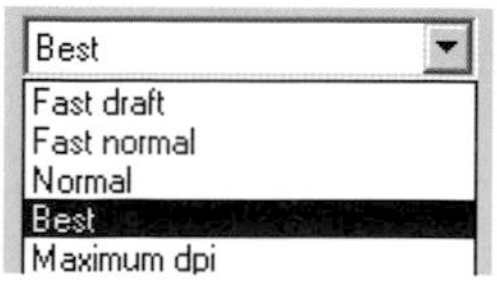

Print Quality Available quality settings depend on the paper used. The highest-quality setting produces the best results, at the expense of decreased speed and increased use of ink. Sometimes a lower quality setting produces results close to maximum. We use HP printers only at the setting *Best*.

Paper Size Most often, you will find your paper size listed. In some cases, you may need to create a custom paper size. Select *User Defined* and follow the instructions.

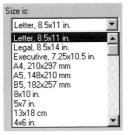

Orientation (found on the BASICS tab) Choose Landscape or Portrait mode.

Print Options Print Preview: Usually, we leave it off.

Saved Settings

In most cases, you will use only a few papers with few variations in your settings. Save these settings and recall them later. It will save time and also avoid costly errors (ink and paper are expensive).

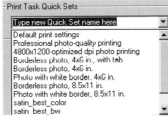

Color Management

For the 8750/8450, we always turn printer CM off. The driver is then set to *Managed by Application.* The only exception is printing black-and-white on the 8750 / 8450 printers (see our Chapter 7 "Black-and-White Prints").

Ink Monitor

With HP printers, you cannot continue printing until the machine stops. When you get an ink low warning, you may try to squeeze three to five prints out of the cartridge and then replace ink. When you get an *Ink Low* message, however, be sure you have a replacement ink cartridge available. The printer will be out of that particular ink really soon.

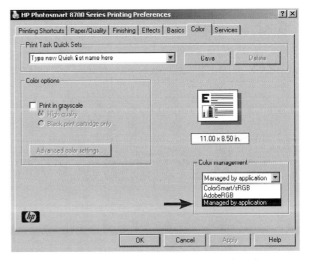

Figure 5-38: When doing color management in Photoshop, set "Managed by application" in the printer driver

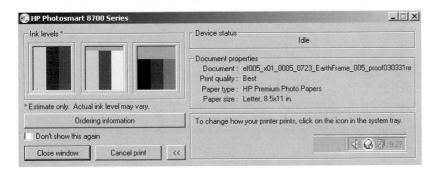

◄ *Figure 5-39:*

Ink monitor of the HP Photosmart 8700

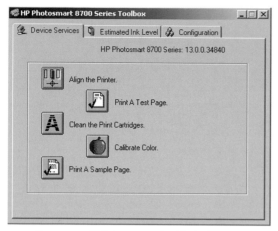

Figure 5-40: Maintenance tools with the HP 8700

Maintenance tools

Align the Printer: Check if you see banding.

Clean the Print Cartridges: Use this option also if you encounter banding in prints

Calibrate Color: As we understand it, the printer does an automatic calibration when you replace cartridges, (which includes the heads).

Printer and Option Information: We rarely use these options. You may reduce the amount of ink laid down on a paper when using thinner paper, which has a tendency to warp. So far, we have not experienced this.

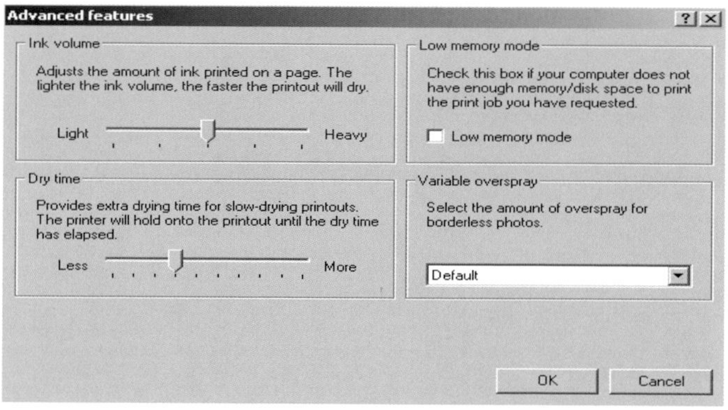

Figure 5-41: ▶
Here, you may reduce the amount of ink laid
down on paper.

HP Photosmart 8400-Premium High-Gloss Film(tricolor+photo+black).icc
HP Photosmart 8400-Premium High-Gloss Film(tricolor+photo+gray).icc
HP Photosmart 8400-Premium Paper(tricolor+photo+black).icc
HP Photosmart 8400-Premium Paper(tricolor+photo+gray).icc
HP Photosmart 8400-Premium Plus Photo(tricolor+photo+black).icc
HP Photosmart 8400-Premium Plus Photo(tricolor+photo+gray).icc
HP Photosmart 8700-Premium High-Gloss Film(tricolor+bluephoto+black).icc
HP Photosmart 8700-Premium High-Gloss Film(tricolor+bluephoto+gray).icc
HP Photosmart 8700-Premium High-Gloss Film(tricolor+photo+black).icc
HP Photosmart 8700-Premium High-Gloss Film(tricolor+photo+gray).icc
HP Photosmart 8700-Premium Paper(tricolor+bluephoto+black).icc
HP Photosmart 8700-Premium Paper(tricolor+bluephoto+gray).icc
HP Photosmart 8700-Premium Paper(tricolor+photo+black).icc
HP Photosmart 8700-Premium Paper(tricolor+photo+gray).icc
HP Photosmart 8700-Premium Plus Photo(tricolor+bluephoto+black).icc
HP Photosmart 8700-Premium Plus Photo(tricolor+bluephoto+gray).icc
HP Photosmart 8700-Premium Plus Photo(tricolor+photo+black).icc
HP Photosmart 8700-Premium Plus Photo(tricolor+photo+gray).icc

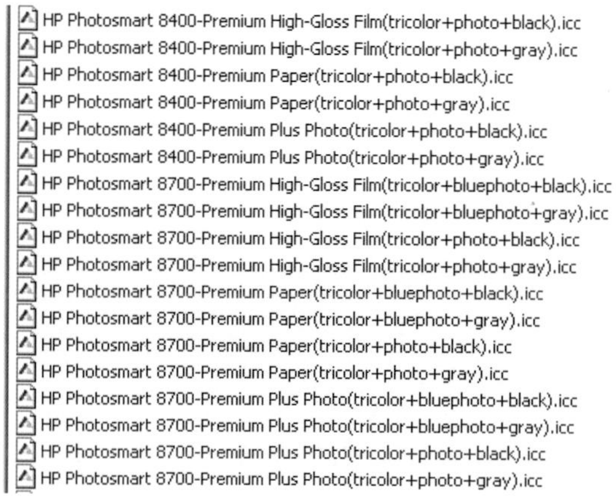

Figure 5-42: List of generic profiles provided by HP
for the Photosmart 8400.

Profiles for the 8440 and 8750

HP provides good-quality generic profiles for their own papers. You may improve prints by using custom-made ones. Most profiles come specifically targeted to certain print quality settings. Check that your choice of profile (in the client application, e.g., Photoshop) not only matches the paper type, but also print quality settings.

HP Designjet 30 / 90 / 130

These Designjet printers are affordable, professional printers that can print 13", 18" and 24" wide, respectively.

The inks

HP archival dye inks, so called *Vivera inks*, are use by the Designjet 30 / 90 / 130 printers, each using the same ink cartridges and ink sets. They are: Black, Cyan, Magenta, Yellow, Light Cyan and Light Magenta

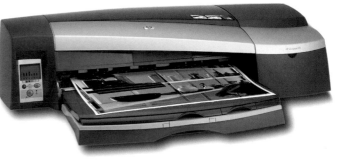

Figure 5-43: HP Designjet 90 (Courtesy HP America)

Overall, the cost per print is much lower than with the Photosmart 8750 or 9450 printers, due to the much larger capacity of the ink cartridges.*

* *As a general rule, the larger the ink cartridge is the cheaper the is per print*

Note: Because these printers use only one type of black ink, they are not an ideal choice for high quality black-and-white prints. However, these printers may be used to deliver acceptable black-and-white quality. However, Epson K3 or HP 8750 printers may be a better choice when superior black-and-white prints are your goal.

Driver settings recommendations

Stated once again, what is covered here should not be viewed as a replacement for the printer manual. And, as usual, we assume that you do all color management in a print application like Photoshop (when printing color prints). We will cover the model Designjet 90 in more detail, but most of it will also apply to the other two models.

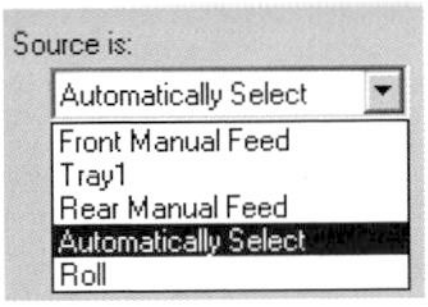

Paper selection (feed) Most users prefer single-sheet feeding with this printer (from the paper tray). We do not recommend using *Automatically Select,* as the printer occasionally does not automatically recognize the correct paper.

Paper Type Try to find a very close match (see Figure 5-45). Incorrect paper type setting can cause serious print discrepancies as quite a few driver internal settings are set by the paper type selection. As with other printers, the menu will only show HP papers suited for this printer. If you use a third-party paper, refer to recommendations the paper manufacturer provides for the printer settings.

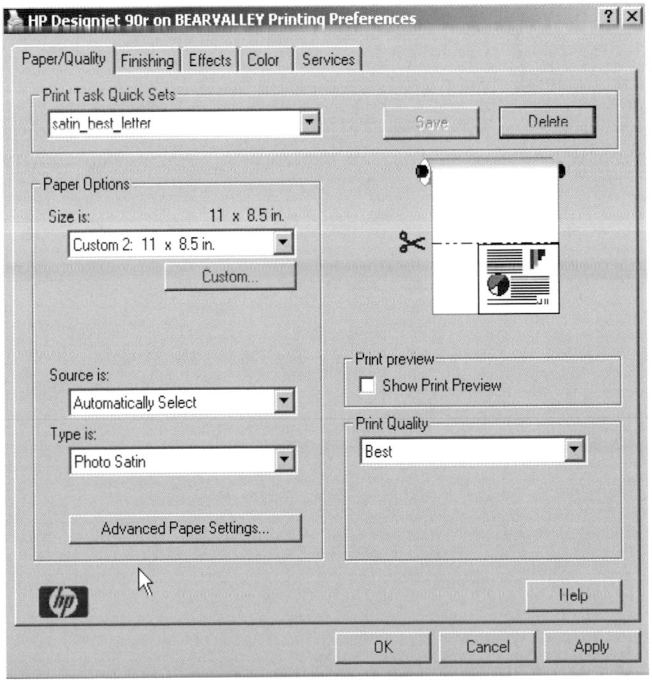

Figure 5-44: Designjet 90 Paper dialog

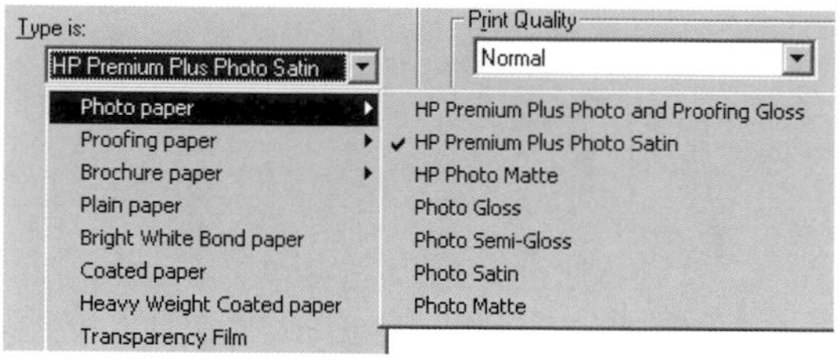

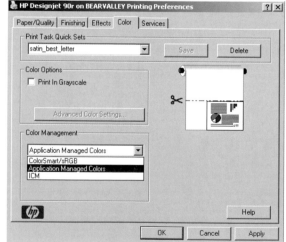

Figure 5-46: Select the paper you are using

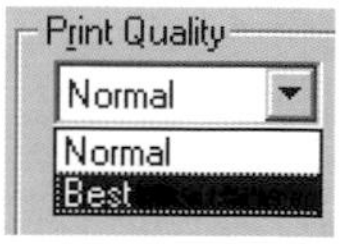

Print Quality The available quality settings depend on the paper used. The highest quality setting will often produce the best results, at the expense of speed and ink usage. A lower quality setting may produce results very close to maximum quality. We prefer using HP printers only at their *Best* setting.

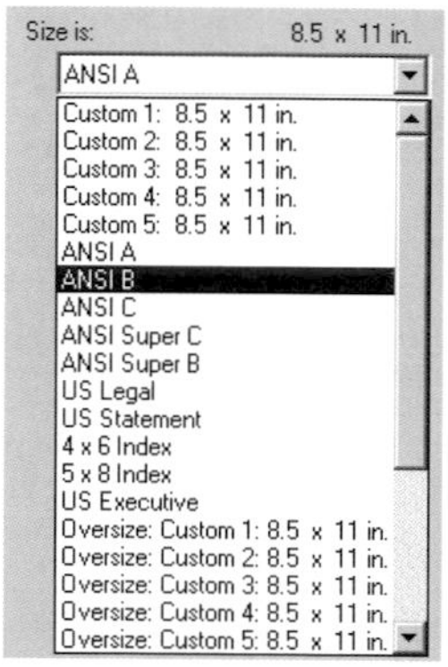

Paper Size You will usually find your paper size listed. But, in some cases, you may need to create a custom size. Just select *User Defined* and follow the instructions.

Orientation (found on the Finishing tab): Choose Landscape or Portrait mode.

Print Options Print Preview: We normally keep this off.

Saved Settings

Most fine art printers use only a few different papers with slight variations in their settings. We strongly recommend that you save the settings and recall them later quite easily, avoiding costly mistakes (ink and paper!).

Color Management

For the Designjet 90, we always turn printer CM off. This sets the driver to *Application Managed Colors*. The only exception is printing black-and-white (see our Chapter 7 "Black-and-White Prints").

Ink Level Monitor

The Designjet 90 has an LCD panel that continually shows the levels of all six inks. When you get an *Ink Low* message, be sure you have a replacement ink cartridge available. The printer will be out of ink soon.

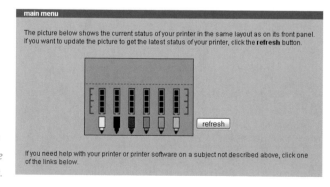

Figure 5-47: CM settings in the driver

Figure 5-48: ▶
Designjet 90 LCD panel continually shows the
fill levels of your inks.

Maintenance tools

When you call up a maintenance utility, a Web page appears.

> **Note:** For Windows-based computers, use MS Internet Explorer as your default browser. Do not connect the printer through a hub (though some may work).

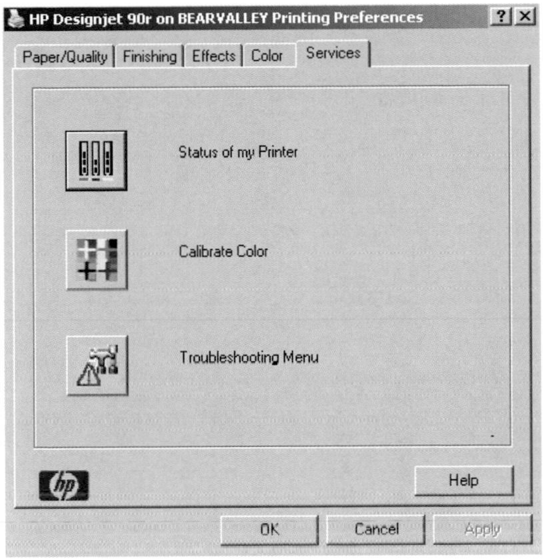

Status of the printer: Shows the printer status (what else :-).

Calibrate Color: **This needs to be done** for all paper types, and also must be redone after switching inks or heads.

For color calibration, HP uses a browser interface that assumes on some PCs that Internet Explorer is the default browser. In any case, and also for maintenance, connect the printer directly to a USB port on your PC, as it may not work properly with some USB hubs. Then locate the printer with the dialog shown in Figure 5-500:

Click on Next, and the browser will be launched with the maintenance page. Select calibrate color:

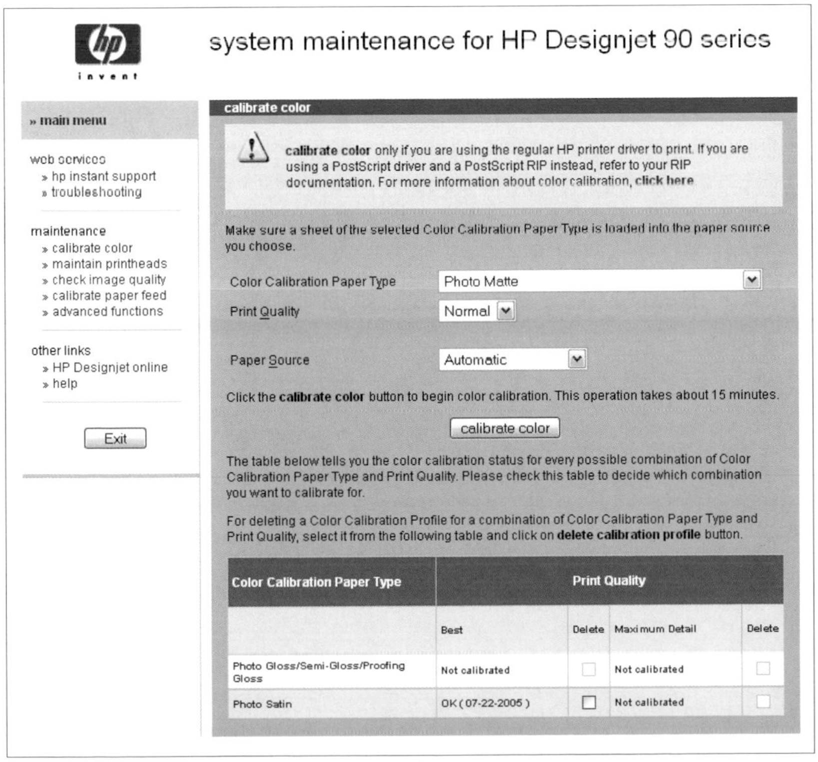

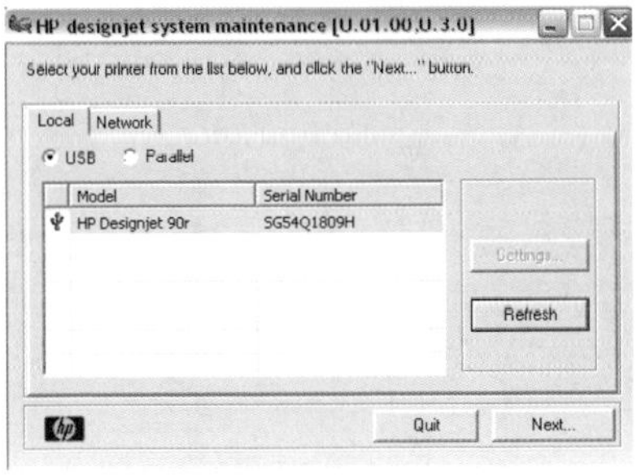

Figure 5-49: Maintenance tools for the Designjet 90

Figure 5-50: First, select the printer you want to calibrate.

◀ *Figure 5-51:*
Dialog for color calibration

The page shows which paper you have calibrated and when. Actually, this is not true color calibration. The printer does, however, measure ink density for each print head (for each color) and adjusts accordingly. For this purpose, an ink pattern is printed.

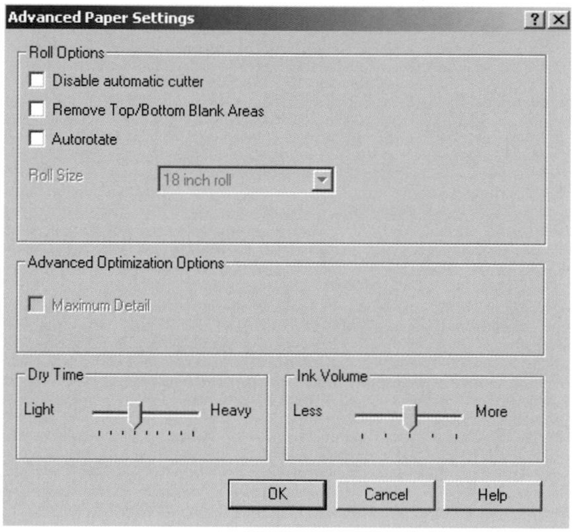

Printer and Option Information We rarely use these options. Check your manual to be sure when you may need them.

Profiles for the Designjet 90

HP has provided good generic profiles for their own papers. Color fidelity may be further improved by using custom-made ones. Most profiles are specifically targeted to certain print quality settings. Check that your choice of profile in the client application, e.g., Photoshop, matches your print quality settings.

Figure 5-51: "Advanced Paper Settings" may be used to reduce the amount of ink laid down.

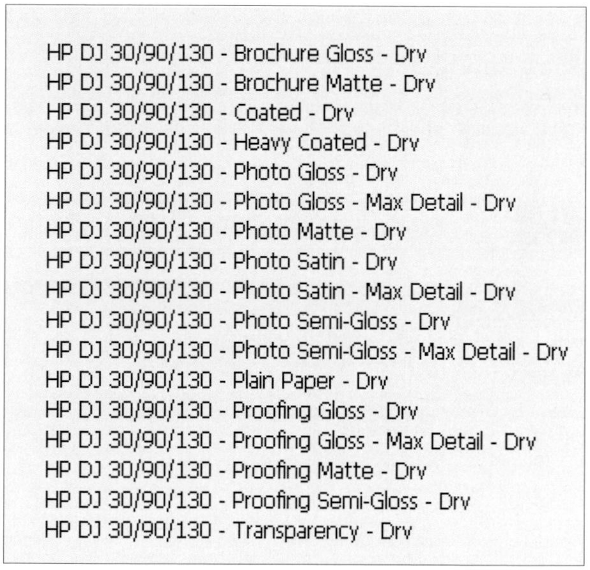

Figure 5-40: ▶
Manufacturer-supplied profiles for the Designjet 90

HP DJ 30/90/130 - Brochure Gloss - Drv
HP DJ 30/90/130 - Brochure Matte - Drv
HP DJ 30/90/130 - Coated - Drv
HP DJ 30/90/130 - Heavy Coated - Drv
HP DJ 30/90/130 - Photo Gloss - Drv
HP DJ 30/90/130 - Photo Gloss - Max Detail - Drv
HP DJ 30/90/130 - Photo Matte - Drv
HP DJ 30/90/130 - Photo Satin - Drv
HP DJ 30/90/130 - Photo Satin - Max Detail - Drv
HP DJ 30/90/130 - Photo Semi-Gloss - Drv
HP DJ 30/90/130 - Photo Semi-Gloss - Max Detail - Drv
HP DJ 30/90/130 - Plain Paper - Drv
HP DJ 30/90/130 - Proofing Gloss - Drv
HP DJ 30/90/130 - Proofing Gloss - Max Detail - Drv
HP DJ 30/90/130 - Proofing Matte - Drv
HP DJ 30/90/130 - Proofing Semi-Gloss - Drv
HP DJ 30/90/130 - Transparency - Drv

5.8 Some recommendations for printing

Though we already mentioned some of the following recommendations, we want to repeat some of them here:

▶ **Print regularly**
Inkjet inks tend to dry up fast and may clog up the nozzles of your print heads. For this reason, you should use your inkjet printers regularly, e.g., once a week, or at least every two weeks. Nozzle clogging seems to be somewhat worse with the Epson printers, obviously due to the pigmented inks. If you really have no inkjet print to do, simply run a nozzle cleaning cycle with your printer.

▶ **Check your inks and run a nozzle check before you start a large print.**
It is annoying if you spoil an expensive sheet of paper due to clogged
nozzles, or because there is not enough ink to complete your print.
Therefore, it is well worth checking your inks.* If you have plenty of ink
for your print and have not printed for some days, run a nozzle check,
usually offered as part of the printer's maintenance utility (see page
152/153 and page 161 for the Epson maintenance tools or page 168 for the
HP tools) to make sure that your nozzles are not clogged. Nozzle clogging may show as banding, or as color shifts or stripes in the print.

All of the printers we discuss here will show the status of all the inks.

▶ **Clean your paper before you print.**
Often, inkjet papers come with some paper dust on it. Therefore, you
should clean the paper before inserting it into the printer. You may use
a large cosmetic brush** or a small, soft broom.

    This prevents the dust from clogging your print heads or your print-
er's rollers. It is also very annoying if tiny paper fragments stick to the
paper when the print is done and fall off afterwards, exposing plain
paper spots with no ink.

    Some papers are more susceptible to this problem than others. We
had some experience with this phenomenon with Hahnemühle papers
(e.g., PhotoRag).

**that is not used for anything else!*

▶ **Give your prints ample time to dry before touching and framing.**
Actually, you should never touch the printed area of your prints, at least
not with your bare hands. Wear cotton gloves when handling your
prints or printing papers.

▶ **Cover up your printer when not in use.**
Cover up your printer with a dust cover in order to avoid dust settling
on and in your printer.

▶ **Keep your spare inks cool.**

▶ **Keep your spare paper dark, dry, and cool, and store it horizontally.**

▶ **Make sure your printer is correctly set up for your paper.** With some
printers, you have to set up your printer if you use thick paper. You may
have to set this either within your printer driver, a lever on the printer,
or you may have to use a special paper feed.

▶ **Make sure you use the proper profile for your paper and your printer
settings.**
As stated when describing how to produce a printer profile, the profile
is specific not only to the printer, the inks used and the paper used, but
also to the printer settings. Printer settings, e.g., print quality settings,
should be reflected in the profile name. Make sure that you select a
printer profile that closely corresponds to your settings in the printer
driver.

Technical data of the fine art printers described

Table 5-1a: Short data sheet of the printers described in this chapter

Function:	Epson R800 / R1800	Epson R2400	Epson Pro 4800 / 7800 / 9800	HP Photosmart 8450 / 8750	HP Designjet 30 / 90 /130
Print size	A4 / A3+	A3+	A2 / A1 / A0	A4 / A3+	A3+ / C / A1
Maximum paper thickness		1.3 mm	1.5 mm		0,038 mm
Borderless printing	+	+	+	+ / +	
Maximum resolution (dpi)	5,760 × 1,440	5,760 × 1,440	2,880 × 1,440	4,800 × 1,200	4,800 × 1,200
Printing technique used	Piezo	Piezo	Piezo	Thermal	Thermal
Inks	Pigment, UltraChrome Hi-Gloss	Pigment, UltraChrome K3	Pigment, UltraChrome K3	Dye, Vivera	Dye, Vivera
Number of inks (simultaneous use)	6 + GO	8	8	9	6
Number of black/gray inks	1 (PK/MK)	2 + 1 (PK/MK)	2 + 1 (PK/MK)	3	1
Ink colors	C M Y K R B	C c M m Y K lk llk	C c M m Y K lk llk	C M Y	C c M m Y K
Minimum ink droplet size	1.5 picoliter	3.5 picoliter	3.5 picoliter		
Ink cartridge size	13 ml	14 ml	110 ml / 220 ml		
Roll paper / roll paper feed.	included	included	included	–	included
Interface	USB 2 + Firewire	USB 2 + Firewire	USB 2 + Firewire, LAN (optonal)	USB 2 + LAN	P+USB 1 / P+USB 1 LAN (optional)
OS support	Win + Mac	Win + Mac	Win + Mac	Win + Mac	Win + Mac
Special features	Gloss-Optimizer		LCD status display	LCD-Panel	Densiometer, LCD for ink status and printer status
Approx. price (US $ + tax) (street price)	$380 / $550	$870	$1,900 / $3,500 / $5,500	$210 / $450	$740 / $1,1000 / $1,300

Acronyms used:

> GO = Gloss optimizer
> P = Parallel interface (IEEE 1284)
> PK = Photo Black
> MK = Matte Black
> c = Photo Cyan (Light Cyan)
> m = Photo Magenta (Light Magenta)
> lk = Light Black
> llk = Light Light Black

Technical data of some new fine art printers

Table 5-1b: Short data sheet of the printers described in this chapter

Function:	HP B9180 Photo	Canon PIXMA Pro9500	Canon iPF5000	Canon iPF9000
Print size	A3+	A3+	17" / A2	60"
Maximum paper thickness	1.5 mm	1.2 mm	1.5 mm	1.5 mm
Borderless printing	+	+	+	+
Maximum resolution (dpi)	4,800 × 1,200	4,800 × 4,800	2,400 × 1,200	2,400 × 1,200
Printing technique used	Thermal	Thermal (Bubblejet)	Thermal (Bubblejet)	Thermal (Bubblejet)
Inks	Pigment, Vivera inks	Pigment, Lucia	Pigment, Lucia	Pigment, Lucia
Number of inks (simultaneous use)	8	10	12	12
Number of black/gray inks	1 + 1 (PK + MK)	2 + 2 (PK + MK)	2 (PK + MK) + 2 (Plk + Mlk)	2 (PK + MK) + 2 (Plk + Mlk)
Ink colors	C c M m Y K lk	C c M m Y PK MK lk R G	C c M m Y K lk llk R G B	C c M m Y K lk llk R G B
Minimum ink droplet size	1.5 picoliter	3 picoliter	3 picoliter	3 picoliter
Ink cartridge size	28 ml		130 ml	
Roll paper / roll paper feed.	–		included	included
Interface	USB 2 + LAN	USB 2	USB 2 + LAN	USB 2 + LAN
OS support	Win + Mac	Win + Mac	Win + Mac	Win + Mac
Special features	LCD status display	PictBridge Photoshop plug-in as driver interface	16-bit driver Photoshop plug-in as driver interface	LCD status display
Approx. price (US $ + tax) (street price)	$2,200	$750	$2,200	not yet available

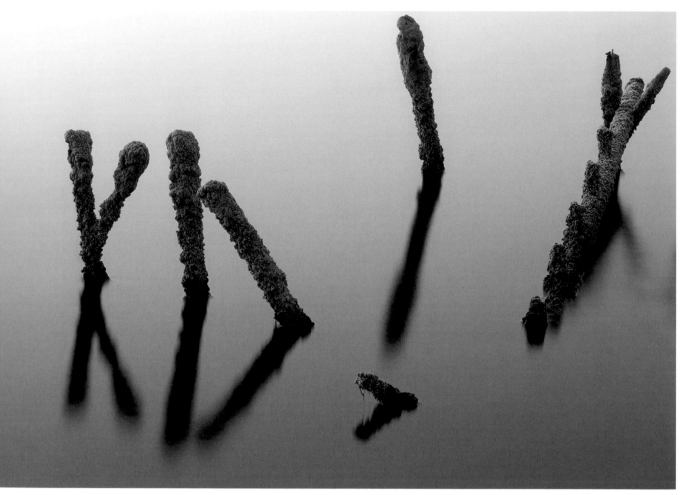

Camera: Canon 1DsX

Printing Packages and RIPs

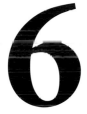

You may achieve excellent prints when printing from Photoshop or another color-management application using the standard printer driver of your operating system. In most cases, this printer driver is supplied by the printer manufacturer. The process for doing this is described in Chapter 5.4–5.8.

In some cases, however, you may need additional options, e.g., when you not only want to print a single image, but also a DTP-built page with text, raster images, and line-art graphics. In other situations, you may look for greater control over printing settings than the standard printer driver provides, or you may want to use fine art papers that the driver does not support. In this case, a Raster Image Processor (RIP) may help.

6.1   What is an RIP?

An RIP takes the input, and from it, produces a raster image that can be sent directly to a printer. It does all the color conversion, such as from RGB to the printer's primary colors,* the dithering, the required resolution adaptation, and more. It's what a standard printer driver does, and usually more, e.g., supports standard ICC profiles. There are two types of RIPs:

▶ RIPs that only do rasterization of the input
▶ RIPs that do additional print-language translation, e.g., from PostScript to an internal printer language

which, in photo inkjet printers, are usually 6–9 different colored inks.

For fine art printing, the first type of RIP is acceptable in most cases, and is often considerably cheaper. PostScript-enabled RIPs make sense when you use the RIP for contract press-proofing. Using a PostScript printer, the second type of RIP is already integrated into your printer's hardware. This integrated RIP, however, may not provide all the features and controls offered with separate RIPs.

Most RIPs are *optional equipment*; you must pay extra for them. Both HP and Epson offer separate software RIPs for some of their inkjet printers. There are many other RIPs offered by third-party companies which are frequently less expensive, more universal, and offer better quality or flexibility for a particular task like black-and-white printing.

HP has discontinued its software-based RIP and replaced it with an "EFI Designer-Edition RIP" described in section 6.3.

Why use an RIP?

Above, we have listed the main reasons for using a separate RIP:

▶ More control over printing parameters
▶ Support of high-level printer languages (often PostScript or PDF)

An RIP also provides the following useful features:

▶ Smoother workflow than printer drivers**
▶ Better dithering and/or up-sizing algorithms
▶ More control of ink lay-down
▶ Additional ICC profiles for some fine art printers, third-party inks, or press printing
▶ Support for profiling
▶ Support for special third-party inks (often for black-and-white printing)
▶ Optimized placement of several images on the same page
▶ Special features for black-and-white printing***
▶ Special features for CMYK proofs (contract press-proofs)

*** *e.g. network-printing, hot-folders, and different job queues for different job types*

*** *Such as special black-and-white profiles for printing, as well as, soft-proofing.*

Not all of these features are provided by all RIPs, and not all features may be needed. For this reason, there is no single solution for all users. We will describe some of the RIPs we have used, and the particular features useful for our kind of work.

6.2   **Printing using a printing package**

When direct-printing with the printer manufacturer's printer driver is not quite good enough, but an RIP is too expensive,* a printing package may be the answer. These printing packages are stand-alone applications that help to prepare an image for printing by calling up a printer driver and passing the image along for printing. They do no actual dithering (also called *screening*), which an RIP or a printer driver can do.

* though there are some moderately priced RIPs around.

Nevertheless, printing packages may be helpful when doing printer-specific up-sizing or down-sizing of an image, and can even do some sharpening. They also may replace Photoshop as the printing application, and do color management, rather than leaving it to the printer driver. These packages sometimes come with additional profiles, or aid in creating printer profiles. This software also features image placement, i.e., several images on a single output page. While we rarely use them for fine art prints, printing packages may be useful for test prints or for contact sheets.

Often, these utilities offer additional image-enhancement operations. As a rule, we don't use these features. According to our experience, good RAW converters plus Photoshop are usually superior. Qimage is one such printing utility. There are other printing packages, but we have little or no experience with them.

Qimage

Qimage by Digital Domain Inc. [50] is a low-priced image-printing package for Windows. It includes free lifetime updates and upgrades. For the budget-conscious artist, Qimage also offers a Lite version. According to our experience, Qimage Lite is sufficient in most cases, although the price of the Pro version is reasonable enough for us to recommend.

Qimage Pro is priced about $50 and may be downloaded from the Internet. Qimage Lite costs $ 39.

While no native Mac version is currently available, Qimage may now be run using Boot Camp that, paradoxically, runs Windows even faster than a Windows-based PC . Below is a list of features in Qimage we consider useful:

▸ Supports a broad range of inkjet printers from HP, Epson, and Canon
▸ Fully color managed; works with ICC profiles
▸ Provides batch-processing of images (printing, scaling, format conversion, etc.)**
▸ Allows placing several images on one output page
▸ Automatic image scaling for optimum prints. Offers several different scaling algorithms
▸ Offers optional sharpening
▸ Offers selective color correction and fine-tuning
▸ Has an image-oriented browser for selecting files for printing

** You may, for example, do batch printing as well as image scaling and format conversion in batch mode.

The user interface is somewhat dated and requires a bit of learning, partly due to the large number of settings involved. This, however, provides a lot of flexibility.

There are a number of features in Qimage that we do not use, for example image editing, RAW conversion, Flash Card import, or import via TWAIN (scanner).

You may download a fully functional version of Qimage from the Web and test it for 30 days. If you purchase a license (via the Web), a license-key is sent by e-mail. Installation is simple: click on the installation file. Although there is little to set up, you should check if the monitor profile is correctly selected (Qimage accesses the Windows system default profile).

Qimage is not actually a true RIP. Instead of doing its own dithering and color translation, it uses the manufacturer's printer driver for actual output to the printer. While this suggests limitations to the program, it supports a large number of printers.

Qimage performs several important printing tasks:

▶ It does up-sizing or down-sizing of the image to an optimal printer's native resolution.* It offers several different sizing algorithms, and is quite good at it

▶ It does some sharpening (may be activated or deactivated)

▶ It offers some helpful administration tasks such as saving and loading printer driver settings

▶ It allows placing several images on one output page, which may be useful for producing contact sheets

After starting Qimage, browse to your image folder. Qimage will build up thumbnails and display all images in the folder in thumbnail view (see Figure 6.1). This may take a few minutes when accessing a folder with many images. Once in the proper folder, you may hide the Folder Browser (toggled by F4).

Before actually beginning printing (building print jobs), select these three settings:

▶ Printer setup (click 🖨 or File ▸ Printer/Page Setup)

▶ Page setup (page size, orientation, borders, etc.), (Page Formatting)

▶ Set up for interpolation and sharpening (Edit ▸ Preferences ▸ Interpolation)

Qimage knows the optimal image resolutions for the printers support by the program and will up- or down-scale the image accordingly before passing them on to the actual printer driver.

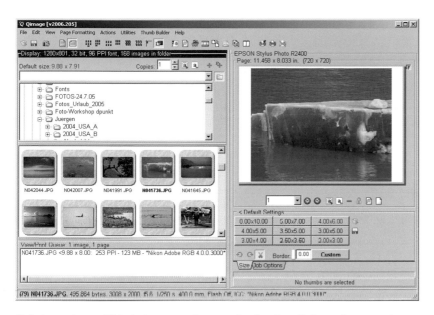

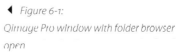

◀ *Figure 6-1:*
Qimage Pro window with folder browser
open

Printer setup This brings up the standard print dialog of your printer (printer driver of the operating system), where you may select all settings. These settings are stored by Qimage and may be saved under a special name.

→ *We had some reports of users of Qimage that indicated that Qimage will not print Lab-mode images in a proper way.*

Interpolation and sharpening Select your interpolation method for up-sizing and down-sizing. Qimage offers various methods and indicates their respective quality and speed (Qimage Lite shows a simplified dialog). You may also activate sharpening (lower right side). We usually choose "Smart sharpening".

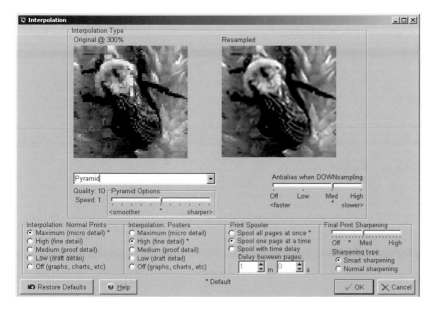

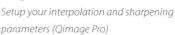

◀ *Figure 6-2:*
Setup your interpolation and sharpening parameters (Qimage Pro)

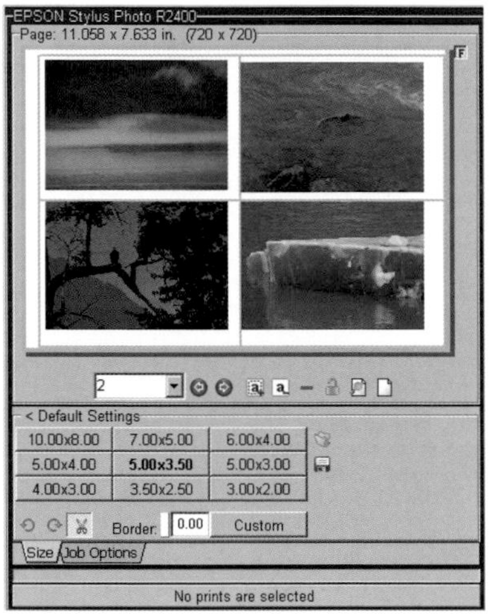

Figure 6-3: Image placement on your page

Additionally, check the color management setup. By default, Qimage uses the monitor profile set by the operating system. Here you can define the rendering intent used for printing (see Chapter 3.2, page 62/63).

To print an image, merely drag your image icon onto the empty page icon (Figure 6-1). You may still modify placement on the page. Alternatively, you may select the image thumbnail and just click ✚. (✚ calls up a preview of the image).

When selecting several images and clicking ✚, they are automatically placed on the page, using the current image size selected in the page window portion. As many images as possible are assigned to a page while automatically creating additional pages (print jobs) as needed. You may delete individual images from a page or modify placement.

Images printed with Qimage show a somewhat more crisp appearance, compared to printing from Photoshop. This should be attributed to the optimal scaling done before passing the composed page on to the printer driver, as well as to sharpening done by Qimage (you may deactivate sharpening). If you must upsize significantly, the up-sizing algorithms of Qimage definitely help achieve a good result, and you usually get by without a third-party up-sizing package, even when up-sizing significantly.

Digital Domain ([50]), the maker of Qimage, offers a number of printer profiles for selected Epson and Canon printers. We have yet to test them, as we prefer to use proven manufacturer's profiles (as listed in Chapter 5) or our own custom profiles.

Digital Domain also offers a simple printer-profiling package (Profile Prism) that uses your flatbed scanner for reading the printed color patches.* It is not as accurate as a professional printer-profiling package.

6.3   Printing using an RIP

As mentioned, there are a number of good RIPs for fine art printing on the market. We begin with a good, reasonably priced RIP, and later move on to RIPs focused on more professional-level press work (CMYK) proofing.

Quad Tone RIP

Some personal history: We've known Roy Harrington for some years, meeting as members of the *Gallery House.* Roy is a passionate 4 × 5 black-and-white landscape photographer who has produced inkjet black-and-white prints for some time now. In Spring 2003, Roy bought our Epson 7500.** He began experimenting with different black-and-white quad-tone ink sets. Here, he was not alone. But, because Roy also knows programming inside and out, he began to write his own quad-tone driver for his inks and the

7500. From this project evolved the new tool called *QuadTone RIP*. When Roy told us that he gets as good a result from standard Epson Ultrachrome inks (Epson 2200/7600/9600) as from his own ink mix, we became curious, as we believe Roy understands digital black-and-white printing at a highly expert level.

QuadTone RIP (QTR for short) is available for Mac OS X and Windows. On the Mac, QTR works like a printer driver. On Windows, it is actually a set of batch programs outputting through the standard Windows printer driver. Handling on Windows originally was not as smooth as with Mac OS X, but with version 2.3, it got a new front-end graphic user interface that makes handling (printing) with QTR easy and convenient. QTR is a shareware program and, for $50, offers a lot for little money. You may download QTR from the Web and test it before you buy.

QTR focuses on black-and-white printing. It does not offer PostScript support, but only TIFF (uncompressed or LZW), making it small and simple. You may also output color images, however, they are automatically converted to black-and-white.

QTR supports a number of Epson printers, desktop and large-format, with several different ink-sets, e.g., UltraChrome, UltraChrome K3, Neutral K7, QuadBlack, and Ultratone. The package includes additional tools for ICC black-and-white profiling, as it is not easy using standard ICC tools. For black-and-white profiling however you need a spectrophotometer. There are also tools that allow to produce your own tone curves for black-and-white printing.

At about $50, the QTR package is very reasonably priced and, in our opinion, well worth the money.

You have to download the Quad Tone RIP form the Internet at:
http://harrington.com/QuadToneRIP.html

→ *A quite useful feature of the QTR package is a supporting application that allows to produce black-and-white profiles, that may be used for black-and-white soft-proofing and printing using 'Let Photoshop Determine colors'. For more on this see Chapter 7.5.*

Installation

QTR comes with an installation script making installation quick and easy. On Mac OS X, you must be sure that *GIMP print* is installed before installing QTR. If it is not, you may simply install it from your Mac OS installation disk, using *Optional Installs.mpkg*. When you reach Custom Install, select Printer Drivers, and check *Gimp Printer Drivers*.

The QTR install script will install the RIP. Next, you must install the ICC profiles for your printer. These profiles come with the package.

The driver will **not** show up immediately in your printer list. First you must add 🖶 a new printer using your Mac *Printer Setup Utility* (🖨). There, select the printer (already installed and online) you want to use for your black-and-white printing using QTR, and use *QuadTone RIP* from the Print Using list. Additionally, select your printer model from the drop-down list (see Figure 6-4).

That does it. From now on, you may use QTR like a regular printer when printing from an application, e.g., Photoshop.

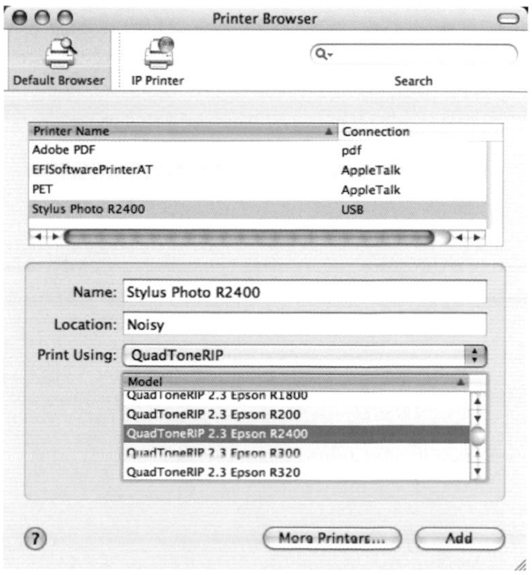

Figure 6-4: Select 'QuadToneRIP' from the 'Print Using' list and choose your printer model

Printing with QTR under Mac OS X

We use Photoshop as our printing application (selecting Print with Preview) and leave color management to the printer (see Chapter 5.3, page 132). If however, we have a black-and-white profile for our printer (+ paper + inkset + driver settings combination), we will use *Let Photoshop Determine Colors*.

In the setup of the printer driver, first select Printer features and then select your media type and Dither Algorithm (which we leave at *Ordered*). For our Epson R2400, QTR not only offers Epson papers, but several others: Ilford Heavy, Transparencies, and Glossy Film.

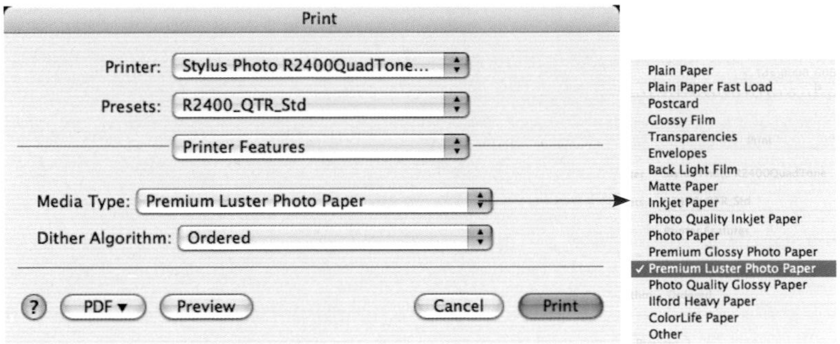

Figure 6-5: ▶
First select your media type.

While in driver settings, go to tab QuadTone RIP (see Figure 6-6). Here, you do your setup for black-and-white prints:

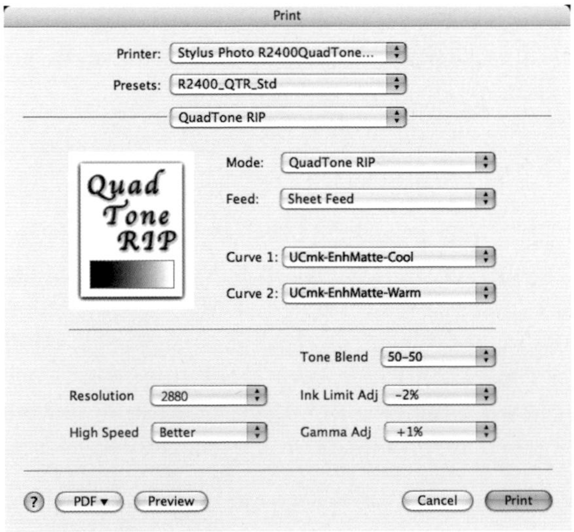

Figure 6-6: ▶
Under the tab "QuadTone RIP," you do your actual setup for the black-and-white print.

Curve 1 and 2 boxes determine your ink+paper profile (including your color hue). There are curves for a cool color, as well as curves for a warm color. You may mix this color hue via the *Tone Blend* drop-down list. A 50-50 blend, as in Figure 6-6, will result in a neutral tone. *Ink Limit Adj* and *Gamma Adj* give still more control of the print. A higher or lower *Gamma* value will darken or lighten an image in the print, without requiring editing of your original image.

Printing with QTR under Windows

With Windows, QTR does not run as a driver. Since QTR 2.3, however, there is a convenient front-end application called *QuadToneRIP Graphical Interface* (QTR GUI). It will be installed in your Windows Quick Start list. If you want to generate your own curves, e.g., for new inks or papers, you would also install the *Curve Creator*.

QTR offers a *Monitor folder* (a Hot folder).* When you drop an image into this folder, is will be printed by QTR automatically.

To print an image the simplest way, call up QTR GUI and do your initial setup. Then select the image you want to print (Image ▸ Select Image) and set the scaling (if necessary). QTR can only print TIFFs that are Grayscale or RGB, uncompressed or LZW. Sixteen-bit TIFFs will be internally converted to 8-bit. In most cases, this is no real restriction in fine art printing. The program takes most versions of TIFFs produced in Photoshop.

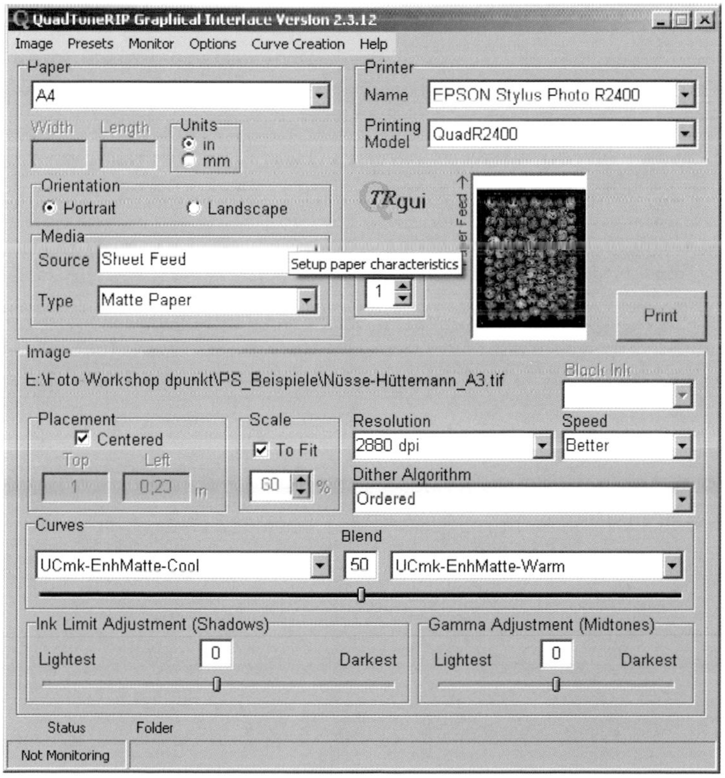

◀ *Figure 6-7:*
QTR Graphic Interface for Windows

QTR has good black-and-white profiling and linearization, although its manual is a bit weak. For more details on profiling, linearization, and curves adaptation, see the various QTR tutorials and help files.

ImagePrint by Colorbyte Software

ImagePrint by ColorByte ([67] 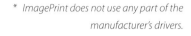) is a very popular RIP for fine art photographers. The main benefits of ImagePrint are:

*ImagePrint does not use any part of the manufacturer's drivers.

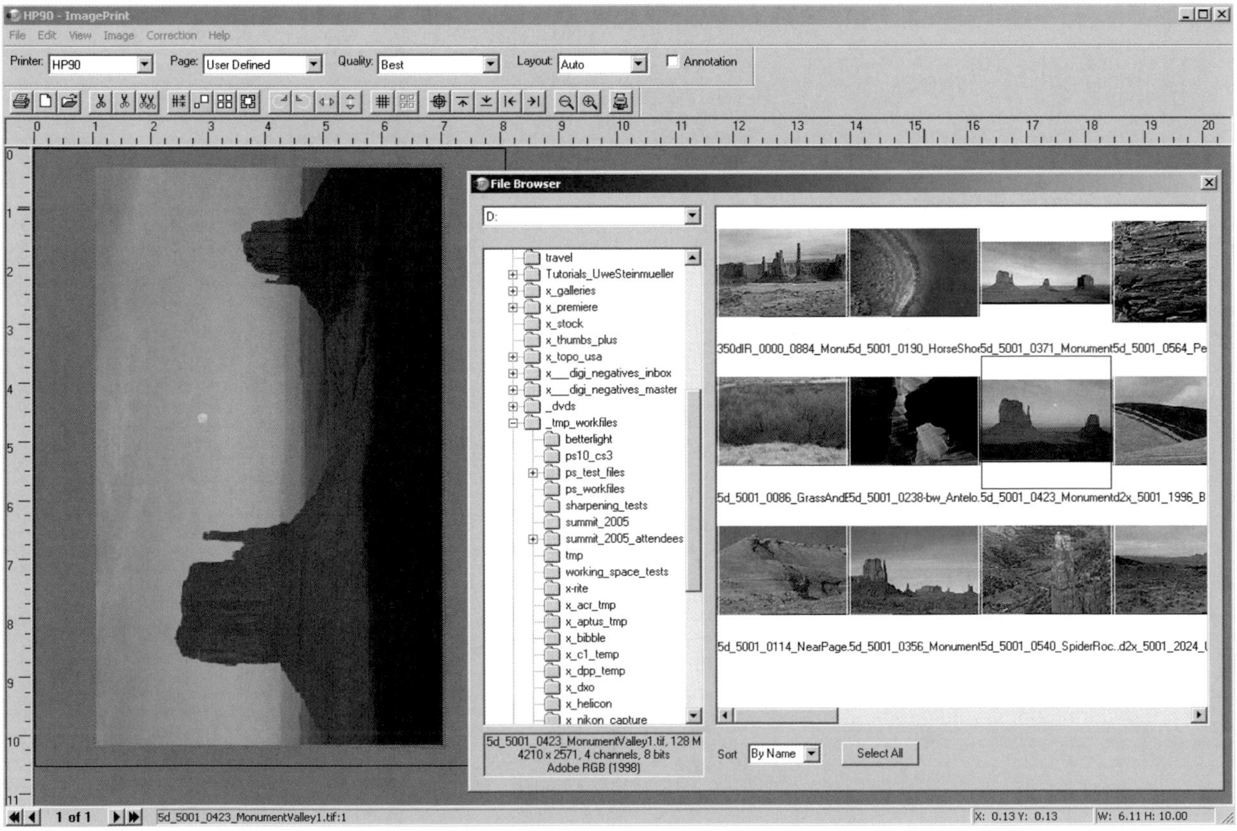

▶ Excellent print quality*

▶ 16-bit capability

▶ Very good profiles for many papers are included, as well as profiles for different lighting conditions. This is important, as creating good profiles can be quite time consuming

▶ Very good black-and-white printing, with very low levels of metamerism

▶ Easy to use compared to other RIPs

Figure 6-8: ImagePrint user interface

We have used ImagePrint for the Epson 7600/2200 and also for the HP Designjet 90, and have been very pleased with the results. Like most RIPs, ImagePrint allows you to select one or more images (for fine art you will usually print one image at a time), position it on the paper template, resize, and finally print.

Color Management with ImagePrint

ImagePrint is fully color-managed, yet it also provides extra control over printing. Here we will cover the basics, as far as we use them ourselves. You may also make image corrections in ImagePrint, but we prefer performing these operations in Photoshop.

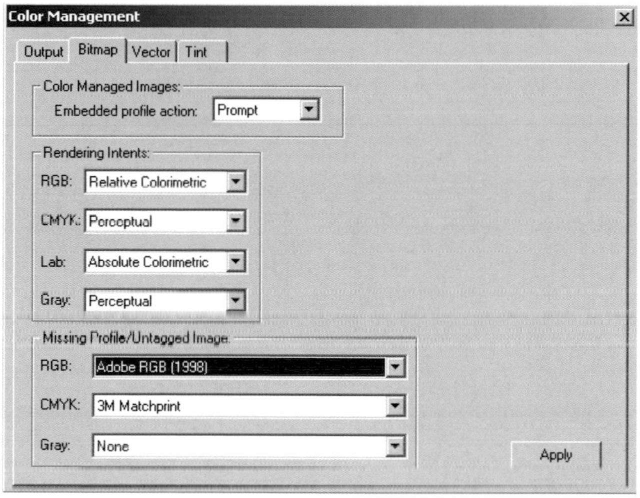

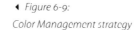

◀ *Figure 6-9:*
Color Management strategy

We want ImagePrint to notify us about the embedded profile, and use mainly *Relative Colorimetric* rendering intent for color images. For grayscale images, we use the *Perceptual* rendering intent.

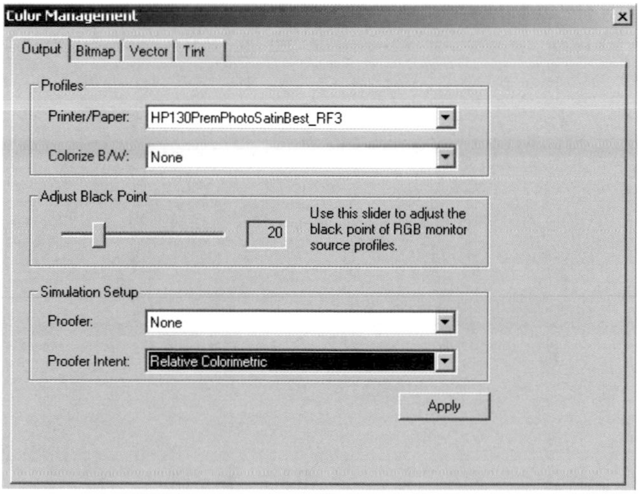

◀ *Figure 6-10:*
Output options

The key property is the profile for the paper. ImagePrint has two different kinds of profiles:

▶ Color profiles for different papers and viewing light conditions (often five variations). The user can also create new profiles

▸   Grayscale profiles for black-and-white printing on various papers. These profiles can only be created by ColorByte.

In special cases, you can have a black-and-white profile plus a color profile to use the colorizing feature, although we have no hands-on experience with this.

The Adjust Black Point slider is important, as you can define the level of black definition for your prints. We did tests, found a good setting, and left it at that level for subsequent prints. The simulation tab is set to "none" because we are not simulating any other target printers.

For black-and-white prints, ImagePrint features a powerful tint control:

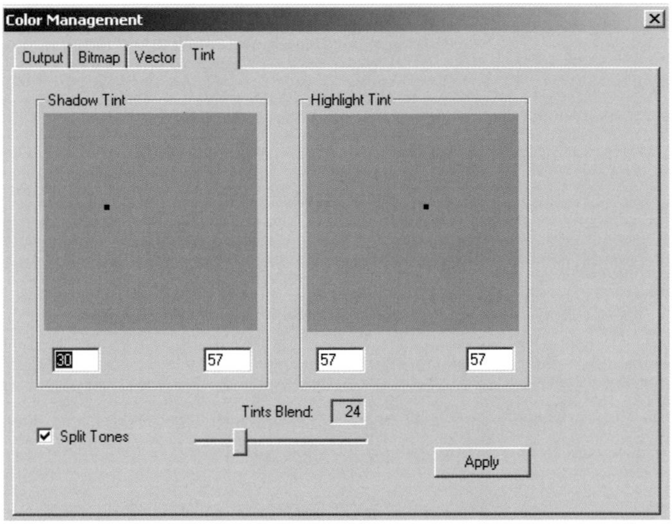

Figure 6-11: ▸
*You may select different tints for Shadows
and Highlights*

We use the same tint for the entire image, but ImagePrint allows so-called *split toning,* where the shadow part of an image receives a different tone than the highlight part. Using an extra slider, you can also control where the split should be for a particular print.

For the HP Designjet 30/90/130 printers, ImagePrint also supports in-printer color calibration (these printers have their own density sensors):

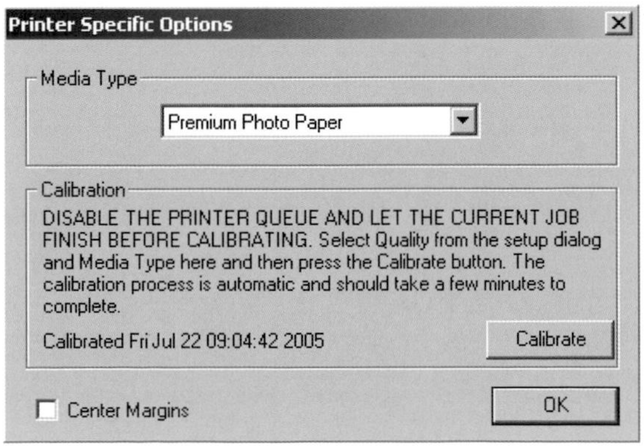

Figure 6-12: ▸
Calibrate dialog

EFI Designer Edition

EFI [68] is well known for its PostScript RIPs (Fiery print controllers) for color laser printers. *EFI Designer Edition* is a software RIP. Running under Windows (XP and W2K), as well as Mac OS, it is suited not only for fine art printing, but also produces highly reliable proofs of images for press printing. It provides an *Ugra/Fogra Media Strip* (a color-controlling tool well established in Europe's press industry). It includes several profiles for this kind of proofing and for a multitude of different papers mainly for professional inkjet printers from Epson, HP, Canon, Encad, and Roland (and others. It offers Adobe PostScript 3 compatibility, as well as PDF and tagged TIFF (RGB, CMYK, and Lab).

EFI may be installed as a virtual printer driver and thus used by any application on your system. It also supports "hot folders." When you drop an image (PostScript or PDF file) onto its hot folder, the image is added to the print queue and processed according to the rules defined for that folder. Thus, the virtual printer may also be used in a network if the folder can be shared. It is fully color managed and provides extended profile options. You may add linearization files to profiles. Additional tools help build linearization files and build connection profiles (these are combined profiles allowing simulation of the printing behavior of device B on device A).

With a price tag of about $650, EFI Designer edition definitely is not a throwaway application but still reasonably priced.

EFI Designer Edition (EFI-DE for short) offers three different printing modes:

▸ **Proof** (simulating a press print on your inkjet printer)

▸ **Photo print** (very much like printing from Photoshop, but with the additional advantage of batch/spool processing)

▸ **Black-and-white print** (converting an image to black-and-white on the fly)

You may also export a job (rendered as TIFF).

EFI-DE comes with a good installation script, so installation may be completed in a few minutes. We had to update this version online (just another click) to get support for our Epson R2400.

To setup the RIP, select Preferences ⚙ and set the parameter for:

▸ **Printer** settings
▸ **Paper profiles** settings
▸ **Color** (including color output mode. *Photo* for fine art printing)
▸ **Output.** Here, you define the RIP's resolution and what kind of additional control information should be included for the print.

* *EFI offers several versions of the EFI designer Edition described here. Their main difference is the maximum print size (related to printers) you may use: version M (printers up to A2), version XL (printers up to 24"), version XXL (printers up to 60").*
If you only want to print photos (images), you may go for "EFI Photo Edition", which is a bit less expensive.

➔ *HP offers the EDI Designer Edition as an optinal RIP for his lines of professional printers.*

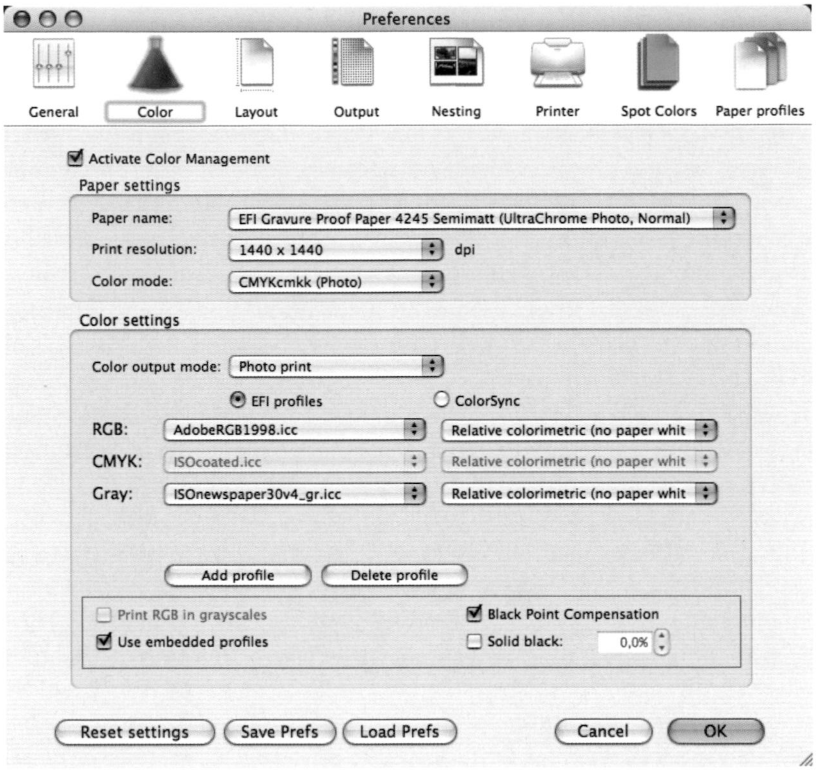

Figure 6-13: ▶
Color setup for your printer

Additionally, using the tab General, setup where your hot folder will be and where exported and preview images should go.

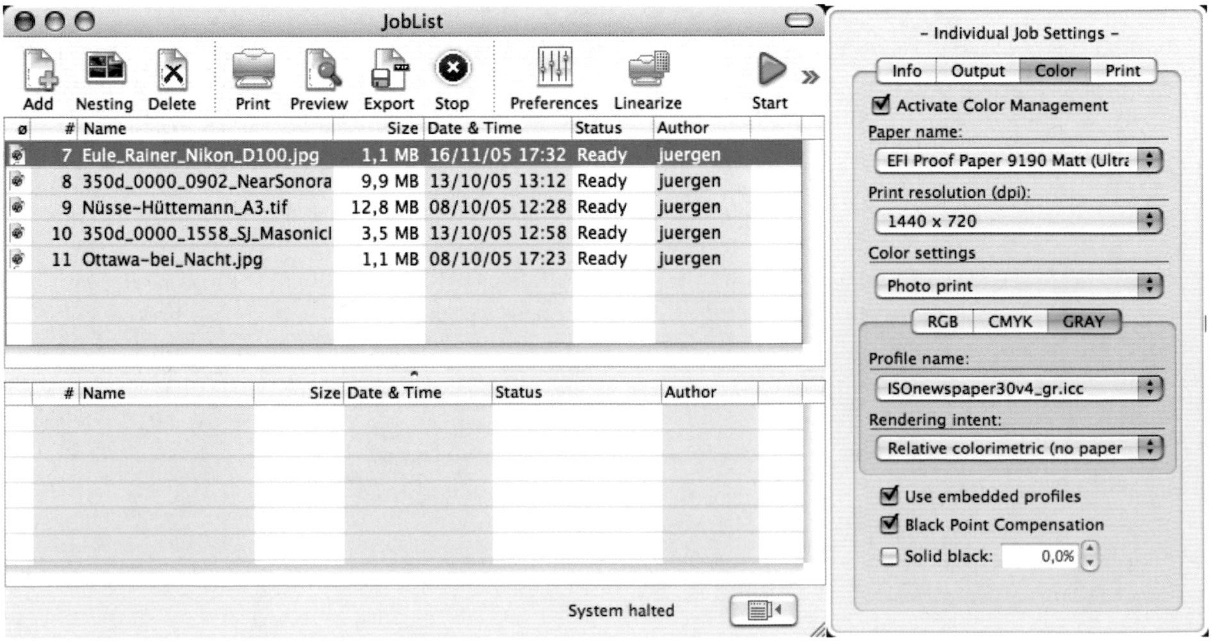

Figure 6-14: Job list of EFI Designer Edition.

For fine art printing, we prefer using drag-and-drop, dragging the image file onto the open job list. Selecting a job and clicking ⬚ will show the details (right palette of Figure 6-14). Here, you may still change some of the job parameters (as long as printing has not started).

EFI-DE does an acceptable job in fine art printing; you may even improve profiles by building a linearization file for a printer and paper using the *Ink Assistant* 🖨. Here, you adapt gamma and individual ink curves, but only for CMYK inks. You may also build custom ICC profiles. EFI-DE offers a pass-through option for printing a target and allows importing the new profile (you still need a separate profiling package). However, apart from color management (which is important), there is no special support for fine art printing, though for test prints the nesting feature comes in handy.

The program's real strength lies in doing a proof before sending your files to a printer for press printing. If your image is part of a DTP document, PostScript and PDF support are quite important. The Ugra/Fogra media-wedge is another plus for these types of jobs. If bought separately, it makes up about half the price of the EFI-DE package.

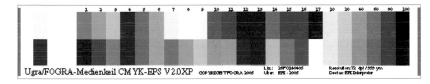

◀ *Figure 6-15:*
Ugra/Fogra Media-Wedge may be used as a control strip for printed colors.

In Europe, this may be used to verify the color/print quality of a press print. You may also proof using spot colors, and there is a *Color Editor* to define additional spot colors. For press proofs, the virtual printer driver is convenient, as you may print from any DTP application to a (supported) non-PostScript inkjet printer.

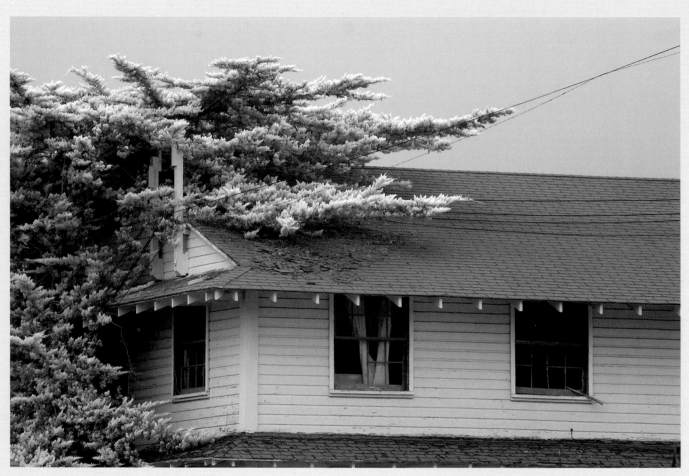

Camera: Canon 350D (infrared modification)

Black-and-white Prints

Even while all digital cameras originally capture the image in color, black-and-white printing still has its charm and followers and many of those, who loved traditional black-and-white in the traditional wet darkroom will be looking for digital black-and-white prints as well.

The charm of black-and-white prints comes from its abstraction, from its strong graphic impression, from the reduction of the image to the essential.

It may seem very easy to print in black-and-white – even easier than in color. But that is not the case. For good black-and-white prints you will have to do a good color to black-and-white conversion – just changing the color mode won't do the trick. Then you need to use the right print modes to achieve a neutral or tinted print. There are also some considerations when selecting a printer suited for optimal Black & White prints. We will deal with all these issues in this chapter.

7

At first glance, printing black-and-white seems easier than color. Unfortunately, this is not the case. The main reasons are:

▸ Finest tonal gradations in B&W prints are more important
▸ Unwanted color casts
▸ Toning of the prints
▸ Metamerism (one of the major problems of black-and-white inkjet prints)
▸ Excellent black levels are difficult to achieve

The key issue with most inkjet printers is that they only feature one black, which leaves two options:

▸ This will get you very grainy-looking black-and-white prints with few good highlights

▸ Using all colors to print black-and-white: potentially introduces various color casts and also can create strong metamerism. Prints look greenish outdoors and/or can have a magenta cast under tungsten light

* Epson Stylus Pro 2200, 4000, 7600, 9600

The previous generation of UltraChrome™ Epson printers* featured at least two blacks. With these printers, you could get good black-and-white prints using the ImagePrint RIP. Using just the Epson drivers would still result in prints that show quite a bit of metamerism and bronzing.**

** Meaning a slight green color cast with daylight and/or a slight magenta color cast with fluorescent lighting.

There were some third-party ink sets on the market that could transform your inkjet printer into a pure black-and-white machine. Well known are the Piezography inks by Jon Cone, but there have been some issues with ink clogging in the past.

In 2004, we saw the first off-the-shelf printers from HP, e.g., the Photosmart 8450, which featured color printing with an additional (or optional) three shades of black inks. In 2005, HP launched the Photosmart 8750, an improved and larger version of the 8450, and from Epson the new UltraChrome™ K3 ink sets (where K3 stands for the three blacks). Now, for the first time, we can create quite amazing black-and-white and color prints on the same inkjet printer. Only the Epson printers cover the range from 17" up to 44" printers, while HP is limited to 13" for printers with three blacks. Here are some options for good black-and-white printing:

Note: In fact, the lighter blacks are very important in these printers, as they produce smoother results in building up darker tones, and adding more lighter blacks than lighter tones with sparse darker blacks.

▸ HP Photosmart 8450 or 8750
▸ Epson R2400, 4800, 7800, 9800
▸ Epson 2200, 4000, 7600, 9600 with ImagePrint or QuadTone RIP
▸ Custom third-party ink sets or even homemade diluted inks with third-party RIPs (like StudioPrint or QuadTone RIP). We know photographers that use up to seven inks. Many use the classic Epson 2000, 7500 or 9500 printers.

We do not cover the use of custom and third-party inks in this book. Here, you are better off checking out specialized forums on the net. We discuss solutions that work off the shelf and additionally allow you to print color and black-and-white using the same printer.

7.1   Workflow for black-and-white prints

The workflow for black-and-white prints is not much different than that for color. Some leave the image in RGB color mode, while others convert files into grayscale images.

Tonality is everything in a good black-and-white print. Some may prefer a stark contrast, while others search for ultra-smooth gradations and open shadows.

One of the major issues in black-and-white printing is good, soft-proofing. Until recently, it was quite a hassle to find a decent solution. Fortunately, Roy Harrington (creator of QuadTone RIP [70]) offers a solution (see Chapters 6.3 and 7.5).

The problem with soft-proofing black-and-white images lies in the fact that there are hardly any black-and-white profiles around (standard profiling packages create color profiles).

From color to black-and-white

There are nearly as many ways to convert a color image to black-and-white as there are avenues leading to Rome. Some newer digital cameras even shoot in black-and-white. We do not recommend it, as a computer-based conversion will give you more control. You may also convert your color image to black-and-white either in your RAW converter, as described in our e-books[*] or in Photoshop. When you convert using Photoshop, simply converting from RGB to Grayscale (Image ▸ Mode ▸ Grayscale) in most cases does not achieve optimal results.

* *See [8] and [9].*

A better way is using the Channel Mixer of Photoshop:

1. Activate your Channels Palette and determine which of the RGB channels carries the most information (don't look at the channel icons; examine your image and deactivate the RGB channel first). In our example of Figure 7-1, it is Red and Green, which often is the case.

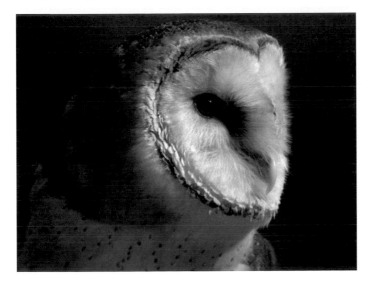

◀ *Figure 7-1:*
Original color image

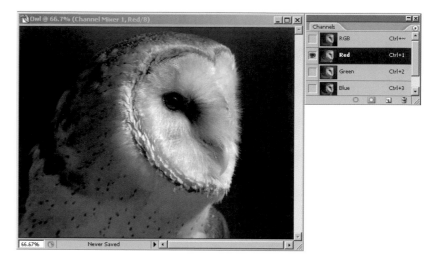

Figure 7-2: ▶
*Look for the channels with the most
information*

2. Create a new Channel Mixer Adjustment Layer (Layer ▶ New Adjustment Layer ▶ Channel Mixer).

3. Enable option Monochrome and start pushing the slider of your most important color (channel) slowly to the right. You may now mix your three channels. The sum of all three should add up to 100 %. Basic values of Red = 60 %, Green = 40 % and Blue = 0 % will give you a good start. In many cases, no further adjustment is necessary (We extracted these values from Clayton Jones' paper on black-and-white conversion).

    This technique involves a bit of trial and error. You may even set a channel slider to a negative value. Carefully check your image while adjusting the sliders.

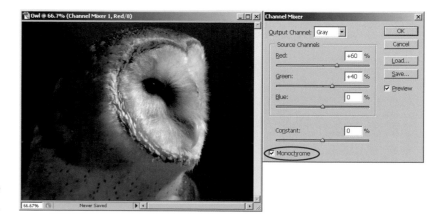

Figure 7-3: ▶
*Tune your channel sliders until the image
looks OK.*

4. If the image looks good, click OK. Though the image now looks black-and-white, it is still in RGB, which has some advantages for further optimizations.

5. You may still apply additional fine-tuning, e. g., using Levels and Curves. We recommend using adjustment layers for this! Fine-tuning a black-

and-white image is a bit different than color, but the same tools may be used.

As mentioned previously, there are a number of additional ways to convert from color to black-and-white, and you will find quite a few Photoshop plug-ins for this task.*

* For example, we like to use B&W Studio by PowerRetouche [38] or ConvertToBW Pro [31] and recommend both, but these are just two of the many converters or plug-ins available for this purpose.

7.2 Printers with black-and-white-enabled drivers

Again, some new printers feature three black inks and produce very good black-and-white prints.

Black-and-white with Epson UltraChrome K3 printers

We show these principles with the Epson R2400 driver dialogs. We understand the other printers are virtually the same.

Again, we use Photoshop as a printing application. We open the image and select File ▸ Print with preview.* When producing color prints, we use the Photoshop Color Handling setting *Let Photoshop Determine Colors* (see Chapter 5.3, page 132); for black-and-white prints, we use *Let Printer Determine Colors*, meaning do the color management:

* *This means that the printer driver will do color conversion and tonal mapping. This is reasonable only when the driver offers a special black-and-white mode.*

◂ *Figure 7-4:*
With black-and-white-enabled drivers, let the printer driver do the color management

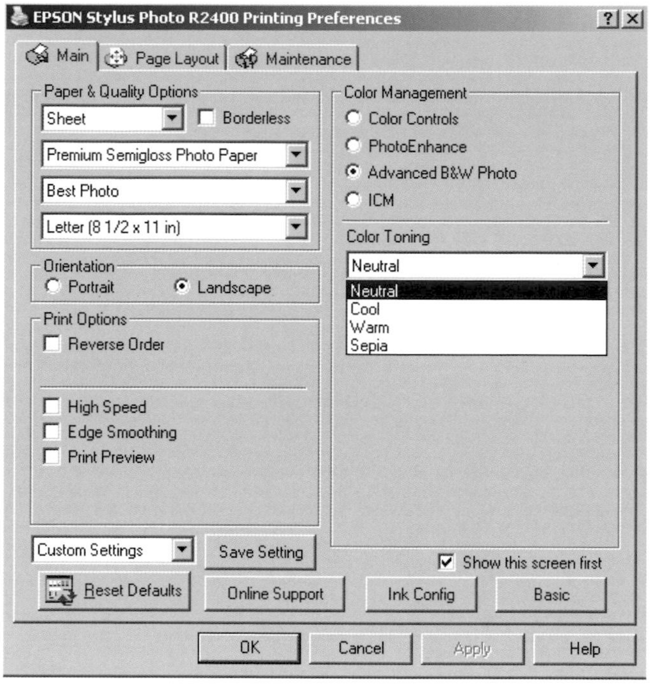

Figure 7-5: ▶

Printing in black-and-white

with the Epson R2400 driver

Set the driver to Advanced B&W Photo. There are four standard options available: neutral, cool, warm and sepia. It is best to start with neutral. We liked the results very much. If you want to fine-tune toning and settings, select the Advanced B&W Photo dialog.

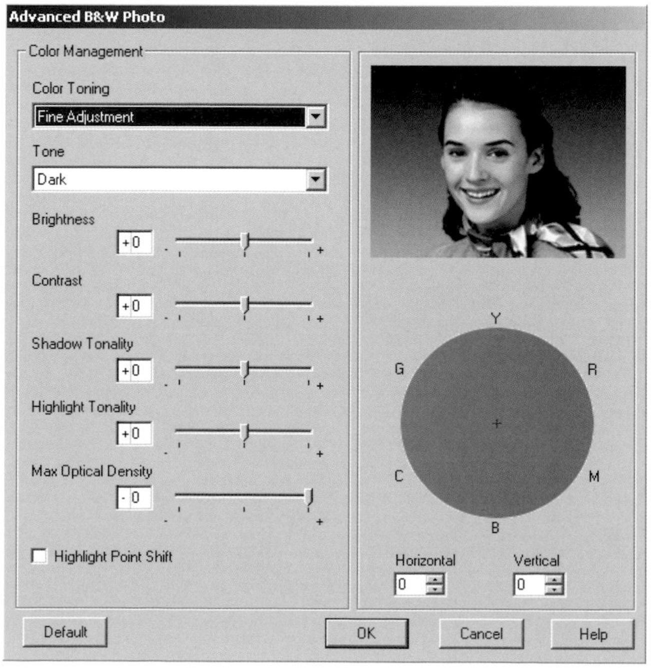

Figure 7-6: ▶

R2400 "Advanced B&W Photo" dialog

Aside from the actual toning, you may first want to set a tone (e.g. "shadow brightness") you like:

We found the default setting of Darker too dark, and changed the setting to Dark.

Be very careful using toning that is too strong, as you may get into a zone in which prints may show some metamerism.

If you use the Advanced B&W Photo setting for the K3 printers, you should not handle color management in Photoshop, but leave it to the printer. You have to gain your own experience in how the image on the screen is related to the print in terms of tonality, as this workflow is not really color managed. We assume that the driver treats a photo as a grayscale image, and then performs its toning. Later in this chapter, we have a note on soft-proofing black-and-white prints.

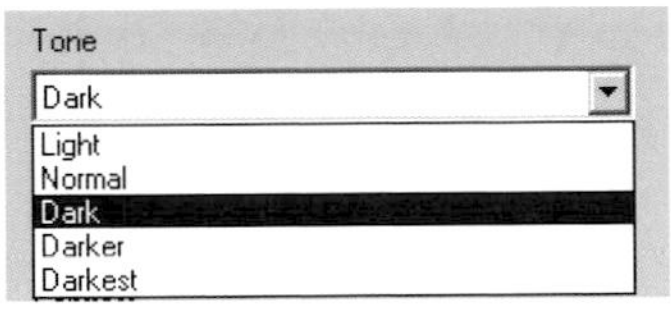

Figure 7-7: Tone settings

Black-and-white prints with HP Photosmart 8750/8450

HP shipped the first consumer/prosumer inkjet printers with three black inks.

In 2006, HP introduced the "HP Photosmart Pro B9180" using pigment inks and two tints of black ink.

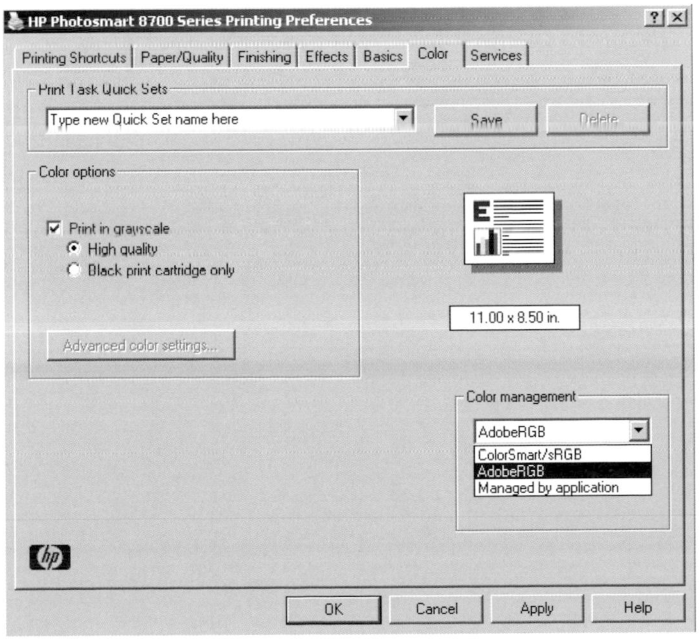

◀ *Figure 7-8:*
Setting the 8750 for black-and-white printing

▸ Select Print in Grayscale and also High Quality.
▸ Set Color Management to sRGB or Adobe RGB.

Using the 8750 for black-and-white, you should not handle color management in Photoshop, but leave it to the printer. Again, you have to gain your own experience in how the image shown on the screen is related to the print in terms of tonality, as this workflow is not really color managed either.

7.3   Special software (RIPs) for black-and-white printing

If your printer has only one black ink, it is quite difficult to achieve a neutral image without a color cast. In this case, a RIP specialized for black-and-white printing may help. The same is true when printing with multi-black third-party inks (e.g. quadtone inks).

Colorbyte's ImagePrint

* This means that the printer driver will do color conversion and tonal mapping. This reasonable only when the driver offers a special black-and-white mode.

ImagePrint earned Colorbyte [67] the reputation of producing very high-quality black-and-white prints from an Epson UltraChrome™ printer generation (2200, 4000, 7600, 9600) with only two blacks. It also uses special techniques to prevent major metamerism for black-and-white prints.

We recommend using ImagePrint for black-and-white only on printers that use at least two blacks. The black-and-white prints for the HP DesignJet look very good, but also show strong metamerism when you view the images outside in daylight. You can compensate for this by using the right tint.

We have covered ImagePrint previously (see Chapter 6.2, page 172), therefore we concentrate here only on the features needed for black-and-white printing.

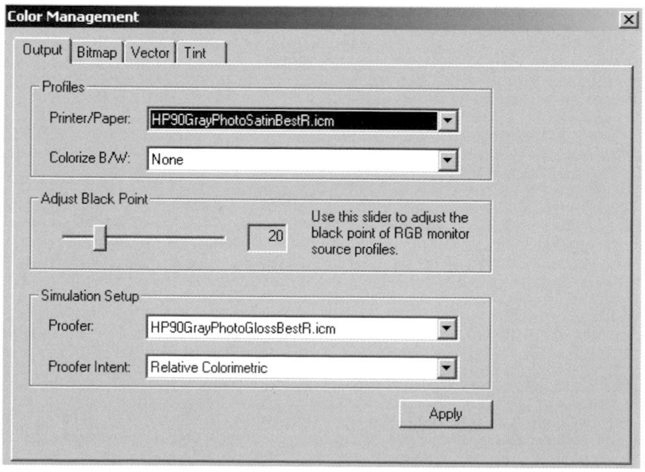

Figure 7-9: ImagePrint 6 black-and-white color management settings

By selecting an ImagePrint 6 grayscale profile, ImagePrint is set for black-and-white printing. These grayscale profiles can only be created by ColorByte. Fortunately, ColorByte covers many different papers.

You should also find which black point you prefer for your black-and-white prints.

Photographers actually have very different preferences as to how a black-and-white print should look (even varying from image to image). Some like them cool, others warmer. This factor creates a need for print toning, and also to compensate for the original black tones of the printers.

ImagePrint has very sophisticated controls for toning images:

The tint control allows more different tones than you may need for typical printing. It even allows tinting shadows differently than the rest of the image by so-called *split toning* (see Figure 7-10). You should experiment with your printer to find the ideal tint, and stay with it for future prints.

If you work a lot in black-and-white, you should check out ImagePrint for your workflow. A free demo version may be downloaded from the Internet. It will embed a watermark into your printed images.

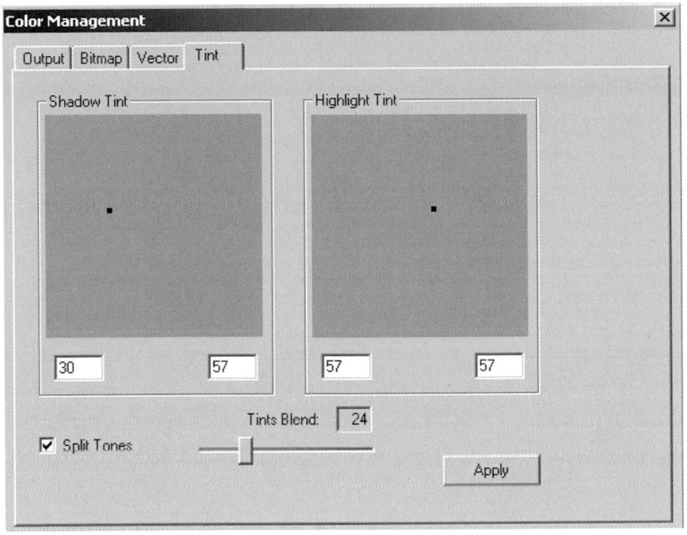

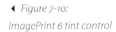

◀ *Figure 7-10:*
ImagePrint 6 tint control

QuadToneRIP

The large-format black-and-white photographer Roy Harrington looked for a simpler and less-expensive alternative to ImagePrint that he also could adapt to customize black-and-white ink sets. So he created his own RIP: QuadTone RIP.

We have seen some very good prints made by Roy with QuadTone RIP. We covered QTR in our Chapter 6: RIP. We will not get into details here, but you may also want to check out this software (you can download QTR from [70] and try the software before you buy.*

* *See Chapter 6.3 "Printing using a RIP" for more details.*

Other solutions

▸ Using StudioPrint RIP [69] (non-PostScript) supporting third-party ink-sets, as well as quadtone inks. It provides a very good linearization process.

▸ Jon Cone's Piezography Neutral K7 ink-set [87]with several different black inks and profiles to support them.

▸ InkJetControl™ (see [66]) is software dedicated to black-and-white printing, and comes together with OpenPrintMaker™.

We prefer to use either black-and-white-enabled printer drivers for printers that have several black inks or use a RIP, such as QTR or ImagePrint (see Chapter 6.3 "Printing using a RIP"). Some photographers swear by "'Black Only" (BO) printing, using just a single black ink for their prints. The results they achieve for their kind of images are very good. The advantages of this technique are its simplicity and low cost.**

* *Clayton Jones offers a nice feature-page at [30].*

7.4   Soft-Proofing for black-and-white prints

Soft-proofing your black-and-white prints will save you a lot of print iterations (meaning paper, ink, and time).

Roy Harrington came up with a solution as part of his QuadTone RIP package (QTR). The package comes with a target and a program to create black-and-white profiles. Additionally, you need the GretagMacbeth Eye One spectrophotometer and a version of Profile Maker's Measure tool (a demo version will do).

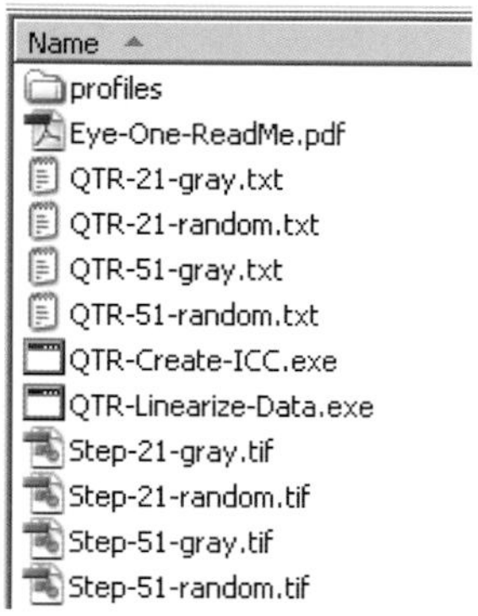

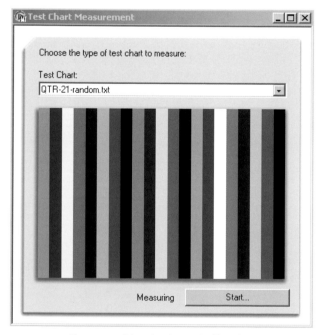

Figure 7-11: QTR tint control

1. First, you print the 21 gray target on your printer with the exact specified black-and-white settings (all black-and-white settings, paper type, toning, dpi, etc.) for your black-and-white capable printer (see beginning of this chapter). Let the print dry overnight for optimum results.

Figure 7-12: ▶

B&W target with 21 gray patches

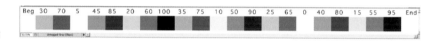

2. Next, launch the Profile Maker Measure tool and select the 'QTR-21-random.txt' reference chart (see Figure 7-13):

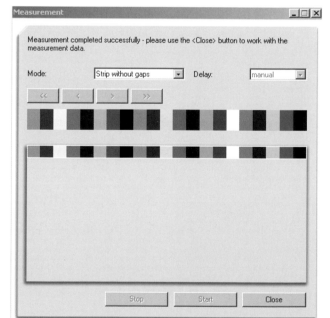

Figure 7-13: Select the chart in ProfileMaker

Figure 7-14: Read the strip

3. Start the measurement and read the line with the Eye One in *Strip mode*. As there are only a few patches, this will be quite easy and quick:

4. Finally, export the Lab values to a text file. Give it some descriptive name describing your driver settings (e.g. "*Eps_semigloss_neutral.txt*"):

5. Now just drop the text file onto the "*QTR-Create-ICC*" application and it will create a black-and-white ICC profile "*Eps_semigloss_neutral.icc*" for you: install this profile into you system profile folder.

Soft-Proofing setup in Photoshop

Now you can use this black-and-white profile for your soft-proofing in Photoshop. Following Roy's instructions exactly we print with Photoshop settings shown in Figure 7-15 using Photoshop's function Print with Preview (See also Chapter 3.10 on soft-proofing):

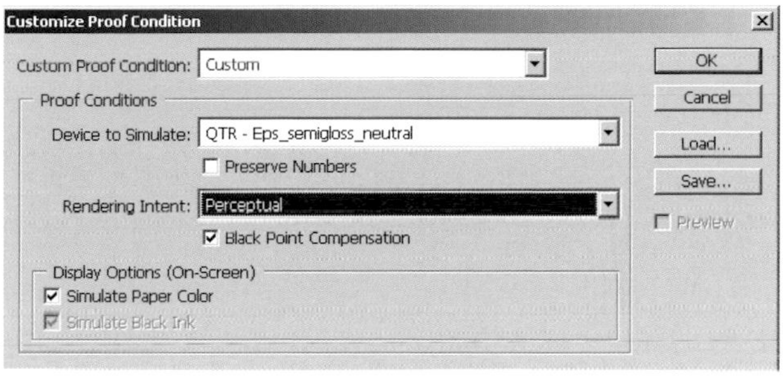

Because these are real ICC profiles, you can even use them as profiles in the printing dialog for Photoshop or other CMS-aware printing applications.

Thanks to Roy Harrington, this problem now also has a simple, elegant solution. If you have a licensed version of QTR, then feel free to share these profiles with other QTR users.

Figure 7-15 Set up your black-and-white profile for a soft-proof

Some comments from Roy Harrington posted in our news group:*

"As the article demonstrates, the basic procedure for these grayscale ICC profiles is very much like color profiling methods and produces a profile that is used very much like color profiles.

All standard profiles have two parts: one set of curves used for printing and to convert Lab values (i.e. colors to numbers for the print driver). The other set is used for soft-proofing that show the actual color (Lab) that is produced for numbers that are sent to the driver.

On first glance, these two sets of curves are just the inverse of each other. But in fact, they can be and usually are slightly different. In color, the obvious difference is the mapping for out-of-gamut colors. In soft-proofing the idea is to map a color to the best the printer can do and then map back to what color that actually is, so you can see it on your screen.

Grayscale profiles do nearly the same thing. There is no gamut limitation – black is mapped to Dmax and white to Dmin with *perceptual intent* mapping everything in between. This direction is pure grayscale; the result being the grayscale values that are sent to the driver (QTR, Epson ABW). The soft-proof side, however, is gray to Lab values and therefore color mapping. So, in the soft-proof, you see the actual tint of the print. In the soft-proof setup you can also Simulate Paper Color and/or Simulate Black Ink that will show those colors.

The profile making procedure actually creates two functions in one ICC profile. Usually, one would use them both – print with the profile and soft-proof with the same profile. But the soft-proof setup has a check box

* For the 'Digital Outback Open Forum' see www.outbackphoto.com/tforum/ viewboard.php?BoardID=1

that asks whether or not you will be printing with the profile. Preserve Color Numbers *OFF* means show the output using the profile in printing. *ON* means: Show the output as if you are not using the profile in printing.

As in all soft-proofing no screen output is identical to a print. The idea is to get a view easier for you to make a visual jump to what a print will look like.

There was also a question about the Measure Tool settings. It should be set to: Spectral OFF, Reflective ON."

7.5   Papers for black-and-white prints

➔ *In Appendix B you will find some URLs for resellers of fine art papers.*

Finding the correct paper for black-and-white prints is even more complicated and demanding than good papers for color. Why? The classic black-and-white prints are based on silver-based, photographic paper quality levels that are not that easy to match. As with color, there are three sorts of papers that photographers prefer:

▸   Matte fine art papers
▸   Satin papers with a very soft gloss finish
▸   High-gloss papers

As we discussed earlier, you cannot reach the same contrast and Dmax (maximum color density) on matte papers as is possible on glossy papers. On the other hand, some matte papers, with their soft cotton surfaces, look just great. Here, we only list papers we know and consider very good:

Matte Fine art Papers

➔ *As matte papers are even more sensitive to dirt and sweat form finger prints, don't touch the paper without wearing cotton gloves and even then avoid touching the printing area.*

▸   **Hahnemühle Photo Rag / (Satin):** A very popular but somewhat expensive paper; you have to watch for scuffing and cotton dust.

▸   **Somerset Velvet Photo Enhanced:** A very nice paper that is one of our favorites.

▸   **Moab Entrada Natural:** Excellent, reasonably priced paper.

▸   **Epson Ultra Smooth:** A top paper that is also archival. Watch for cotton dust, however.

▸   **Crane Museo II:** Very fine paper.

▸   **Arches:** Paper with a very good reputation, although we have not yet had a chance to check it out.

Satin or soft gloss papers

Most of these papers have a slightly plastic feel. More an issue in open portfolios than behind glass.

▶ **Epson Premium Semimatte:** Nice surface for a satin paper.

▶ **HP Premium Plus Satin:** Very nice satin surface.

▶ **Epson Premium Semigloss:** Comes close to the Epson Premium Semimatte paper, but maybe not quite as nice.

▶ **Crane Mueo Silver Rag:** A very fine paper for back-and-white prints. We really like it.

We expect new papers in this category to show up in the very near future, as the demand for fine art inkjet papers increases.

High Gloss papers

▶ **HP Premium Plus Gloss:** Very nice glossy paper surface.

▶ **Pictorico Photo Gallery Hi-Gloss White Film:** Very special paper, that has an ultra smooth surface and also a lot of contrast and depth. It is rated to be highly archival.

Clayton Jones' article "The Great Paper Chase" [30], is another good resource on papers for black-and-white printing.

A new generation of fine art papers very suitable for black-and-white printing came to the market in 2006 – e.g., Hahnemühle FineArt Pearl, Innova FibaPrint Gloss, Crane Museo Silver Rag, and Premiere Art Platinum Rag. We recommend to give them a try!

More information on black-and-white printing

Clayton Jones [30] has a very instructive Web page on fine art black-and-white printing. Uwe Steinmueller also provides a series of papers on black-and-white photography and printing, and also provides a forum on "Digital B&W processing and printing".*

See www.outbackphoto.com/artof_b_w/index.html

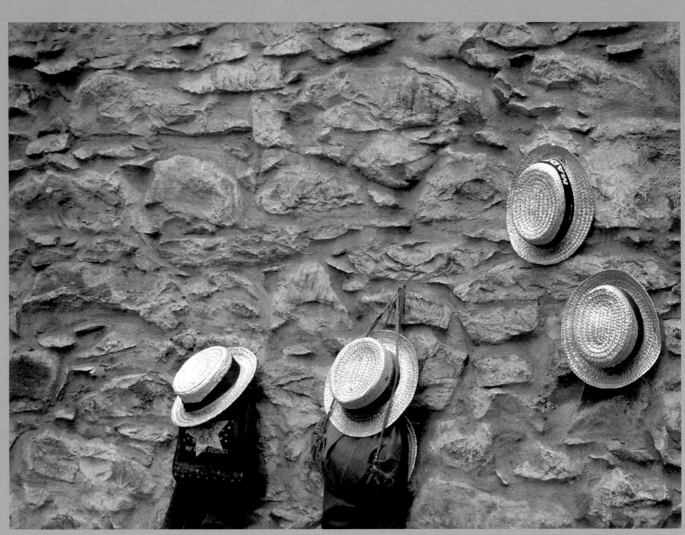

Camera: Nikon D1X

Image Judgement

An image for fine art printing will likely be evaluated and judged many times, starting with the first inspection after downloading from the flash card of your digital camera or after scanning. Typically, only very few of these photos will make it to fine art printing. Before you begin actually printing, you should give the image an additional close inspection, looking for minor faults like dust spots, or dead or hot pixels. Do this at least at a zoom level of 100 %. Next, we recommend you make a test print on lesser-quality paper and possibly a somewhat smaller-sized print.

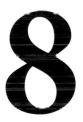

Repeat a close inspection, increasing scrutiny for minor deficiencies. It may even be helpful to use a magnifying glass. You may be surprised how many minor deficiencies you will find. Often, you can overlook minor defects, otherwise you'll have to go back and patch them in Photoshop.

A test print done on a paper different from the final print is useful for the purpose described above, but not for examination of the proper colors. This inspection is next.

8.1   Critical image judgement

It may be helpful to use a magnifying glass for closer inspection. But this is more for seeing the printing dot pattern in a more technical way than to see the impression the print will have.

In the first inspection of your prints you should look for obvious flaws in your print – tiny dust spots you didn't notice in your digital image, some dust or tiny paper fragments that came on when printing, or for stripes or banding.

The final inspection is for the correct colors of your print. Chapter 9.7 discusses using standardized daylight D50 for a proper inspection of colors, because that's the light today's color management systems target and rely upon. When you have a normal ICC profile, its colors are based on D50 light. Today, only a few profiling systems support other lighting, although this will be a feature any good package will have in the future.

You might argue that the print will probably not be viewed under D50 light, since most *normal* lamps have a somewhat different light spectrum. Nevertheless, your first inspection for correct colors should be done using a D50-compliant lighting. How do you achieve that? There are a number of ways – some simple and cheap and also more expensive ones:

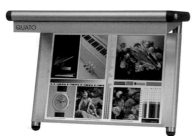

Figure 8-1: Lightbox XL for viewing A3+ sized prints (Courtesy Quato Technology, Germany)

▸ The professional way would be to use a D50 lightbox (viewing box) as seen in Figure 8.1. There are boxes that serve for viewing and judging transparencies, as well as prints (incidental light).

With some boxes, you may even dim the light to a level at which you can compare the print to an onscreen image side by side, both with the same brightness level. This kind of box is the proper choice for print shops and final press work. With a price tag of about $500–$1,000, they aren't cheap and they take up valuable space on your desk top. Some of them offer different light sources, providing D50, D65 and D75.

▸ Use of a D50-compliant luminary. This method is usually less expensive, about $100–$150. The point of these lamps is their D50-compliant light source and neutral white reflector.

There are several companies offering such daylight lamps: SoLux TrueColor Task Lamp ([62], see Figure 9-2), the Ott-Lite TrueColor light ([60]) or the Sol-Source by GretagMacbeth ([55]).

We use the Sol-Source.

When you wish to inspect large-scale prints, you will probably want to use color viewing lamps like GRAPHICLITE 100 by GTI Graphics Technology ([54]) as they are used in printing companies. They consist of any array of fluorescent tubes with a color temperature of 5,000 K.

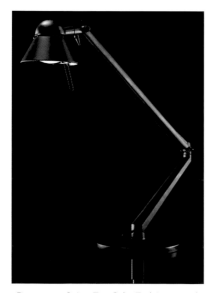

Figure 8-2: SoLux TrueColor Task Lamp with a light spectrum close to natural daylight (4,700 K/D50) (Courtesy VP-Tailored Lighting Inc.)

▸ Buy a D50-compliant bulb or tube, and use it in a lamp with a neutral white or a pure silver reflector. Your investment will be about $15–$25, including the lamp fixture.

We recommend avoiding fluorescent tubes, at least in small-scale solutions, as their light spectrum is not even and typically shows several spikes (see Figure 9-14 on page 212). SoLux and Ott-Lite offer these kinds of bulbs/tubes. Some also recommend Philips TL-950 5,000 K fluorescent bulbs or Philips Colortone F40T12/C50 as reasonably priced alternatives.

◄ Figure 8-3:

Three types of "daylight" bulbs. While the left two are more suited for image and color inspection, the bulb on the right is filtered and halogen based (SoLux MR 16, 4700 K), and may also be used for illuminating a print on the wall.

▶ Inspect your print in bright daylight. As the spectrum of daylight changes through the day, the best time for this will be around noon. Though the least-expensive solution, it is also the least reliable one. If you must rely on daylight, you should at minimum use the light indicator strips described in section 8.2.

In most cases, your lighting does not really have to be exactly 5,000 K, but should be reasonably close to it. A light source in the color temperature range of 4,500 to 5,500 Kelvin is probably close enough. An even and balanced color power spectrum is probably more important, as color power spikes (e.g., from most fluorescent tubes) may skew some colors. This is why we prefer daylight-balanced halogen lamps.

Before you begin a color inspection, the print should be completely dry. The time required for this depends on the type of ink and paper used, but one hour should be the minimum time, as the color will change slightly during the drying process.

If you intend to coat your print (see Chapter 9-5), we recommend doing a second inspection after coating and drying of the coating. Coating will influence the appearance of colors.

For a critical color inspection, your environment should be color neutral. Avoid colored wall papers nearby or any other colored reflection from nearby objects. Use a neutral white, gray or black background for your image. Environmental colors influence your color perception! It is well worth first using a bright light, or working close to the lamp, for inspection and using a normal-intensity light for color judgement. *Normal* here meaning about 150–400 lux, about the standard office-light intensity.

For final color inspection, you should provide a light situation similar to one the print will probably be viewed under. This, again, may influence your colors, plus some metamerism may occur. In some cases, you must go back in the entire printing process to slightly correct an image. Some newer versions of printer-profiling packages allow for this eventuality, when gen-

* e.g., PULSE ColorElite ([59]), as well as
GretagMacbeth ProfileMaker 5.x ([55]))

erating a printer profile.* You should gain considerable experience for this kind of color and profile fine-tuning.

If you experience *bronzing* (black being slightly copper colored) or metamerism, using a specialized RIP may help (see Chapter 6.3).

8.2   Control tools

You may not have a D50 or D65 light box or other light source (e.g. a lamp) that complies to the lighting standard for image inspection. In this case, there are a few simple control tools available that may help judge lighting conditions. They are called *light indicators* and consist of some patches printed with colors showing strong metamerism. While this is undesirable in many conditions, here it helps. When patches show different colors (stripes), this indicates that your current lighting is off natural daylight (4,700–5,500 K). If, instead, the different patches display the same color, your lighting is (probably) close to the lighting standard of 5,000 K:

Figure 8-4: ▶

GATF RHEM Light Indicator strip, showing under unsuitable lighting (left) and lighting, that is close to the view standard of 5,000 Kelvin (right)

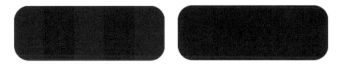

You may order these patches from several sources, e.g., from the GAIN store [53]). Bruce Fraser includes such a patch-strip at the end of his excellent book on color management [3].

Still more accurate is a spectrophotometer, such as Eye-One Pro, the colorimeter Eye-One Display 2 by GretagMacbeth ([55]), PULSE ColorElite or the MonacoOPTIX by X-Rite ([59]). Most of today's hardware-based monitor profiling tools come with a device that allows measurement of the color temperature of lighting. Some of the more expensive light meters also provide this.

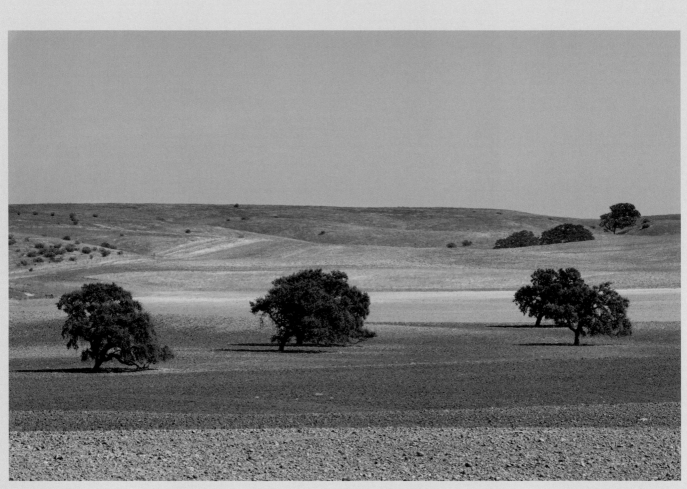

Camera: Nikon D2X

Presenting Fine Art Prints

Even when you have a beautifully printed image, there is still work to be done. The image must be prepared for presentation. A nice image looks better when it is well-matted, and a framed image looks best of all. This chapter will cover presentation techniques, focusing mainly on matting.

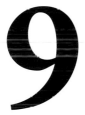

Matting and frame may be strongly influenced by your personal taste – or that of a buyer or gallery. There are virtually millions of ways for matting – single matting or double matting with different colored mats or use no matting at all – and of framing or direct mounting on various kinds of boards. Here, we will mainly restrict our discussion to the technical side and will not go into any discussion on taste.

9.1   Presentation options

Here are some of the most common options for displaying prints:

▸ Portfolio binders
▸ Portfolio books
▸ Portfolio cases with matted prints
▸ Single-matted prints
▸ Final-framed prints

All but the first option require that you mat your prints.

9.2   Portfolio binders

Many different kinds of portfolio binders are readily available. A cheap looking portfolio binder can make an entire portfolio appear cheap. Also, plastic sleeves come in various quality levels. Some sleeves are less transparent than others. Sleeves protect portfolio prints, but can also detract from a print's true quality with milky plastic or light reflections on the sleeves.

If you use transparent sleeves for your images, they should be made of polyethylene, polystyrene or polypropylene but not polyvinyl (PVC) or cellophane as the latter two contain softening agents.

For galleries, top quality binders are preferred, along with a suitable layout for your portfolio prints. Some of the digital tools for Photoshop simulating frames can be a good place to start. Finally, you should find a layout for your signature that fits to your work. All materials for portfolio binders should be archival (acid free, will not yellow). Below are some of the binder brands we use:

▸ **Itoya Art Profolio Evolution** ([79]): Inexpensive and simple. Adequate to store images. Probably not the correct choice to display in a gallery.

▸ **Prat** ([89]): Higher-end portfolios. Quite expensive.

See our paper on the "Unibind Photo Book Creator" at www.outbackphoto.com/portfoliowork/ pw_54/essay.html

▸ "Unibind Photo Book Creator" is also a fine solution where the binding of the portfolio is provided by Book Creator.* This reasonably priced device can bind up to about 30 pages (12" × 12" maximum).

9.3   Matting

True matting

Note: For your matting, mounting and framing work all materials should be archival (P.A.T.-certified).

The most common form of fine art print presentation is matting. While there are many different styles of matting, we cover some methods commonly used by fine art photographers.

▸ **Back Mat:** This may be regular mat board or archival foam board.

▸ **Mats:** The two principle styles are *single matting* and *double matting*. We mainly use single, natural-white mat boards.

The color of the mat board should harmonize with the colors of the image. Picking one of the image colors and lighten it or darken it a bit is one way to achieve this. At the same time the matting should show a clear contrast to the outer sides of the image to clearly separate image and mat.

More on mats:

▸ Museum boards are 8-ply thick (used often for black-and-white matting)

▸ Most boards are 4-ply (used by us)

▸ Boards need to be archival

▸ Boards are available in many colors (we prefer simple, natural white)

▸ You can use your own mat cutter, purchase precut mats, or order board from a mat-cutting service. Remember that blades need to be very sharp, otherwise they make ragged corners. Change blades often!

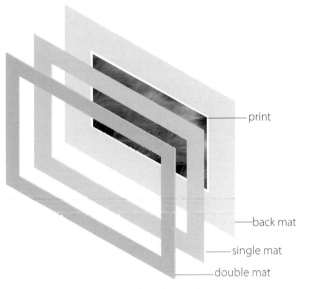

Figure 9-1: Principle and terms of matting

The principle matting process

▸ Always print pictures with white borders at least 1" wide.

▸ Use heavy paper so that your photos do not curl. De-curl prints, if needed. We usually use paper of 250–350 grams in an attempt to avoid curling.

▸ The first step is to mount/hinge the print onto the back board. We hinge the print to avoid possible side-effects of heat or glue.

Thin or large prints need to be cold/heat-mounted. Testing is suggested to see how your paper behaves. We will later show a procedure to hinge a print.

Using readily cut mats or letting the mats be cut by a matting service might be a good start if you do not have the right tools and some experience in mat cutting.

▸ Cut the first mat and place it on top of the print. Here are two principle strategies for cutting the top opening in a mat.
#1: The mat opening is wide enough to show the white boarder, and a possible signature (you may prefer to tone the photo paper to match the mat).
#2: The mat hides the white border of the print.

▸ Optional: Cut a second mat if you prefer double mats.

As when handling fine art papers, wear cotton gloves when handling your mats!

Matworks! helps with your calculations

For the PC, there is a helpful, free program by Giorgio Trucco called *"Matworks!"* ([39]) which you may download from Giorgio's internet site. Matworks! aids in the calculations of mat openings:

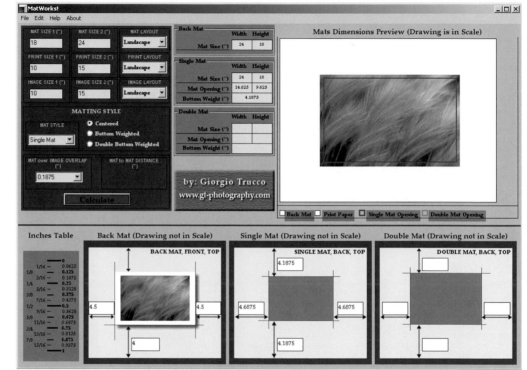

Figure 9-2: ▶
Matworks! main dialog

You enter the following values:

▸ **Back-mat size:** Here, 18″ × 24″

▸ **Size of the print paper:** Here, 13″ × 19″

▸ **Print size:** Size of the actual print on paper you want to display. For our example, it is 10″ × 15″.

▸ **Mat Style:** Here, *Single Mat*

▸ **Weighted or centered:** *Weighted* means that the bottom border will be larger than the top border. *Centered* will keep both borders the same measurement. This depends on your personal taste.

▸ **Mat over image overlap:** The mat overlap can be positive or negative. When positive, the mat covers part of the actual image. If negative, the mat allows some part of the white border to show (consider tinting the photo paper during printing to match the mat color). Revealing a white border has some advantages, as a signature can be written on the photo paper and it will remain visible.

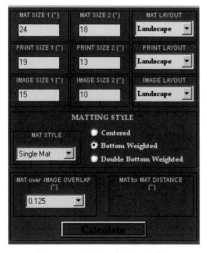

Figure 9-3: *Matworks! input data*

When you hit Calculate, Matworks! calculates all the placements and openings:

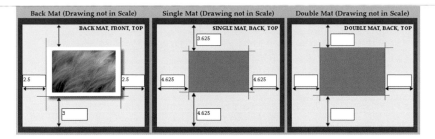

◀ Figure 9-4:
Matworks! output

Matworks! is very helpful when using a standard mat cutter where the openings are marked on the back of a board with a pencil. This next section describes a sample session using a professional mat cutter and more advanced matting techniques.

A mat cutting sample session

Here we show a sample session, where we followed the well-known master printer Charles Cramer in his studio. Charles showed us how he mats pictures, using one of our prints from an HP Designjet 90:

▶ **Paper size**: $13'' \times 19''$

▶ **Print size**: $10'' \times 15''$

▶ **Mat size**: $18'' \times 24''$. We advise using standard mat sizes: $11'' \times 14''$, $16'' \times 20''$, $18'' \times 24''$, $24'' \times 30''$. This way, the mats readily fit standard sized frames. Of course, there are situations where you may choose to deviate from these standard sizes.

▶ **Single matting**

Matting step-by-step

We again stress that all materials used are archival![*]

1. Cut two $18'' \times 24''$ mat boards (using identical material).

2. Place the print onto the back-mat (centered or weighted) and secure it in place using post-it notes.

3. Mount/hinge the print to the back-mat. Charles uses a so-called *T-hinge* (⎯⎯◢⎯▭):

*   *implying lignin-free, acid-free (better still if "buffered") and must not chemically interact with the print in any way.*

> **Note:** For the HP satin paper, we may glue the print at the top of the paper, since the back is very rough and tape may not adhere securely.

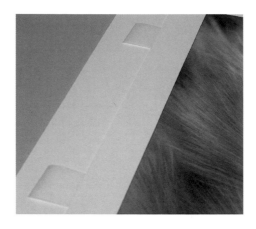

Figure 9-5: ▶
Transparent tape mounted to the back of the
print (glue toward the top)

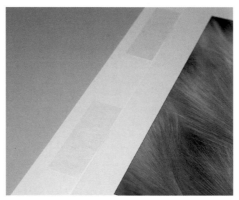

Figure 9-6: ▶
Use tape to hinge the transparent tape to the back mat

4. Add protective photo corners.
    In fact, these photo corners do not actually hold the print, but leave
    room for a print to move (allowing for changes in heat and humidity).
    The photo corners also serve the purpose of helping to avoid excessive
    tension on the T-hinges during transport.

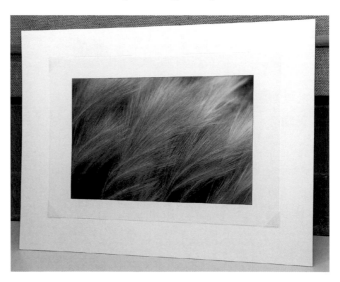

Figure 9-7: ▶
Stabilize the print with photo corners

5. Measure the opening of the single mat.

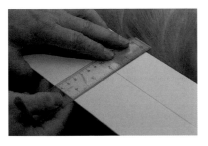

◀ *Figure 9-8:*
Measuring the border width

We are now ready to cut the mat. Charles uses a
40″ × 60″ Speed-Mat cutter (Uwe has a 32″ × 40″
model.) These mat cutters are expensive, but make
cutting mats more fun. Additionally, these wall-
mounted cutting systems save considerable space.

With the Speed-Mat, it is not necessary to mark
the opening on the back, as you can set all four cor-
ner stops of the Speed-Mat itself. The mat board is
then inserted, and cut on all four sides without
changing the mat board position.

6. Smooth the cuts with a burnishing bone.

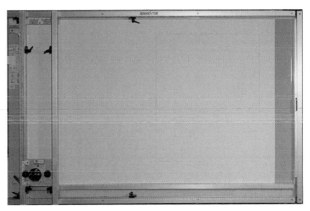

Figure 10-9: *Speed-Mat cutter*

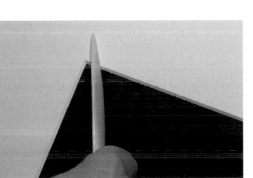

◀ *Figure 9-10:*
Smoothing using a burnishing bone

7. Sign the print if you wish.

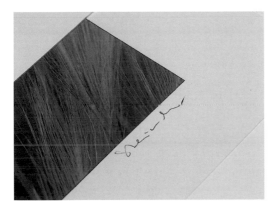

◀ *Figure 9-11:*
Signature on the print

In this case, we sign both the print[*] and the mat, because we will hide the white border with our mat. Of course, for signing on the print, use pigment ink pens that are archival.

8.   Fasten the back-mat and the mat together with tape.

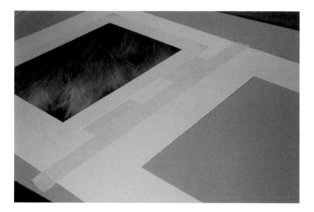

Figure 9-12: ▶
Fasten back-mat and mat

9.   Sign on the mat. We prefer to use a normal soft pencil for the signature on the mat.

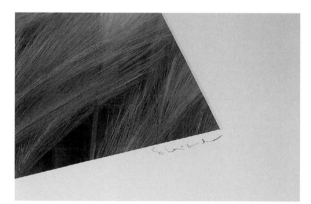

Figure 9-13: ▶
Signature on the mat

These steps are not difficult, but close attention must be paid to each small, yet important, detail.

Faux matting

When we talk about "faux matting", it means a separate mat is not used; rather, a mat-like image is printed surrounding the original print. This, quite naturally, is not of the same quality as a true mat but, may be satisfactory in some cases. When using a good faux mat, one may have to look closely to see the difference. When a framed print includes a glass cover, a disadvantage of faux matting is that the faux mat will provide no separation between the print and the glass. A print in contact with the glass is a poor solution.[*]

* There should at least be a distance of 2–3 mm from print to glass. You may use small matting board strips to achieve this. These strips may be hidden by the side of the frame.

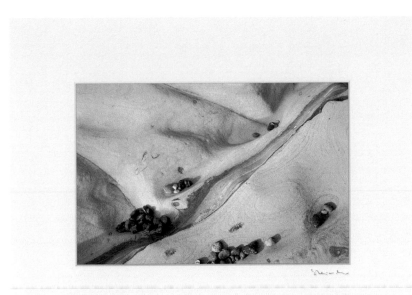

◄ *Figure 9-14:*
This faux matting was done using QuickMats 3

Faux mats can be created in Photoshop or other drawing programs. Specialized Photoshop plug-ins are available for this purpose (e.g., QuickMats by John Hartman [33]), but with a price tag of $ 229, may be too expensive for many users. An inexpensive alternative is ShutterFreaks' "Photoshop Frames for Printing", available for about $ 20 (see [40]). It offers a set of actions for creating frames and mats within Photoshop.

One advantage of faux matting is that it is easy to select a mat color that matches a color found in the image. To do this, determine a dominant color from the image and use the same color for the mat background color. In most cases, a more appealing mat is achieved if the color saturation of the mat is reduced to a slightly lighter color.

9.4   Framing a print

For optimum permanence, it is advisable to frame pictures using a glass or acrylic cover. This not only helps to present an image in an appealing way, but also protects it from dust and other kinds of contamination. Glass, acrylic, or Plexiglas, also filter some of the destructive UV components of light (partly by reflecting it). In addition, air flow over the print is greatly reduced, thus adding protection from the bleaching effect of air pollutants, such as ozone.

Like matting, framing is a matter of personal taste. Fortunately for the fine art photographer, there are literally thousands of different types of frames. For this reason, we will focus only on basic framing techniques, and not on the types of frames.

The normal framing process involves:

1.   Attaching the print to a backing board

2.   Overlaying the attached print with a mat, if one is used. This is done using archival-quality framing tape.

3.   This sandwiched package is then covered by an acrylic or glass front panel (at least we recommend this) and mounted into the frame. To improve the UV-filtering function of your glass or Plexiglas, use museum-quality materials. This may filter up to 99% of the UV rays, but is substantially more expensive (three to five times as much) than standard glass or acrylic.

4.   Tape this sandwich into the actual frame, again using archival-quality tape.

     Alternatively, the backing board, print, mat and glass front sandwich may be fixed into the frame with spring clips on the back of the frame. However, even when using spring clips, we recommend adding tape on the back to create an (almost) air-tight package.

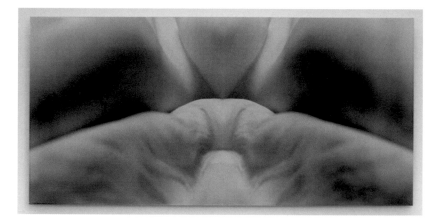

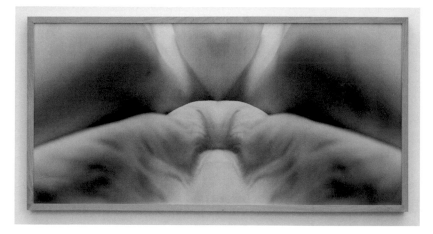

Figure 9-15: ▶
Print cold-mounted on an aluminum board
(top) and frame-mounted (bottom) create a
different impression
(prints: Gottfried Hüttemann, Germany)

If the image has been printed on canvas rather than on paper, the canvas should be mounted on a board, or artist stretcher bars should be used.

Frames are available in many styles, materials and sizes. Ensure that the material is acid-free, if longevity of the print is an issue, and that any part of the frame coming in contact with the print will not chemically alter the print.

About costs: it is advisable to use one of the numerous standard frame sizes.* One disadvantage of this is that those sizes do not match printing-industry paper sizes. This is no real problem if a larger frame and a mat that matches the frame size is used. However, the aspect ratio of most standard sized frames differs from the aspect ratio of photos shot with today's digital cameras (which is either 3:4 or 2:3 – if you did not crop part of the original image), or even with traditional 35 mm film format (which is 2:3).

e.g. 8" x 10", 11" x 14" or 16" x 20".

Some further points to consider when framing a print:

▶ Allow your print ample time to dry before it is framed. We consider 24 hours to be the minimum drying time, but we prefer two to three days.

▶ **All** material used must be archival or museum quality.** This applies to backing boards, mats, adhesive materials, and even the paper used to seal the print against dust and air flow at the back of the print. To ensure that the materials used are conservation quality, look for material that has a P.A.T. certification.

*** acid-free, lignin-free*

▶ If a wooden frame is used, do not let the print touch the wood (wood contains some acid and lignin), but separate it from the wood using buffer paper.

▶ Never let the print come in contact with the glass, as some inks or coatings may react with the glass or permanently stick to it. Should condensation occur, water on the glass could damage the print. Either a mat or a frame spacer should be used to provide sufficient print clearance.

When there is not a demand for large quantities of frames, it is advisable, and often less expensive, to use the services of a framing shop. A framing shop can provide standard-sized and custom-sized frames. When print preservation is desired, the framing service must be clearly instructed to use only archival-quality materials.

➜ *A nice paper on framing of fine art prints may be found at the internet site of the "Fine Art Trade Guild": www.fineart.co.uk*

Not only are there many different types of frames, but there are also many more ways to mount a print. Mounting prints on foam, fiber boards, or even aluminum boards are good alternatives that give a print a more modern touch. Foam boards are available in various sizes and thicknesses from art supply vendors. They may easily be cut to your required size with a sharp blade or a mat cutter.

When a print is mounted on a board, a borderless print, or one cut to be borderless, will probably look best. A mounted print without a glass cover may display colors better than a print with standard glass, as the glass may give your print a more bluish appearance (see Figure 9-15 lower image). This may be prevented by using more expensive, specialized glass.

There are several methods of mounting prints:

▶ Hot-mounting techniques
▶ Cold-mounting techniques
▶ Spray mounting

Since proficient mounting requires some experience, it should be left to a photo service, frame shop or bookbinder. The investment in tools and the time to learn mounting is worth the expense only if one intends to mount a large quantity of prints.

9.5 Coating a print

With canvas-based prints, usually no frame, glass or acrylic cover is used. In this case, it is recommended to cover the print with a protective coating. The same is true when mounting a print on foam board or other type of board to display it with no covering at all. For prints presented outdoors, coating is an absolute must. There are two specific problems with coating:

1. There are few coatings on the market that have a proven record for being truly archival (conservation quality).*

2. The coating will, to some extent, influence colors. For this reason, if color confidence is an issue, you should use an ICC profile based on a coated print. Print the image on the preferred paper, coat it, then profile this combination.

One product, recommended by several photographers and having a test certificate by WIR, is PremierArt Print Shield ([90]). It is offered as a spray or a liquid that may be rolled on or otherwise applied to prints.

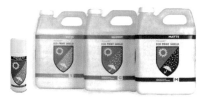

Figure 9-16: PrintShield by PremierArt is one of the proven post-coatings and available in several packaging sizes and for matte as well as for gloss papers.

When coating, be sure the coating is suited for the kind of ink and the type of paper surface used with the print. Some coatings are only suited for dye-based inks, while only a few coatings are suited for mat or semigloss prints.

There are several ways to apply the coating, such as with a brush, a roller (we prefer a foam roller), or by spraying. Applying the coating with a brush or roller gives the surface a somewhat artistic special touch. In any case, it must be done very carefully, while avoiding dust. There is a genuine risk of spoiling a print when coating. It is advisable to test the coating method using a scrap print, before experimenting on a prized photo. Carefully clean the print prior to coating, and be certain that it is thoroughly dry. A good rule of thumb is to wait a minimum of one day after printing a photo prior to coating.

When framing a coated print, allow the coating ample time to dry before framing or storing.

When working with a spray-on coating, wear a face mask, goggles, and gloves, and work in a well-ventilated area. Maintain a stable room temperature of about 64°–77° Fahrenheit (18°–25° C).

Laminating a print

Lamination effectively seals and protects an entire print from humidity, soiling, and atmospheric pollutants. With pigmented inks, laminating also provides a highly homogeneous gloss. In theory, laminating should improve lightfastness, however, studies show that this is not always the case, even in instances that followed the high-quality techniques used by some museums.

High-quality lamination requires specialized tools, therefore the services of a reputable print shop may be preferable for this process.

In our opinion, laminating may give the photo a somewhat *plasticky* appearance.

9.6 Displaying a print in true light

Lighting is a prominent concern when shooting a photograph. Light is also an important factor when presenting a photograph, as the impression of a printed image is very much influenced by its external lighting.

As mentioned previously, digital color management assumes that Daylight 50 (D50) will be used for image viewing (or inspection). Prints produced by our inkjet driver (or any other color-managed printing technique) are fine-tuned and color-corrected while viewing them under D50 illumination. Employing different lighting management systems may lead to incorrect coloration and/or "metamerism".*

Metamerism is an effect wherein two colors appear identical when viewed in one type of lighting, but look different when viewed in another type of lighting (or vice versa). The degree of metamerism may depend on the inks used, the ink mix used, the weaving pattern (dithering) employed, and a variety of other factors. But even when there is no noticeable metamerism, colors may change when viewed under different lighting.

* where some colors may look the same with one kind of lighting and may visually differ with another lighting.

The characteristics of light

When hanging your own prints or consulting with a customer about how they intend to display a print, it is important to understand the qualities of various forms of light.

Let's have a look at a few common types of lighting:

▶ Daylight (D50)
▶ Tungsten Light
▶ Sunlight
▶ Fluorescent Light

Figure 9-17 shows the various light characteristics of typical types of lighting, and suggests how the appearance of an image can change according to the lighting used.

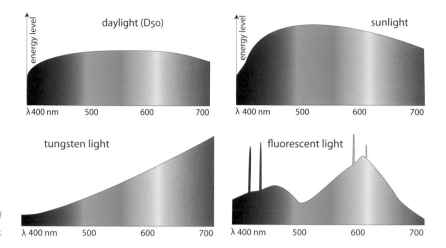

Figure 9-17: ▶
Light spectrum characteristics of typical
lighting options

Daylight generates the most even and continuous spectrum of light. Because of this, daylight is used as the reference by which all other forms of light are compared.

Fluorescent light is clearly the least desirable type of lighting among those mentioned – at least standard fluorescent tubes.[*] However, there are still worse lighting conditions, such as metal-halide (mercury) lamps.

It is advisable to display prints under lighting conditions that are close to daylight-like lighting whenever possible. Since natural light is inconsistent, even in a perfectly located room, the use of carefully placed lamps are essential.

Full-spectrum lamps or "daylight lamps" may be purchased from several lighting manufacturers.[**] Some manufacturers claim that their daylight lamps are superior, providing a more uniform light spectrum than their competitors, thus coming closer to ideal daylight.

Spotlights can provide optimal lighting for a picture. Halogen systems with a UV filter provide warm, natural-looking light. Avoid white fluorescent lamps which will cast a cold, rather dead light.

The optimal light intensity for print illumination is about 200–500 lux. This intensity is equivalent to the average lighting in an office building. You can measure lux with a traditional light meter, although we prefer to use a digital model.

* There are some fluorescent tubes (e.g., some sold by "www.justnormlicht.com") that come closer to the daylight characteristics.

** such as SoLux [62] and Ott-Lite [60]

For more on daylight bulbs and tubes, see Chapter 8.1.

Using an Eye-One Pro spectrophotometer you may analyze the spectrum of your lighting as well as the lux values using the free application Eye-One Share .

Protecting prints from light damage

Exposure to light may decrease the longevity of a print. As stated in Chapter 2, the more energy emitted by a light source, the more destructive it will be. Thus, intensity and frequency (i.e., which part of the color spectrum) are factors to be considered. Brighter lighting will cause prints to fade faster; shorter wavelength lighting (with higher ultra-violet components) will do the same.

Galleries and museums are acutely aware of the damaging effects of light and are very cautious when choosing lighting.

In addition, if you market your prints, your customers may not be aware of the detrimental effects of natural and artificial light, and would most likely be grateful if you were to inform them.

9.7   Storing prints

Most of the guidelines and conditions that apply to the storage and preservation of traditional photographs also apply to digital prints. For optimal longevity, store prints in a dark, dry environment which is as cool as possible. A relative humidity of 25–35 % is optimal. Specialized, sub-zero, cold storage systems are available, and are optimal for longtime archiving of valuable prints. (See [46] for essays on this topic).

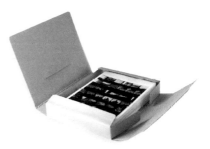

Figure 9-18. Use closed archiving boxes with buffered materials (P.A.T certified) for storing your prints (Courtesy Monochrom [85]).

Whenever possible, avoid temperature and humidity fluctuations. When using a closed, air-tight container, you may add silica gel packages to absorb excess moisture. Flat, horizontal storage should be your preference. Avoid stacking prints directly on top of each other. Protect them from light, dust, high humidity, atmospheric contaminations, and from physical damage. This is best done by using envelopes or protective sleeves. The sleeve, envelope and the container (e.g., an archive box) or album all should be acid and lignin free and buffered. Regular PVC-based envelopes or sleeves should be avoided. As with framing, use P.A.T.-certified materials, if possible.

Photographic albums

Storing prints in photographic albums is sometimes preferable to using archive boxes, particularly when frequent access is required for exhibitions and showings. For optimal print preservation, albums should be fabricated from acid-free, lignin-free, buffered materials. When using plastic protection sheets, select polyethylene, polystyrene or polypropylene. Avoid using plastic protection sheets made of polyvinyl or cellophane,.

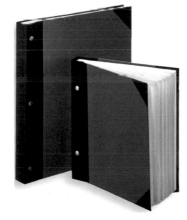

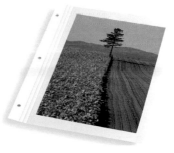

Figure 9-19: Albums/portfolios with direct printing onto the album pages (Courtesy of Monochrom [85])

Using an album slipcase will provide enhanced protection against dust and light, thus increasing the longevity of the contents.

The hinging of a print on an album sheet can be cumbersome. Fortunately, several companies offer printable album sheets constructed of high-quality inkjet paper. These printable sheets are usually sold with pre-punched holes, and may be easily inserted into the album by unscrewing a few screws. Albums of this type are available in a range of sizes up to 19.3″ × 25.6″ (49 × 65 cm).

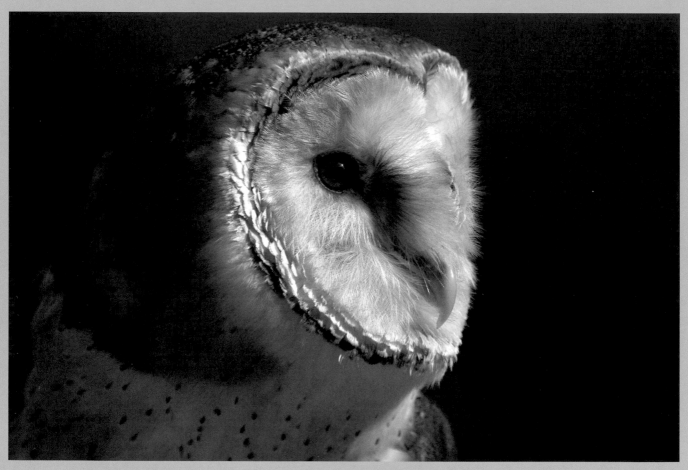

Camera: Nikon D100

Glossary / Abbreviations

absolute colorimetric • See *rendering intent.*

ACR • see *Adobe Camera Raw.*

Adobe RGB (1998) • A color space defined by Adobe. It is well-suited for digital photographs and has a reasonably wide gamut, larger than sRGB, and includes most printable colors.

artifacts (or artefacts) • An undesirable effect visible when an image is printed or displayed, such as moiré patterns, banding or compression artifacts. Compression artifacts (JPEG artifacts) may result from too severe JPEG compression. Also over-sharpening may produce artifacts.

banding • Noticeable tonal level jumps in an area, where a continuous tone level would normally be. Banding is one type of *artifact.*

black point • The density (or color) of the darkest black a device may reproduce. Black levels beyond that are clipped to the black point.

bronzing • Some inks (usually black inks) have a reflective property that results in a slightly bronze appearance under certain lighting conditions. This should not be confused with *metamerism.*

calibration • Adjusting the behavior of a device to a predefined state. Calibration, in many cases, is the first step when *profiling* a device.

caliper • refers to the thickness of a sheet of paper expressed in thousandth of an inch.

camera RAW format • See *RAW.*

candela • Unit of measurement for luminosity. Luminosity is specified in candela per square meter (cd/m²).

cd • See *candela.*

CF • *Compact Flash* – a type of data storage used in memory cards for digital cameras.

CIE • *Commission Internationale de l'Eclairage.* This is the international scientific organization which defined the CIE Lab standard.

CIE LAB • See *Lab.*

characterization • See *profiling.*

CMM • *Color Matching Module* – the internal color engine of a color management system. It does the color translation from different (source) color spaces to the PCS (*Profile Connection Space*), and from the PCS to the output color space. Well known CMMs are Apple's *ColorSync* for the Mac and Microsoft's ICM as an integral part of Windows. Adobe provides its own CMM module with applications, such as Photoshop and InDesign. It is called ACE (*Adobe Color Engine*).

CMS • *Color Management System.*

CMYK • A color model based on the four primary printing colors *cyan, magenta, yellow* and *black* (Black is also called the *key color, thus K*). Used in print production, they form a subtractive color model. Though many inkjet printers use CMYK inks (and often more additional colors), they, in fact, present an RGB interface to the user.

CRT • Cathode Ray Tube – a component in monitors incorporating glass tubes for display.

clipping • The loss of certain tonal values usually found in the color or tonal limits of a color space. Clipping occurs, for example, when converting images from 16-bit-mode to 8-bit or when converting from RGB to CMYK. In these cases, usually some saturated colors are clipped to become less saturated colors.

color gamut • See *gamut.*

colorimeter • An instrument used to measure the color of emitted light. Often, one is used while profiling monitors.

color model • The way colors are described by numbers. RGB, for example, uses a triple, denoting the amount of red, green and blue. CMYK uses a quadruple for the percentage of cyan, magenta, yellow and black. There exist other colors models, such as Lab, HSM, Grayscale (a gray value) or Bitmap (with pixel values of 0 or 1, white or black, respectively).

color space • A range of colors available for a particular profile or color model. When an image resides in a particular color space, this limits the range of colors available to that image. It also defines *how* the color values of an image are to be interpreted. There are *device-dependent color spaces* (e.g., those of a scanner or printer) and *device-independent color spaces* (e.g., Lab, Adobe RGB (1998) or sRGB).

ColorSync • Apple's implementation of ICC-based color management (part of Mac OS 9 and Mac OS X).

color wheel • A circular diagram that displays the available color spectrum (at a particular brightness level).

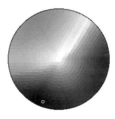

color temperature • A measure on the spectrum of the wavelength of white (light). The unit used is Kelvin (K). Lower color temperatures correspond to a red or yellowish light, higher temperatures result in a bluish tint. The term "temperature" stems from a blackbody radiator emitting (white) light when heated to a specific color temperature; for example:

candle light, fire	1000–1800 K
tungsten	2600–2700 K
halogen lamp	3400 K
moonlight	4100 K
D50 daylight illuminant	5000 K
sunny and blue sky	5800 K
D65 daylight illuminant	6500 K
flash	6500 K
cloudy sky	7000–8000 K
neon light	8000–9000 K
sunny mountain snow	up to 16000 K

chroma • The technical term for *saturation*.

curves • A tool in Photoshop that allows control (change) of tonal values in an image. The curve diagram below represents the relationship between input and output. By modifying this curve, corresponding tonal values of the pixels in the image are changed.

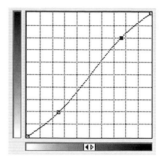

CS1, CS2 • Adobe Creative Suite 1 & 2. The full suite includes Photoshop, InDesign, Illustrator, GoLive, and Version Cue. The Premium suite includes Acrobat. CS2 also includes Bridge.

D50 • Daylight at 5,000° Kelvin. This is the standard light (*illuminance*) in the printing industry (prepress) for evaluating colored prints.

D65 • Daylight at 6,500° Kelvin. This is the standard (*illuminance*) that is closer to the light emitted by CRT or LCD monitors.

device profile • See *ICC profile*.

dithering • A technique used to simulate many different colors and/or halftones yet utilizing only a few primary colors by placing dots in a certain pattern. Viewed from an appropriate distance, the image is perceived as a continuous-tone image.

Dmax • specifies the maximum of a density range of a scanner, a slide or a print. Density range is the difference in density between the lightest and the darkest areas of an image.

dot gain • Halftone dots grow slightly in size when printed (e.g., due to ink spreading). This is called *dot gain*. Coated paper has a dot gain of 8–20 %, while with uncoated paper it may grow up to 28%. Photoshop may take dot gain into account when producing output for printers by reducing a dot size appropriately to compensate for its future dot gain.

DPR • *Display Permanence Rating* – a time period a print should last before a noticeable fading of the image occurs. For comparable figures, it is important to know under what conditions this measurement was taken.

dpi, DPI • *dots per inch.* Used as a measurement of print resolution with regard to ink or toner dots per inch on paper or printing plates. Most printing techniques (e.g., inkjet printers or offset presses) simulate a halftone value or a non-primary color of a pixel, using a pattern of tiny dots. With such printing techniques, the dpi value of a printing device must be considerably higher (by a factor of four to eight) than the *ppi* (*pixel per inch*) value of the image.

ECI • *European Color Initiative.* This organization defines standardized means to exchange colors (color images) on the basis of ICC profiles. You may find some specific color profiles on their Web site (see www.eci. org).

ECI-RGB • An RGB work space for those images destined for prepress work in Europe. Its gamut is somewhat wider (slightly more green tints) than that of Adobe RGB (1998) and also covers nearly all colors intended to be printed.

EPS • *Encapsulated PostScript.* A standard file format, usually including vector graphics or a mix of vector graphics and bitmap images. Often, EPS files contain both the actual graphic information and, additionally, a preview image.

EV • *Exposure Value.*

Exif, EXIF • A standardized format for camera metadata (e.g., camera model, exposure value, focal length, etc.). These data are usually embedded in the image file and may be used for searching or by applications to act in an intelligent way on the data; for example, PTLens uses the focal-length value from EXIF data to correct lens distortions.

Firewire • (IEEE 1394) a fast, serial interface for cardreaders, digital cameras, scanners and other peripheral devices. Firewire allows for transfer rates of up to 40 MB/s (1394a) or 80 MB/s (1394b).

gamma • (1) Relationship between tonal values (or input voltage with a monitor) and perceived brightness. There are two gamma values in broad use:

(A) 1.8, the Apple standard for the Mac and preferred in prepress work.

(B) 2.2, the Windows standard. For photographs, we recommend using 2.2, (even on Apple systems) for monitor calibration and profiling.

(C) The degree to which a *color space* or device is non-linear in tonal behavior.

gamut • The total range of colors (and densities) a device can reproduce (e.g., a monitor or printer) or capture (e.g., a scanner or digital camera). *Color gamut* is the range of colors a device can reproduce (or capture) and *dynamic range* refers to the brightness levels a device can produce or capture.

gamut mapping • The way colors are remapped when an image is converted from one color space to another. If the destination space is smaller than the source space, color compression or color *clipping* occurs.

gray balanced • A color space is called *gray balanced* if equal values of the *primary colors* result in a neutral gray value. This situation is preferable for work spaces.

gsm • *gram per square meter* (g/m²) – a measurement (*grammage*) for the paper weight.

highlights • Areas of an image with no color or gray level at all.

histogram • A visual representation of tonal levels in an image. With color images, it is advantageous not only to see luminance levels but also tonal levels of each individual color channel: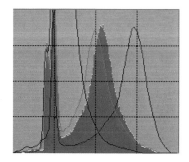

HSB, HSL • Adaptions of the RGB color model. Colors are described by a *hue*, *saturation* of the hue and *lightness* (HSL) or *brightness* (HSB).

hue • Hue is normally referred to as *color tint.*

ICC • *International Color Consortium.* A consortium of companies that develop industry-wide standards for color management – e.g., ICC profiles. For more information see www.color.org.

ICC profile • A standardized data format to describe the color behavior of a specific device. ICC profiles are the basis of color management systems. They allow CM systems to maintain consistent color impression across different devices, different platforms and throughout a complete color-managed workflow.

ICM • *Image Color Management* or *Integrated Color Management* – the Microsoft implementation of the color management module in Windows.

IPTC • *International Press Telecommunication Council.* In photography, IPTC is a metadata format that describes the image. It provides fields, e.g., for copyright notices, rights usage terms, a title (caption) and keywords.

intent • See *rendering intent*.

IT-8 • A family of standard targets used by profiling devices, such as scanners or digital cameras.

JPEG • *Joint Photographic Experts Group.* This ISO group defines a file-format standard for color images. The JPEG format uses lossy compression, offering various trade-offs between high quality (at lower compression) and lower quality that results in a higher compression but smaller files.

Lab, LAB, L*a*b*, CIE LAB • A perceptual-based color model defined by the *CIE*. Colors in this model are defined by L (*Luminance*) and two color components, **a** and **b**. "a" (or "A") is the axis ranging from red to green while "b" (or "B") ranges from blue to yellow.

LCD • *Liquid Crystal Display.* A display technique used for flat-panel monitors (TFT monitors).

lpi, LPI • *lines per inch.* The measure used to define printing resolution (or screen frequency) with typical halftone printing methods, such as offset printing.

luminance • Amount of light (energy) emitted by a light source, e.g. by a monitor. The unit used with monitors is *candela per square meter* (cd/m²).

lux (lx) • Unit for measuring the illumination (illuminance) of a surface. 1 lux = 1 lumen/m², 1 lux = 0.093 foot candles.

metadata • Data that describe other data objects. EXIF and ITPC data are examples of metadata as part of digital photographs.

metamerism • The phenomenon that two color samples composed of a different mix of primary colors may look the same (produce the same color sensation to a viewer) with some lighting and may produce different color sensations when viewed under a different lighting.

mil • Measurement of thickness, especially in paper. 1 mil = 1/1000 inch = 0.0254 mm.

P.A.T. • *Photographic Activity Test*, a testing standard (ANSI NAPM IT9.16-1993, ISO 14523-1999, DIN ISO 9706) for material in archiving and preservation. Material with a certificate to be PAT-compliant should show a good longevity and should be well suited for archival and museum usage.

PCS • *Profile Connection Space.* This is an intermediate color space used when converting colors from a source space to a destination space (say, from one profile to another). According to the ICC specification, it can be either *CIE-Lab* or *CIE XYZ*.

perceptual intent • See *intent*.

ppi, PPI • *pixel per inch*, used to specify the resolution of a digital image. See also *dpi*.

primary colors • Those colors of a color model used to construct the colors of the pixels. For RGB, the primary colors are red, green and blue. CMYK primaries are cyan, magenta, yellow and black.

profile • See *ICC profile*.

profiling • The act of creating a device *profile*. Usually a two-step process, whereby the first step is to linearize the device. The second step measures color behavior of the device and describes it with an ICC profile. The entire process is also called **characterization**.

PS • *Photoshop*.

RAW (camera RAW format) • See *ICC profile*.

RC • *resin coated paper*, used for photographic prints in the wet darkroom, as well as for inkjet prints

relative colorimetric • See *rendering intent*.

rendering intent • A strategy to achieve color space mapping when converting colors from a source to a destination color space. ICC has defined four different standard intents:

(1) *Perceptual* compresses colors of the source space to the gamut of the destination space (where the source space is smaller than the destination space). This intent is recommended for photographs.

(2) *Relative colorimetric* does a 1:1 mapping when the colors in the source space are all present in the destination space. Out-of-gamut colors of the source are mapped (clipped) to the nearest neighbor of the destination space. This intent may be used for photographs if most of the colors in the source space are available in the destination space. In this instance, most colors of the source are mapped 1:1 into the destination. The *white point* of the source space is mapped to the *white point* of the destination space, as well.

(3) *Absolute colorimetric* does a 1:1 mapping when colors in the source space are present in the destination space. Out-of-gamut colors of the source are mapped (clipped) to the nearest neighbor of the destination space. The *white point* of the source is maintained. This intent is used (only) when *soft-proofing*.

(4) *Saturation*. This intent aims to maintain saturation of a source color, even when the actual color has shifted during mapping. This intent may be used when mapping logos and diagrams, but is not suitable for photographs.

resolution • This term defines the depth of detail an image can reproduce. Resolution is measured in dots per inch (*dpi*) or pixels per inch (*ppi*).

RGB • *Red, Green, Blue*. These are the primary colors of the standard additive color model. Keep your photographs in RGB mode as long as possible, and use RGB for archiving your images.

RH • *Relative Humidity, expressed as a percentage*

RIP • *Raster Image Processor*. A module, either part of a printer or a software application. The RIP converts page information into a raster image or dot pattern for printing.

saturation • (1) defines the purity of color. Saturation may vary from none (which is gray) via pastel colors (some saturation) to pure colors (full saturation) with no gray.

(2) One of the four rendering intents. See *rendering intents*.

spectrophotometer • An instrument to measure the color of emitted and reflected light. It usually is used when profiling printers and measuring the color (light spectrum) of a print or other surface.

soft-proof • Usage of the monitor as a proofing device. For soft-proofing, Photoshop simulates colors an image will have with a different output method (e.g., a print) on a monitor.

sRGB • A standard color space for monitors. It is intended for images presented on monitors or on the Web.

swellable paper • A kind of coated paper used for dye-based inks. Here, when the moist ink hits the paper, the paper swells up and lets the ink sink in (only into the top layer). When drying, the paper again closes up and encapsulates the ink particles.

tagged images • Images with an embedded color profile.

TIFF • *Tagged Image File Format*. A file format for images. TIFF acts as an envelope format for many different image formats and allows several different compression modes, most of them lossless (e.g., LZW, ZIP, Runlength encoding, uncompressed). It allows storing different color depths (from 1 to 32 bits per channel), embedded comments, profiles, and other metadata, as well as layers and alpha channels. It is well suited as an archival format for images.

USB • Universal Serial Bus. A computer device interface for peripherals, such as card readers, cameras, scanners and external hard disks. There are two version of the USB bus, where USB 2 (high speed) is much faster (up to 60 MB/s) than USB 1.x (up to 1.2 MB/s).

USM • *Unsharp Masking*. A method of sharpening an image by increasing the contrast of its edge pixels. The term stems from a traditional film-composing technique.

vignetting • Vignetting is an effect where some areas of a photograph are less illuminated than others. Most camera lenses show "optical vignetting" to some degree, mostly at the outer edges, but stronger when the aperture is wide open. "Mechanical vignetting" may occur if a lens hood is too wide or not properly attached.

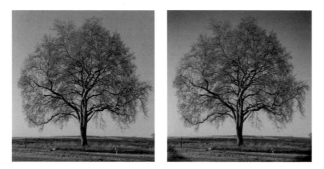

slight vignetting   *very strong vignetting*

wide-gamut RGB • A large color space that covers almost all of RGB. There is no physical device that can reproduce all color of *wide gamut*. This color space is sometimes used for archival purposes when output will be produced for photographic printers or transparent recorders.

white balance • Adjusting the color temperature and color tints in an image, so that there is no color cast, and gray areas show no color tint.

white point • (1) The color of "pure white" in an image. On a monitor, it is the brightest white the monitor can display. In photo prints, it usually is defined as the color of blank white paper.
(2) The color of a light source or lighting conditions in terms of *color temperature.*
(3) The color "white" in a color space; for example, *Adobe RGB (1998)* and *sRGB* have a white point of 6,500° K (*D65*) while *ECI-RGB, Color Match RGB* and *Wide Gamut RGB* have a white point of 5,000° K (*D50*). Most CMYK color spaces have a white point of D50.

white point adaptation • When a color mapping takes place and the source and the destination spaces have different *white points*, with some *intents* (e.g., *Relative colorimetric*) colors are adapted relative to the new *white point.*

WIR • *Wilhelm Imaging Research Institute.* This is a well known research institute that evaluates the image permanence ratings of specific prints.

working space • A device-independent color space (profile). It defines the color *gamut* available to the image using this working space. For photographers, *Adobe RGB (1998)* or *ECI-RGB* (in Europe) are the recommended working spaces.

Resources

B.1 Recommended Books

[1] Katrin Eismann:
Photoshop Masking & Composition
Peachpit, 2005

[2] Tim Grey: *Color Confidence.*
The Digital Photographer's Guide to
Color Management.
Sybex Inc, San Francisco, 2004.

[3] Bruce Fraser, Ch. Murphy, F. Bunting: *Real*
World Color Management
Peachpit Press, Berkeley CA, 2003

[4] Brad Hinkel: *Color Management for*
Photographers.
Rocky Nook, Santa Barbara, 2006.

[5] Harald Johnson: *Mastering Digital Printing.*
Second Edition.
Thomson, Boston, 2005.

[6] Peter Krogh: *The DAM Book. Digital Asset*
Management for Photographers.
(printed book) O'Reilly, Sebastopol, 2005

[7] Andrew Rodney: *Color Management for*
Photographers. Hands on Techniques for
Photoshop Users.
Focal Press, Burlington, MA, 2005.

[8] Bettina & Uwe Steinmueller: DOP2000:
Digital Photography Workflow Handbook:
www.outbackphoto.com/booklets/dop2000/
DOP2000.html

[9] Uwe Steinmueller, Jürgen Gulbins:
DOP3002: *The Art of RAW Conversion. Optimal*
image quality from Photoshop CS2 and leading
RAW converters.
E-book on RAW conversion, using Adobe
Camera Raw, RawShooter Essentials, and other
RAW converters:
www.outbackphoto.com/booklets/booklets.html

[10] Bettina & Uwe Steinmueller: DOP3001:
Photoshop Layers for Photographers:
www.outbackphoto.com/booklets/booklets.
html

[11] Ben Willmore: Adobe Photoshop CS2 Studio
Techniques.
Adobe Press, 2005

B.2 Useful resources in the Internet

Remember that World Wide Web addresses may
change or vanish over time.

[12] Uwe Steinmueller: Outbackphoto.
This is Uwe's website, full of up-to-date information on digital photography, including lots of
informative papers on photography:
www.outbackphoto.com

[13] *Colors by Nature* – some of the color works of
Bettina & Uwe Steinmueller:
www.colors-by-nature.com

[14] Uwe Steinmueller: *A Profile for black-and-white*
conversion:
www.outbackphoto.com/artofraw/raw_08/
profile_BW.zip

[15] Digital Outback Photo: *Our Tonality Tuning*
Toolkit (,):
www.outbackphoto.com/workflow/wf_61/
essay.html

[16] Uwe Steinmueller: *Variation Toolkit* (,) :
www.outbackphoto.com/filters/dopf004_
variations/
DOP_Variations.html

[17]   DOP free Photoshop action "Ring around":
        www.outbackphoto.com/
        DigitalCameraExperiments/dce_003/
        ring_around.zip

[18]   EasyS Sharpening Toolkit (⊞, ⌘) :
        www.outbackphoto.com/workflow/wf_66/
        essay.html

[19]   Digital Outback Photo: Paper on sharpening:
        www.outbackphoto.com/
        dp_essentials/dp_essentials_05/
        essay.html

[20]   *B&W-Ramp*: An image with black-and-white
        values to determine the black-point and white-
        point of your printer:
        www.outbackphoto.com/booklets/resources/
        fap/

[21]   Digital Outback Photo: Essay on *Workflow tech-
        niques using actions and filters in layers*:
        www.outbackphoto.com/workflow/wf_19/
        essay.html

[22]   Paper on *Noise Ninja* – a noise-removal tool
        (⊞, ⌘):
        www.outbackphoto.com/workflow/wf_25/
        essay.html

[23]   Digital Outback Photo: Essay on printing in-
        sights:
        www.outbackphoto.com/printinginsights/pi.
        html

[24]   Uwe Steinmueller: *Printing Insights #027: The
        D-Roller.*
        www.outbackphoto.com/printinginsights/
        pi027/essay.html

[25]   Uwe Steinmüller: *Printing Insights #029.Epson
        R800 Experience Report. A review diary*:
        www.outbackphoto.com/printinginsights/
        pi029/Epson_R800.html

[26]   Digital Outback Photo: Paper on noise reduc-
        tion:
        www.outbackphoto.com/
        dp_essentials/dp_essentials_04/
        essay.html

[27]   Jack Flesher: *Paper Upsizing in Photoshop*:
        www.outbackphoto.com/workflow/wf_60/
        essay.html

[28]   Alain Briot: *The Art of Digital
        B/W #007. Take control of your black & white
        inkjet printing with Inkjet Control*:
        www.outbackphoto.com/artof_b_w/bw_07/
        essay.html

[29]   Outback Photo: *The Art of Digital B&W.*
        Here, you'll find a number of papers on B&White
        photography (conversion, printing, etc.):
        www.outbackphoto.com/artof_b_w/index.html

[30]   Clayton Jones: *Fine Art Black and White Digital
        Printing. An Overview of The Current State of
        the Art.*
        This is a very informative page on black-and-
        white printing:
        www.cjcom.net/articles/digiprn1.htm

[31]   Uwe Steinmueller: *TheImagingFactory:
        ConvertToBW Pro 3.0*:
        www.outbackphoto.com/artof_b_w/bw_08/
        essay.html

[32]   Paul Caldwell: *Workflow Techniques #092:
        Sizefixer by Fixerlabs.* Paper on upsizing using
        Sizefixer (⊞, ⌘):
        www.outbackphoto.com/workflow/wf_92/
        essay.html

[32]   Altostorm Software: Altostorm Rectinliear
        Panorama™ (⊞) corrects geometric image dis-
        tortion:
        http://altostorm.com

[33]   Aian Brios essay on *QuickMats*, a program for
        virtual matting:
        www.outbackphoto.com/portfoliowork/
        pw_25/essay.html

[34]   *Fine Art Trade Guild.* This is the UK trade asso-
        ciation for the art and framing industry. You
        may find some useful hints, standards and rec-
        ommendations on framing of fine art prints
        here:
        www.fineart.co.uk

[35] HP: *Inkjet Photo Prints: Here to Stay.*
www.hp.com/united-states/consumer/sop/pdfs/
Lightfastness_white_paper_update_final.pdf

[36] Harald Johnson: *DP&I – a digital printing &
imaging resource.* A very informative site on
many aspects of digital printing with quite a few
how-tos:
www.dpandi.com
If you want to know more on giclée printing, go
to:
www.dpandi.com/giclee/

[37] onOneSoftware: *plx SmartScale*
This is a Photoshop plug-in for upsizing. The
company also sells *Genuine Fractals*:
www.ononesoftware.com

[38] *Power Retouche* offers several Photoshop plug-
ins. One we sometimes use for color to black-
and-white conversion is *Black & White Studio*:
www.powerretouche.com

[39] Giorgio Trucco is a well-known photographer
and offers *Matworks!* as a free PC tool to calculate matte openings:
www.gt-photography.com/matworks.html

[40] ShutterFreaks "Photoshop Frames for Printing"
– a set of actions that create frames and mattes
in Photoshop:
www.shutterfreaks.com/Actions/ACsBigFrames.
html

Organisations and institutes

[41] ECI – European Color Initiative
www.eci.org

[42] ICC – International Color Consortium:
www.color.org

[43] *IPI – Image Permanence Institute*: This institute
sprang from the Rochester Institute of
Permanence and does research in digital image
quality, light stability tests and on the right conditions for long-term storage of film materials
and digital images (e.g., inkjet prints):
www.imagepermanenceinstitute.org

[44] Wilhelm Imaging Research Inc (WIR).
This institute conducts research on stability and
preservation of traditional and digital color
photographs and motion pictures.
www.wilhelm-research.com
See also:
www.wilhelm-research.com/pdf/
HW_Book_758_Pages_HiRes_v1a.pdf

[45] Henry Wilhelm, Carol Brower:
*The Permanence and Care of Color Photographs:
Traditional and Digital Color Prints, Color
Negatives, Slides, and Motion Pictures.*
This is a 758 page e-book (PDF) that you may
download for free from the WIR Web site:
www.wilhelm-research.com/book_toc.html

[46] *WIR: Sub-Zero Cold Storage for the Permanent
Preservation of Photographs, Motion Picture
Films, Books, Newspapers, Manuscripts and
Historical Artifacts*:
www.wilhelm-research.com/subzero.html

[47] *WIR Display Permanence Ratings for Current
Products in the 4x6-inch Photo Printer Category*:
www.wilhelm-research.com/4x6/4x6.html

Color management tools

[48] ColorVision: Color Management Tools
(e.g. ColorPlus, Spyder2Pro, ProfilerPlus,
PrintFIX, etc.) (⊞,) :
www.colorvision.com

[49] Cromix is a color oriented company. One of its
tools is *ColorThink Pro* (⊞,) offering many
functions like profile inspection and correction,
profile management, and gamut graphing:
www.chromix.com

[50] Digital Domain Inc: *Qimage RIP* (⊞)
and *Profile Prism* (⊞) – a profiling software for
printers, digital cameras, and scanners:
www.ddisoftware.com
Profile Prism (⊞).
ICC profiling tool for cameras and scanners.
They sell printer and camera profiles, as well.
www.ddisoftware.com/prism/

[51] *Dry Creek Photo*: A Web site with much useful information and links on color management for photographers and various test charts and hints on how to prepare an image for digital photo printing:
www.drycreekphoto.com
They also have a useful page for monitor calibration done without special hardware devices:
www.drycreekphoto.com/Learn/monitor_calibration.htm

[52] Epson U.S.: *Profiles for Epson R2400.*
ICC profiles for the Epson R2400:
www.epson.com/cgi-bin/StoreEditorial
Announcement.jsp?cookies=no&oid=59082651

[53] GAIN store: GAIN is a service of the Printing Industries of America/Graphic Arts Technical Foundation (PIA/GATF).
Their store offers a lot of different photographic materials. You may also find the "GATF RHEM Light Indicator":
www.gain.net

[54] GTI Graphic Technology Inc:
www.gtilite.com/color-viewing-lamps.html

[55] GretagMacbeth: *ColorChecker* and several profile packages (e.g. Eye-One Match and Eye-One Photo):
www.gretagmacbeth.com

[56] *Hutcheson Consulting*: Good information on color management. Go to *Free* and you will find several useful images and test targets.
www.hutchcolor.com/Images_and_targets.html

[57] Bruce Lindbloom: Information on *Beta RGB*. You may download the ICC profile of Beta RGB here, as well:
www.brucelindbloom.com/
index.html?BetaRGB.html

[58] *Microsoft Color Control Panel*:
A small Windows XP utility to install and uninstall ICC profiles, set default profiles for devices and for the graphic display of ICC profiles:
www.microsoft.com/windowsxp/using/
digitalphotography/prophoto/colorcontrol.mspx

[59] Monaco Systems (now part of X.rite):
Color-Management Tools (Profiling packages, e.g., Monaco OPTIX for monitor profiling and PULSE ColorElite for printer profiling):
www.xritephoto.com

[60] Ott-Lite Technology offers several TrueColor daylight lamps, as well as bulbs and tubes:
www.ottlite.com

[61] *Pantone*: Pantone offers color guides and color management software, and also third-party inks for various Epson printers, including ICC profiles for various papers:
www.pantone.com

[62] SoLux: Offers different lighting solutions for "natural" light (close to D50):
www.soluxlicht.com

RIPs, test software and test images

[63] Bill Atkinson: A test image for your printer:
www.jirvana.com/resources/printing/
bills_lab_test_image.zip

[64] Bill Atkins: *Bill's Color Profile Downloads.*
Here, Bill offers a number of very good ICC profiles for some Epson printers and several papers for free. There are also helpful comments on profiles:
http://homepage.mac.com/billatkinson/
FileSharing2.html

[65] BabelColor offers several color oriented products, e.g., *BabelColor* (🪟, 🍎), a very nice and reasonable priced tool for measuring color (e.g. using Eye-One Pro) for converting and comparing colors and color gamuts as well as measuring Dmax in a print:
www.babelcolor.com

[66] *Bowhaus* is focused on black-and-white printing. It offers InkJet Control and OpenPrintMaker (RIP software):
www.bowhaus.com

[67] Colorbyte's Software *ImagePrint* (⊞,) is a Software RIP for fine art printing coming with a large library of profiles. They differentiate lighting under which a print will be displayed: www.colorbytesoftware.com

[68] EFI: *Efi Designer Edition* is a RIP supporting TIFF, JPEG, PostScript and PDF: www.efi.com

[69] ErgoSoft: ErgoSoft is focused on Large Format and Printing. The ErgoSoft RIP *StudioPrint* (⊞) is mainly for printing photos. Another useful component offered is ColorGPS for a very extensive profiling of inkjet printers: www.ergosoft.com

[70] Roy Harrington offers *QuadTone RIP* (⊞,), a fine RIP dedicated to black-and-white printing: www.quadtonerip.com

[71] *Imatest*. This is an informative presentation on cameras, lenses, scanners, and printers. Imatest is also an interesting program (test version available) to evaluate image quality of a picture or a print:
www.imatest.com/docs/iqf.html
See also the photography page of Norman Koren including many technique descriptions: www.normankoren.com

Paper, ink, coatings and cutters

[72] Arches Infinity: This company offers fine art papers of various kinds. Here, you also find ICC profiles for papers for several Epson and HP printers (e.g., Epson R800, R1800, 1280, 2200, 2400, 4000, 4800, 7600, 9600, HP 5000): www.archesinfinity.com

[73] Glastonbury Design: *D-Roller* www.d-roller.com

[74] Hahnemühle: A maker of fine art papers of various kinds. You also find some ICC profiles there for their papers for various fine art printers (e.g., Epson): www.hahnemuehle.de/site/us/798/home.html

[75] Hahnemuehle: *A-Z of Paper:* A good glossary for terms about paper (PDF file): www.hahnemuehle.comindex. php?mid=970&lng=us

[76] *inkAID*. A precoating to make uncoated papers suitable for inkjet printing: www.inkaid.com

[77] *Inkjet Art Solutions* sells inkjet printers, papers and inks for these printers: www.inkjetart.com

[78] *Inkjet-Mall*: This company offers a rich selection of fine art papers and inks: www.inkjetmall.com

[79] *Itoya* offers art portfolios: www.itoya.com/Catalogs/Profolio/Profolio_ html/Art_profolio.htm

[80] *Luminous Photo Corp:* They offer several ink sets for inkjet printing, including black ink sets for Epson printers. Luminous (using the label Lumijet) also offers archival inkjet papers: www.lumijet.com

[81] *Lyson:* Lyson offers third-party inks for a range of Epson and HP, as well as some Canon inkjet printers plus inkjet papers. For their inks and papers, they provide ICC profiles and descriptions of how to use them. www.lysonusa.com

[82] *Mediastreet* – an online shop with inks and media for fine art printing. They also offer the "Niagra Continuous Ink Flow System": www.mediastreet.com

[83] *MIS Associates Inc* is an online shop for inkjet inks and media: www.inksupply.com

[84] Moab: A maker of fine art papers of many kinds. You will also find ICC profiles there for their papers and different fine art printers (e.g., Epson): www.moabpaper.com

[85] *Monochrom* – a German supplier of photo-
      graphic material with a good Web site and an
      even better printed catalog:
      www.monochrom.com

[86] *Pictorico* Ink Jet Media: The company offers a
      rich selection of fine art papers (including trans-
      parency film):
      www.pictorico.com

[87] Piezography: The company produces several
      special black-and-white inks (e.g., "Piezography
      Neutral K7") which achieve very fine black-and-
      white prints. Inks are sold online by stores like
      Inkjet Mall.
      www.piezography.com

[88] *PixelTrust*. This is a precoating product to pre-
      pare uncoated papers for inkjet printing.
      Currently, this is only available in Germany,
      and the page is in German.
      www.pixeltrust.de

[89] *Prat* is one of the manufacturers of professional-
      quality presentation materials. Its products are of-
      fered by many online stores:
      www.prat.com

[90] *Premier Imaging Products* offers a number qual-
      ity digital fine art papers under the label
      PremierArt:
      www.premierimagingproducts.com

[91] *Speed-Mat Inc* offers several high quality, al-
      though expensive, matte-cutters:
      www.speed-mat.com/mat_cutter_standard.
      html

[92] *Tetenal*: A maker of inkjet papers of various
      kinds. Also have ICC profiles for their papers
      for different fine art printers (e.g., Epson):
      www.tetenal.co.uk/acatalog/Downloads.html

Index

C